W9-AXC-049

ST. PATRICK

EUROPE

AFRICA

FATHER MATTEO RICCI

Peking

KAGAWA

Nanchang

Macao

PHILIPPINES

Lambarene

Loanda

Ujiji

Zanzibar

Victoria Falls

Kuruman

Capetown

Indian Ocean

FRANK LAUBACH

DAVID LIVINGSTONE

palacios

Their faith knew no barriers . . .

Their lives were their sermons . . .

This is no tale of ordinary men and women, nor a book of theology. It is the human story of courageous, *believing* men and women who lived for their fellow men, and changed history — great religious leaders whose lives hold a valuable message for each of us today.

This is the story of Charlotte Bompas, the "first lady" of the Klondike, who administered to the burly "sourdoughs" during the turbulent gold rush days of '98; of Father Damien, the little Belgian priest who gave his life for the outcast lepers of Molokai; of the great humanitarian David Livingstone; of Wilfred Grenfell, the "miracle doctor" of Labrador.

The scene shifts to the Burmese jungle with the story of Ann Judson, who fought to keep alive the seeds of Christianity planted by her husband, imprisoned and tortured by an Oriental despot; to pioneer America for the exciting story of Jacques Marquette; to Albert Schweitzer's medical mission in darkest Africa; to the old Oregon Trail with Narcissa Whitman.

We journey to Cathay and the court of the "Celestial Emperor" with Matteo Ricci; to modern Japan and Toyohiko Kagawa, beloved apostle of the Kobe slums; to the headhunters of Mindanao where Frank Laubach began his crusade to bring light to the illiterate of the world.

A panorama of the most colorful epochs in history, the most extraordinary people and events unfolds before our eyes. Here are inspiring personal adventure stories universal in their appeal, set against unusual backgrounds, portraying the fascinating customs of faraway places — a book crammed with the excitement of a dozen historical novels and written with the vividness of front-page news.

But these Crusaders lived more than mere lives of adventure. They were men and women of great practical achievement. Though they scorned material things for themselves, they earned for others social reforms that "hard-headed" welfare-planners might well envy. Visionaries? Read in these pages of the lasting contribution of a Grenfell, a Schweitzer, Serra, Livingstone, Marquette, a Laubach and you will know the answer.

The fact is that these Crusaders for God were the supreme realists of their times. In living active Christian lives they not only solved their own spiritual problems but *solved the problems of the world in which they lived.* They provide the answer to present-day skeptics and materialists who belittle faith as an instrument for bettering the world. And they serve as an inspiration to the modern man or woman who seeks not only peace of mind, but peace among one's neighbors.

DANA THOMAS is co-author of the well-known Living Biographies series, with sales here and abroad totaling nearly a million copies. GREAT RELIGIOUS LEADERS is the title of one of his most popular books, and he has contributed to *Reader's Digest, Cosmopolitan, The Journal of Living* and other leading magazines.

Mr. Thomas lives in New York City with his wife and young son.

DANA THOMAS

CRUSADERS FOR GOD

A. A. WYN, INC: NEW YORK

FOR RUTH

Preface

THE MOST extraordinary adventure of the ages is Christianity in action. Yet it has not received the popular attention it deserves. Historians, concerned more with the exploits of kings and statesmen, have tended to overlook the greater story—the achievements of people who dedicated their lives to their fellow man, and who, in so doing, lived lives that surpass fiction.

The fifteen crusaders in this book were chosen for the richness of their contribution, not because they favored any particular interpretation of the scriptural message. Indeed, in translating the philosophy of the gospel into their everyday affairs, they expressed various spiritual influences. They manifested the passion of the Hebrew prophets for social justice, the inspired mysticism of the old Indian sages, the salty, earthy morality of the old Greek philosophers, readapted and transmuted through the teachings of Jesus into a dynamic expression of Christian brotherhood.

Supreme artists of the humble deed, they walked along the road to Golgotha, converting the heart of the stranger by their example. The greatest lesson they taught is this: Christianity really *works*—when one is courageous enough to try it.

D. T.

Table of

Contents

ENDPAPER MAP

BY RAFAEL PALACIOS

Go therefore and make disciples of all nations . . . teaching them to observe all that I have commanded you; and lo, I am with you always, to the close of the age.

MATTHEW: XXVIII, 19-20

1

First Lady of the Klondike

CHARLOTTE BOMPAS

ON JULY 16, 1897, a steamer docked in the harbor of Seattle, Washington. Among the passengers who debarked were a group of men in soiled mackinaws and muddy rubber hip boots who staggered under the weight of bulging duffel bags, moosehide satchels, suitcases, and bundles protruding from sacks and old wrapping paper.

Reporters on the harbor beat approached several of these men and received the surprise of their lives. One of the newcomers held up an old coffee pot. He turned it over and gold dust showered into his hand. Another produced a jar with a jam label, unscrewed the cap, and poured out a fistful of gold dust. Still another of the company took off a boot. Out came the inevitable stream of gold.

The reporters promptly wired the amazing story to their editors. Gold had been discovered in the Klondike, in Canada, just east of the Alaskan border. The first boatload of miners to dock in Seattle had extracted eight hundred thousand dollars from the gold creeks.

Within hours, newspapers in millions of homes broadcast

3

the story of the strike. And for months to come their reports kept Americans thrilled with the happenings. But in their search for headline topics, the editors to a man overlooked the greatest story of the gold rush—the tale of a white-haired Englishwoman of sixty-seven who entered the Klondike, not to dig riches, but to win something dearer to God. And this story of human courage has survived the last windlass set up over the rich placer diggings and the final miner going to his rest.

It is the story of Charlotte Selina Bompas.

The Canadian Northwest has never known a more stubborn person than Charlotte Bompas. She was an artistic, cultured woman who seemed totally unfit for the role of a missionary. Born into a family of means, she spent her early years in Italy, surrounded by the culture of Rome and Florence. At her coming-out party, she danced with the King of Naples. She possessed a talented pen and wrote popular fiction; she was lionized in literary circles.

Yet this patrician lady at forty-four became the wife of Bishop William Carpenter Bompas, an Anglican missionary who lived among the Eskimos and Indians. She married him knowing that she would spend the rest of her life in the sub-Arctic.

Just how much this break with her early life cost her she herself revealed in letters from her mission post. "When this reaches England," she wrote on one occasion, "your summer will be at hand. An English summer! . . . I do not know how I could bear the excitement of this, any more than I could bear to hear a symphony of Mozart or Haydn, or a song of Beethoven or Schubert; these all seem to belong to another state of existence to which I can hardly believe that I ever belonged."

Her introduction to the new country was a shock. She had come prepared for frigid weather, but as she sailed up the Saskatchewan River to Fort Simpson where her husband had his mission headquarters, the heat was of almost tropical intensity. The mosquitoes swarmed into the open, flat-bottomed boat and dropped into her *ribabou* soup. At night she was bitten by sand flies so small that no netting could keep them out.

In administering to his diocese, her husband rode a circuit of three thousand miles. Charlotte put it graphically in a letter: "The length of travel in this country may be compared to a voyage in a canal barge down the Rhine and Danube from England to Turkey. If all the populations between London and Constantinople were to disappear except for a few tents of Indians or a gypsy encampment, and if all the cities and towns were to be obliterated except for a few log huts, that would be a measure of this wasteland."

Upon arriving at Fort Simpson, at the juncture of the Mackenzie and Liard Rivers, Charlotte had to adapt herself immediately to conditions that were unlike anything she had ever known. Her diet consisted almost entirely of tough moose meat. It tasted like shoe leather, and she broke most of her teeth on it. The weather which had been so hot on her arrival changed suddenly to bitter cold. The glare of the sun on the snow was painful to her eyes. "I have to draw down the blinds in the sitting room as we used to do in Naples in the summer days."

And when the snow and ice melted, the roads were so

deeply rutted that when she traveled, she was bounced almost to the ceiling of the wagon.

However, despite her personal discomfort, she got along excellently with the Indians who lived in the neighborhood of Fort Simpson. They were demonstratively fond of their *Yalti Betzani*—the "bishop's wife." Charlotte ran a school for the children; she played the harmonium in church. During the service, a small Indian lad, "Mission Ned," stood by to turn the pages of music, while at her back a chorus of Indian girls sang the hymns.

Charlotte transformed her first Christmas in the Northwest into a heartening experience for the Indians. They had never before seen a Christmas tree. She decorated one with the few resources available, and placed under it toys of her own making—woolly lambs, charmingly painted dolls, ingeniously carved marionettes, drums and aprons, sweaters and leggings. She gave a special Yuletide dinner for Indian wives, who, after cramming their bellies with all the food they could eat, lit up their pipes and smoked blissfully between belches. The holiday was celebrated in weather 34 degrees below zero.

When, after several seasons, it was decided by the Mission Board to move the bishop's headquarters from Fort Simpson to Athabasca, five hundred miles to the south, Charlotte prepared for the arduous journey without complaint. The mission party embarked down the Mackenzie River in open boats navigated by oar and sail, and occasionally towed by men who walked along the banks with ropes. The boats were filled with fox, lynx, and mink skins to be distributed among the Indians at Athabasca. The party ran into furious thunderstorms and had to seek shelter under the oilcloths brought along to protect the furs.

At Athabasca, a settlement surrounded by mountains, Charlotte ran the mission by herself for weeks and even months at a time, while her husband traveled to his outposts. "In my loneliness I talk a great deal to the grand old mountains, and they say much to me."

Despite periods of sizzling heat, the hills and valleys remained packed with ice. The moon shone with an incomparable brilliance. The heavens were painted in splendid colors. Sometimes the aurora borealis was a cool sea-green, sometimes it was vermilion frayed with mist at the edges. Beginning in May, the nights ceased altogether; the sun shone until ten o'clock in the evening, and then the world was flushed with twilight until dawn. In the bloom of evening, the geraniums, violets, and gooseberry bushes took on colors Charlotte had never seen before.

In her dealings with the Indian children, Charlotte employed the utmost tact. Schooling was irksome to an Indian boy. When he caught sight of his father going hunting, a hunger for freedom seized him, and he slipped out of the classroom to follow his parent. The girls, too, looked upon the closed door with resentment. But the missionary was a born teacher, and her pupils eventually became devoted to her.

Charlotte encountered whims on the part of the adults as well as the young. A squaw sent a message to one of the mission help: "Tell the big minister's wife that my husband killed a beaver, and I will give it to her for that petticoat she had on the other day. And if she will be good to me, I will be faithful to her all the winter, and when I get a bear

or beaver and maybe grease, I will always give her some."
(The Indian woman received the petticoat.)

Life in the Canadian Northwest was dangerous. When
Charlotte was fifty-six, an uprising of Indians and half-
breeds broke out along the Saskatchewan Valley. Resentment over the penetration of the white men into Canada,
fear that their lands would be snatched up and that the
buffalo, their chief source of food, would be exterminated
by these settlers, were the chief reasons for the rebellion.
The entire countryside was terrorized. Supplies for the mission areas were cut off and some of the bishop's outposts
were attacked. The Northwest Mounted Police and Canadian militia finally put down the rebellion after hard fighting at Fish Creek and Cut Knife Creek. But meanwhile
there had been much unnecessary suffering.

Like so many other missionaries who have exposed themselves to a harsh environment, Charlotte was physically frail.
Yet she continued to live among the Indians in temperatures
that shot down to 50 below and climbed to almost tropical
levels. She traveled down ice-locked rivers, slept in tents, ate
unpalatable food, rode by wagon over rocky roads. From
time to time her health broke, and on three occasions the
bishop sent her to England for a rest to protect her from the
excessive demands she made on herself. During one of her
absences, he wrote to her: "I tell the Indians and everyone
else that I have sent you home against your will. I told them
that Christ died for them long ago and that one martyrdom
is enough. There is no occasion for you to die for them as
well, however willing you might be."

Nevertheless, at the first opportunity, Charlotte returned
to her husband. On her third voyage back from England,

she met with a misadventure that would have tried the courage of a woman many years younger. The bishop had moved his headquarters to Forty Mile Creek, a settlement on the bank of the Yukon River between the Canadian Rockies and Alaska. As the steamer on which she was a passenger proceeded up the Yukon River, the waters receded to a dangerously low level at Fort Yukon in United States territory.

The captain assembled the passengers and announced, "Our way is blocked by a sand bar below Circle City. We cannot proceed further. You will either have to return with me to port or leave the ship here at Fort Yukon."

Estimating that she would not be able to join her husband until the spring, Charlotte debarked at Fort Yukon, utterly depressed. She reconciled herself to spending the winter months icebound and alone.

But surprising events had been taking place in this region, and they were destined to provide her with one of the most physically strenuous winters she had ever known. The year before in the fall of 1896, gold had been discovered in the Klondike. When word reached the United States, it created a furor. The country was then in the midst of a depression.

At the cry "Gold!" farmers put aside their plows, factory workers abandoned their jobs, tellers left their banks, saloon keepers quit their bars to grab a boat for the Klondike. Burglars put away their tools and decided to strike it even richer legally; debtors seized the opportunity to wipe out their debts at a stroke; streetwalkers bought a ticket to the Klondike and followed the men; hoboes, rich men, playboys, beggars, mothers with young babies rushed off to Alaska. More than fifty thousand people poured money into mining equipment weighing two and three thousand pounds, every bit of which they had to carry with them, in some cases several thousand miles.

People who had not yet lost their sanity warned their relatives and friends that they were rushing headlong into a territory noted for the severity of its winters. Most of the bush-league miners had had no experience in outdoor living. But the rush North continued.

The two chief ports of arrival in Alaska were Dyea and Skagway, north of Sitka. From both, winding mountain trails led into Canada and the Klondike gold creeks. All summer a procession of steamers arrived at these ports. Passengers, in their haste to be among the first ashore, dumped their luggage into scows, rafts, and barges and swam to the dock. High tides washed away many of the provisions, leaving the owners impoverished.

The "new frontier" was dominated by underworld characters, one of the most notorious of which was "Soapy" Smith, a tall, dignified looking confidence man who ran Skagway with a six-shooter and a squad of killers. He was on hand to greet the arrivals with a shell game at the dock. Many of the newcomers were lured into his game and swindled of their savings.

On the Fourth of July, "Soapy," in the role of Skagway's "first citizen," led a patriotic parade through town. In his top hat and trim Van Dyke beard, he looked like a statesman out of an American history primer. But a few days later he put a bullet through a townsman who had organized a meeting to wipe out his reign of terror. As the citizen toppled to his knees, he pressed the trigger of his own pistol. "Soapy"

Smith's eyes went cold as a flounder's, and his fifty-cent cigar fell from his lifeless lips.

The chief route by which the emigrants passed into the Klondike was over Chilkoot Mountain Pass on the Alaskan-Canadian border. This became a cemetery of broken hopes. Hordes of gold seekers hired mules, steers, horses, goats—anything on four legs—to transport them and their equipment up the thirty-five-hundred-foot heights of snow and ice. Some even tried to make it pushing bicycles with packs slung over the seat. Rains turned the lower trail into a quagmire. Hundreds of animals were injured and abandoned on the spot; others, when they struggled to the summit, were so exhausted as to be useless. And men, made heartless by a craving for gold, pushed them over the precipice and continued the descent unencumbered, deserting equipment necessary for survival in the Northland.

Blizzards trapped swarms of climbers on both slopes of the pass. Hundreds were buried alive in an avalanche of snow. Those who survived hauled themselves to the shores of a lake on the Canadian side of the pass. There they pitched tents and slept the sleep of exhaustion. When they recovered their energy, they chopped down trees and assembled clumsy craft of all shapes and sizes to take them down the Yukon River, past the dangerous White Horse Rapids, to their goal—Dawson City.

Only one out of five of these amateur miners—"Cheechakos," they were called—who had started out so determinedly reached the gold reefs. All the way from Dyea and Skagway to Dawson City, notched trees, crosses, and old tin cans marked the graves of those who had died on the way.

When Charlotte Bompas arrived at Fort Yukon, the countryside buzzed with news, rumors, and gossip about the incredible doings at Dawson City and at Lousetown, a settlement a few miles down the river.

"People have gone plumb crazy in those places, Ma'am," one party who had just returned from the boom town told Charlotte. "Think of it! They're paying sixty dollars a month to real-estate sharks to live in one-room shacks shot through with cracks in the roofs and walls. And they're using whisky bottles for windows!"

And another eyewitness reported, "There's so much money out there, fathers are giving their children gold nuggets instead of nickels to buy a piece of candy with!"

Friends of Charlotte's had established a mission in Dawson City long before it had turned into a mining town. Charlotte had a premonition; she felt that somehow she could be of service in this boom town, and she decided to pay it a visit. She traveled by wagon, and upon entering Dawson City discovered that the people at Fort Yukon had not exaggerated conditions.

Thousands of miners—from Africa, Australia, Norway, Finland, Syria, as well as the United States—paraded along freshly laid out streets fringed with log cabins from which stovepipes protruded at rakish angles. Groceries and supplies were stored on platforms built on stilts ten feet high, beyond reach of the prowling wolf dogs. In the crowded dance halls, "professors" pounded the piano while sweaty, foul-smelling "sourdoughs" danced with girls and slipped gold nuggets down their backs.

Everywhere Charlotte turned, there seemed to be gold dust. Men and women carried it around in little moosehide

sacks—"pokes." The pokes flaunted by females were orna-
mented with beads. In each of the fifteen thriving saloons,
after a round of drinks, men shot their pokes down the bar.
The cashier weighed out the correct amount on scales that
gleamed garishly above counters covered with rich red
carpetry. In the weighing, a good deal of the dust slipped
onto the sawdust floor, and the sweepers who cleaned up
each night after closing collected a fortune.

"A man's got to pay for that job," a grinning sourdough
told Charlotte. "Why, one fellow cleaned up forty thousand
dollars in leavings this summer!"

And she heard about a miner who fell in love with a
dance-hall girl. "I will marry you," she told him, "if you pay
me my weight in dust." The infatuated sourdough promptly
called for scales and in front of the cheering patrons of a
saloon weighed out fifty thousand dollars.

Certain scenes moved the missionary deeply—evidence
that these adventurers hadn't completely severed their ties
to home. When the mail arrived from the States, the crowds
around the post office were so great that men stood in line
for two and three days to receive their letters. Charlotte
met several miners who paid fancy sums for a position close
to the mail booth, and one fellow who hired a substitute
for fifty dollars to hold his place while he grabbed a bite to
eat and a few hours' sleep.

Newspapers, at first, were scarce. When one new arrival
brought a newspaper from the States, a resident purchased
it from him for one hundred and seventy dollars. Then he
placed posters all over town announcing that he would hold
a public reading of it. He charged a dollar admission and

filled a hall five times, reading every news item from first page to last.

This was a heartbreak city for hundreds. Many a man, on reaching the gold fields after intense suffering, set up his windlass and sifted through tons of gravel without realizing anything for his efforts. Yet a neighboring claim might yield a fortune.

The physical labor involved in placer mining frightened away many a "cheechako" who had come North under the impression that he could pluck gold as easily as daisies in the fields back home. The ground of the Klondike beneath a depth of five feet was frozen all year round. For winter mining, the surface had to be stripped of the frozen tundra, and even during the summer, it was necessary to dig pits and build fires to burn in them all night. Each morning the sourdough would dredge the few inches of gravel that had been thawed out by the fire. The ore was then separated by sluicing or panning. Sometimes it took weeks to reach pay dirt.

One young man who came North, however, "struck gold" in a highly individual manner. Arriving too late to profit from the diggings, twenty-one-year-old Jack London collected the characters and theme for a series of stories that were to make him famous.

Charlotte Bompas visited the sourdoughs and their families in their rickety cabins, not only in Dawson, but in settlements along the entire Klondike Valley. She tried in her quiet way to eliminate the rougher edges from their environment. She held classes for the children, knitted sweaters for new babies. To men discouraged by worthless claims, or remorseful at having abandoned their wives and good jobs in the States, she contributed solace and advice.

With the coming of winter, Charlotte heard alarming reports from tradespeople. The migration had taken place in such an impulsive, disorderly fashion that not enough provisions had been put in to provide for the winter. "I don't know what we'll do until spring," one grocer told Charlotte. "Our boom towns may yet turn into faminevilles."

"But how have you been caught short like this?" she exclaimed. "Can't you get provisions by ship from the States?"

The grocer shrugged his shoulders. "Several supply vessels on their way up-river have been blocked by sand banks since early this fall. The river is rising now, but it will soon be frozen solid with ice."

As the first real cold gripped the air, word went around that a vessel loaded with supplies had managed to get through the sand bars and was speeding to make port before the river froze solid.

The Klondike was tense with excitement. Food was on the way to tide seven thousand men, women, and children through the winter! Everything depended on the arrival of this steamer. Daily, miners and their families scanned the river as the thermometer dropped ominously and more and more packs of ice floated past Dawson and Fort Yukon. Would the vessel get through?

And then late one afternoon, after Charlotte had dismissed her pupils and had settled down to her sewing, there was a sudden commotion in the streets. The steamer had been sighted. Charlotte rushed down to the river bank. As a crowd of sourdoughs watched anxiously, the steamer docked. The captain stepped ashore and was greeted by a committee of miners.

A few minutes later, the leader of the welcoming committee mounted a platform of hastily piled-up boxes and faced the crowd. He was white-lipped. "Folks," he said, "I have a disappointment for you. There has been some misunderstanding of our needs here. This boat hasn't brought food. It is packed from stem to stern with barrels of whisky!"

This was the final blow. Merchants in the States, eager for a quick profit and unaware of famine conditions up north, had estimated that what the Klondike needed more than anything else was a shipload of barleycorn!

Anger mounted in the stunned crowd. Voices roared out, "Lynch the captain! String him up!"

A rush toward the skipper was stemmed by Royal Canadian Mounted Police who had been dispatched by the government to keep order in the Klondike.

Charlotte returned to her dwelling sorrowful and apprehensive. She felt as if she were living through an episode that might have come out of the Bible, a terrible parable illustrating in terms of human suffering the irony of man's search for riches.

In the weeks that immediately followed, the prices of the meager food supplies left soared to dizzy heights. One miner who had hoarded a dozen eggs sold them for two hundred and fifty dollars apiece. A plate of bacon and beans in a restaurant cost ten dollars. A cucumber cost five dollars. Milk sold for thirty dollars a gallon. A gallon of kerosene cost fifty dollars. Soon these provisions were unavailable at any price.

Miners went from shack to shack with bags of gold dust trying to buy food. They were turned away. Who wanted more gold? Men with fifty thousand dollars in their pokes crawled along the gold creeks starving to death. Prolonged undernourishment and frigid temperatures brought on epidemics. Teeth fell out from scurvy. Pneumonia was prevalent. Daily the deaths mounted.

In the crisis, the white-haired lady of sixty-seven became a tower of strength to the miners. She was one of the few people in the Klondike who had had extensive experience in weathering the severe living conditions of the North. She showed the women how to prepare meals out of scraps. She conducted sewing schools which turned out clothes for the destitute. She nursed the sick. Unwell herself, the burden of her responsibilities wore her down. Not long afterwards, she was to write, doubtless with this tragic winter in mind, "I am encumbered with the weight of years and . . . by infirmities which have beset me of late. I would never have stepped into this country for any other object but to walk humbly with our God."

During the height of the epidemic, she made the rounds of the sick for miles along the valley, taking long trips over the frozen tundra in a dog sled with a robe wrapped around her, suffering severe joltings on the ice hummocks. It was so bitterly cold that a man walking along the street could be suffering from a frost-bitten nose without being aware of it unless someone called it to his attention. Charlotte's blankets at night were fringed with icicles caused by her frozen breath. The lamps in her schoolroom refused to burn because the oil had jelled. "Can you imagine," she wrote, "the cold of the handle of a kettle on the fire being so intense that one cannot touch it, while the water in kettle itself is boiling?"

The miners who were well enough to get about came to the mission church and prayed for the end of the winter to come. A few brought wives wrapped in blankets and little ones toddling along in rabbit skins. Somehow, Charlotte's numb fingers managed to pick out hymns on the harmonium.

To the children she related a story: "There was One who once lived in a world that was as fond of quick, easy riches as it is today. And He said to men in their folly, 'Lay not up for yourselves treasures upon earth, where moth and rust doth corrupt. . . . But lay up for yourselves treasures in heaven.' "

And the children asked her, "Where is this man now? Does he know of the Klondike? Will he help us through the cold?"

"Of course," Charlotte answered. "He is stationed wherever there are gold reefs threatening to wreck men on their voyage to Him."

When that terrible winter came to an end, many a miner returned to the United States a sadder and wiser man. But human nature remained the same. For every man who went home, a new adventurer set out for the North with the spring. Gold had been discovered in still other areas of the Yukon Valley, and a new parade of fortune-seekers arrived —better prepared, fortunately, than the first.

As soon as it was possible to continue on her way, Charlotte Bompas joined her husband at Forty Mile Creek. This was in the heart of other gold fields. Here a typical boom town had sprung up, replete with trading posts, billiard rooms, dance halls, and saloons. So Charlotte continued her mission among the miners, and her name became a byword throughout the Yukon wherever these blunt, restless men gathered. "She is an angel of mercy," they agreed.

One Christmas Day a deputation of miners called on her. They handed her a gleaming nugget of gold. "We present this to you, Mrs. Bompas, in recognition of your being the very first white woman who has ever wintered this far north in the Yukon. You are the First Lady in the region—and in our hearts."

On her seventy-first birthday, Charlotte wrote a letter that indicated the price she was paying for refusing to retire. "I was recently seized with pneumonia, followed by bronchitis. I suffered terribly, had bags of ice all around my body. . . . I have fresh milk provided for me every day now, and new laid eggs—the first time for twenty-seven years in the North that I have had such luxuries."

Yet despite her age and illness, she accompanied her husband on a move to a new mission site when circumstances made a change desirable. At Caribou Crossing just northeast of Chilkoot Pass, where large numbers of miners were congregating, as well as many Indian families, the bishop and his wife took over an old roadside tavern whose floors were strewn with empty whisky bottles. The air within still reeked of alcohol and tobacco. It required several days to clean the floor alone, scrubbing repeatedly with soap and soda. Then they had to clear the rooms of the mice and squirrels in the rafters.

The bishop and two Indian boys hauled timber to a nearby sawmill and fashioned beds, a dining table, and benches. For weatherproofing, the bishop lined the walls with a coarse, strong calico and a covering of thick red paint. Before he had finished, winter was upon them. The cold was so severe that while he was in the process of papering the walls of the schoolroom, the paste froze solid before it could dry.

In this magnificent twilight of their life together, the elderly couple were visited by a fellow missionary who afterwards wrote of the conditions under which they lived. "Their house is built of logs on the sand. The flooring boards are half an inch apart, and so shrunken that it would be easy to rip them up. . . . And the roof! It is papered across the battens. Everything is as crude as indifference to creature comfort can make it, excepting the books, which are numerous, up to date, and as choice as any two excellent scholars could wish."

Charlotte and her husband continued to serve with a compassion as strong as ever. In her moments of relaxation, she read again and again an edition of Dante's poetry that she had brought to Canada thirty years before and had carried with her on all her trips. And the tall, white-bearded old bishop, in his spare hours, studied his books in Syriac and Hebrew.

In his seventy-second year, the bishop began to fail rapidly. He suffered an attack of scurvy and lost all sense of taste and smell. Then one afternoon, while sitting at his writing table, he slumped forward. His labors in the Arctic were over. He was buried among the Indians, to whom he had devoted forty years of life, in their native cemetery a half mile from the mission. "It was all so strange and bewildering," wrote his widow. "I seemed turned to stone."

Other, younger people now conducted the mission at Caribou. Nevertheless, Charlotte remained in Canada, living with her nieces, raising funds for the mission, following its every affair until she passed away a few weeks before her eighty-seventh birthday.

But along the banks of the Yukon River, where half a century ago an army of adventurers gambled to strike a fortune, they still tell the story of this remarkable woman whom many a sourdough learned to value far more than his diggings, who proved that the truly great bonanza is to be found in the golden deed.

2

Saint among the Lepers

FATHER DAMIEN

(Joseph de Veuster)

◇◇◇◇◇◇◇◇◇◇◇◇◇◇◇◇◇◇◇◇◇◇◇◇◇◇◇◇◇◇◇◇◇◇◇◇◇◇

THE CARPENTER had driven in the final wedge of the main hatch battens, the decks had been holystoned, the windlass oiled, the longshoremen had hoisted the last supplies over the bulwarks. The ship was ready to sail from the port of Bremerhaven in the North Sea. Seamen of a dozen different nationalities, sweat pouring down their leathery faces, unfurled the clouds of canvas as they chanted the traditional sea ditty *Whisky for my Johnny.*

On the lee, a group of missionaries stood huddled in their broad-brimmed hats and black cassocks, discussing their new assignment. One of the party remained apart, gazing in fascination at the sea. He was a young man with the broad, placid features of a peasant. His hands were large and calloused.

"Good morning, Father Damien. I gather you have never been to sea before."

The captain of the ship was making the rounds. He

22

addressed the missionary in French with a thick German accent.

The other nodded. His brown eyes, framed in silver-rimmed spectacles, were bold, speculative. He had the frank smile of a man who enjoyed life to the fullest.

"No, Captain. I was brought up in a Flemish village. In twenty-three years the closest I've ever come to traveling on water has been ice skating on the River Lak."

The captain smiled. "Well, you'll see plenty of water the next five months. Nineteen thousand miles of it between here and Honolulu! And all that comes with it as well—the gales off Cape Horn, the doldrums in the Pacific. And then the Islands. Life out there will be quite different from what you've known in Belgium."

The missionary nodded his head. "Yes, it will be as different as night from day."

The captain regarded the young man keenly. "Father, in my line of work one gets to know human nature pretty thoroughly. I can understand how a man can cheat, fall in love, even give his life for another on the battlefield. But what is beyond me—and forgive me for saying it—is why a young man will leave his home and travel nineteen thousand miles to live on an island with a bunch of half-civilized Kanakas!"

The conversation was interrupted by a summons from the first mate who wished to consult with the skipper on an urgent matter.

"Well, Father, the best of luck to you at any rate," concluded the captain. He walked on.

The trip to the Hawaiian Islands in this year of 1863 took at least five months. It was a risky one, especially when rounding Cape Horn. As the ship approached these waters, the sailors filled the open seams on deck with oakum and lashed down everything movable.

One morning when Damien emerged from the hold, he observed through a telescope the rocky slopes of Tierra del Fuego packed with snow. Before the day was over, the *pampero* had struck in force. The heavy green sky opened in wounds of lightning. The wind blew the mizzen to shreds. Seas sixty to seventy feet high wrenched the weather railing from its stanchions.

For nine days the vessel struggled blindly off the Horn. And hardly had the stormy weather subsided than the passengers were exposed to the tropical sun. The ship drifted like a drowsy fish gasping for air. The heat sent the tar spilling from the seams, leaving scars across the deck. But amid the calm, the flying fish sported unconcernedly, and schools of mullet threaded the sea with flashes of silver.

During the trip, the young missionary served as sacristan at Mass. When the supply of altar breads ran out, he consulted the steward and together they experimented with flour until a suitable supply of wafers was baked.

Occasionally, as Damien aired himself on deck, he encountered Captain Geerkin, the ship's master, who conversed with him in his characteristically bluff fashion. One evening as they stood together watching the flames of phosphorus flicker beneath the surface of the sea, the captain spoke of the Islands.

"These Kanakas have little cause to love the white man, Father. When Captain Cook discovered the Islands, there were five hundred thousand natives living on them. Today there are fewer than fifty thousand. In less than a hundred years, nine-tenths of the population has been destroyed by syphilis, consumption, and other germs introduced by the whites. The Kanakas had never led the kind of life to build up any resistance to disease. Just about every second native has a dry, pulverizing cough. It makes fine music against the surf at Waikiki."

"Perhaps," Damien answered, "some of us can make amends for this." His face held a look of determination.

"Let me tell you something," the young missionary said. "My father wanted me to be a merchant. I spent several months preparing for this career."

The captain regarded him with interest. "What made you change your mind?"

"One morning I attended a meeting of the Redemptorist Fathers in Compte-le-Main. I realized at once that I was born to be a salesman of a different kind. I joined the Order of the Sacred Heart. It was a terrible disappointment to my father. He had already given his oldest son, Auguste, to the Church. But my mother understood. Before I left on this voyage, I met her before the shrine of Our Lady of Montagu. It was there we said goodbye, before the Mother who has survived so much sorrow. I haven't prepared for the trip lightheartedly, Captain. I do not expect the future to be altogether a pleasant one. I am prepared to meet with anything on the Islands."

Within a week following this conversation, the first plover alighted on deck, indicating the nearness of land. The snow-veiled summit of Mauna Kea on the Island of Hawaii sparkled amid the thin, pink clouds of sunrise. Within a short while the ship reached Oahu, and pushing through the channel in the foamy white reef, rode into Honolulu harbor, anchoring among sugar schooners and men-of-war.

Damien, accustomed to the monotonous stretches of Flemish plain, to the drab dress of peasant farmers, was astonished at the world he entered. Along streets fringed with algarroba, Mexican creepers, and a variety of other trees transplanted from all parts of the tropics, Kanakas and half-breeds from distant South Sea islands mingled with New Bedford whalers and Chinese merchants from Hong Kong. He was fascinated by the coral houses of the white inhabitants and their lawns that sparkled with heliotrope and passion flowers. He was intrigued with the swarms of cats that followed the Hawaiian women as they shuffled barefoot in their halukas or rode ponies to the shops. What simple, passionate people these natives were; and how they loved flowers! He saw women who looked to be ninety wearing wreaths of blue blossoms in their hair.

Daily, he walked the streets of Honolulu, orienting himself to the temper of its inhabitants. He poked his head into the garishly illuminated shops of Chinese merchants, observed the cosmopolitan character of the diners in the eating places along Nuana Street, Honolulu's Great White Way. He visited the Kanaka quarters, watching the natives dance the quadrille, race their unshod fillies, paddle their outriggers through the surf, haul in mullets in their palm-leaf fibre nets.

And while he took the measure of this colorful, indolent city, Damien reminded himself that but for an accident he wouldn't be here. Only months before, he had been a novitiate at the Monastery of the Sacred Heart in Louvain. His brother Auguste, a fellow member and an ordained priest, had been selected to go with nine other missionaries to the Hawaiian Islands. But an epidemic of typhus broke out in Louvain, and Auguste had caught the disease while administering the Last Rites to the dying. Although he recovered, a long sea voyage for him was out of the question.

Taking advantage of the vacancy, Damien wrote a letter to the Superior-General in Paris, asking to be sent in his brother's place. For a novitiate to communicate with the top official of his order was indeed presumptuous. He awaited the reply with anxiety.

One morning while he sat at breakfast in the refectory, his immediate superior came up to him and said, "You did a very foolish thing in writing to Paris over my head. You are not even ordained. However, your letter has been received favorably. You are to go in place of your brother."

And now, following his arrival in Honolulu, Damien spent two months preparing for his ordination. On the eve of Whitsunday, he was made a priest. The following day he conducted his first Mass in the cathedral in Honolulu. Shortly afterwards, Monseigneur Maigret, the Vicar Apostolic of the Islands, summoned his twenty-four-year-old priest. "Father Damien, for your first assignment I am sending you to Puna, on the Island of Maui. You will be the only white man in your community."

Monseigneur Maigret was of the breed of pioneers. Men like him ploughed through jungles as eagerly as they said Mass. He looked at the young missionary appraisingly. "I don't know what's in store for you on Puna. There hasn't been a priest there for seven years. However, I give you my blessing."

There were other young priests to be sent to parishes as

well, and Maigret accompanied the party of missionaries on an island steamer, saying goodbye to each personally at his destination.

Puna, in the neighborhood of an active volcano, was paved in some areas with lava, hardened and brittle, and sizzling hot only eight inches beneath the foot. Father Damien traveled three days before reaching the outlying villages in the district.

The chapels he constructed in each village were crude affairs. Some were merely straw huts with entrances less than four feet high. There was no glass available for windows, and frequently he could hardly keep the candles lit for the wind. His physical strength was his chief source of influence with the natives. They were impressed when he put his muscles to the ax, cut down trees, and hauled heavy loads that required the strength of three Hawaiians.

To reach his various congregations, he hewed his way through the jungle, and climbed hills on which the lava had been known suddenly to split into enormous cracks. He crossed flooded streams, trekked along the edges of the active crater where a sudden shift of wind poured sulphur fumes into his lungs and killed the birds around him. He traveled with an altar stone and other furnishings for the Mass strapped to his back. Sometimes he went by horseback and sometimes he paddled along rivers in a hollowed-out tree trunk.

For four years he ministered to Puna. When word came to him that a fellow missionary who had been assigned to the adjacent community of Kohala, an area even larger than his own, was suffering poor health, Damien persuaded Monseigneur Maigret to allow him to exchange parishes. It took him six weeks to cover his new territory. On one occasion he started out for a settlement in his homemade canoe, but it capsized in a storm. He swam ashore, changed his clothes, and proceeded on horseback by an alternate route over the mountains. When the slopes grew sheer, he left his horse with natives and crawled on his hands and knees. He arrived at his destination in time to baptize a dying child.

Most of the natives called Father Damien *Kamiano*—"comrade." But on occasion his life was threatened by groups who held secret voodoo rites at which they plotted his assassination. One evening he was awakened by the beating of drums. He dressed and followed the sound, arriving at the entrance of a burial cave. Within, beneath flaming torches, a group of men were huddled about an aged soothsayer who was mumbling incantations over a vessel holding the blood of a dog whose throat he had slashed. When he saw Father Damien, the old voodooist picked up a wooden doll dressed to represent a priest in his cassock. He shook his fist and cursed it.

The entire company had been stirred to a frenzy against Damien. But without hesitating the priest seized the doll and slowly ripped it to pieces. Then to demonstrate unmistakably that no harm could come to him, no matter how thoroughly he insulted the voodoo spirits, he trampled the wooden face with his heel and tossed the pieces into a corner.

This was a deft stroke of psychology. The natives turned upon the voodoo doctor in derision. And from that time on Damien encountered no trouble from this quarter.

One evening after the priest had been at Kohala four

years an island steamer arrived bringing four constables and a physician on duty with the government. (The Hawaiian Islands at this period were under the native rule of King Kamehameha V.) The sergeant of the constabulary nailed a poster to a tree near Father Damien's church. The natives crowded around to read it. It was written in English—a language American missionaries had taught the Islanders.

ALL LEPERS ARE REQUIRED TO REPORT THEMSELVES TO THE GOVERNMENT HEALTH AUTHORITIES WITHIN FOURTEEN DAYS FROM THIS DATE FOR INSPECTION AND FINAL BANISHMENT TO MOLOKAI.

The physician spoke to Damien in his hut. "The police have received orders to track down all natives known or suspected to have leprosy, Father. The disease has gotten out of hand. The people of Honolulu have become so fearful they have compelled the government to buy land on Molokai to establish a leper colony. But a number of the diseased are roaming the forests, or hiding out in caves. We have just launched a drive throughout the Islands to enforce the quarantine laws. And we expect your full cooperation."

A few days later, the police threw a dragnet over Kohala, enlisting patrols of natives to aid in the hunt. Within the next few weeks, suspected parties were herded into the main village from remote areas. Whole families accompanied the proscribed son, daughter, or parent. They spread their mats before Father Damien's church and huddled together, wailing, "*Aui, aui.*" They didn't understand why they shouldn't be permitted to nurse their loved ones at home for the few months or years of life that remained to them. They dreaded the banishment to Molokai.

One morning Damien heard news that a native from his village, refusing to surrender his leper wife to the authorities, had seized a gun and taken his wife to the hills where for three days he had held the constabulary at bay. Plans were drawn up for an assault to blast the couple from their position. Father Damien asked the police for permission to make the climb himself. He hoped to be able to persuade the couple to surrender peacefully.

He was guided by the natives through miles of dense vegetation, past huge trees coiled with creepers and stag's-horn moss. Finally the party reached a sharply rising slope, green with ferns and koa trees and scarred by huge volcanic ridges of lava turned yellow from pools of sulphur. Somewhere on the frowning pali lay the Kanaka with his panic-stricken wife. And a rifle was cocked to shoot anyone who attempted the climb.

Gambling on the hope that Nicua, the husband, would recognize him and withhold his fire, Father Damien openly began the ascent. The sudden "ping" of a bullet, followed by a spiraling of dust a few yards to one side, sent him sprawling on his stomach. However, in a few moments he was on his feet again.

"Nicua," he called. "It is I, Kamiano. See, I am unarmed. I am coming to help you."

Despite the warning shouts of the police below, Father Damien continued the ascent without taking cover, ledge by ledge over the ropy rocks of lava. No more shots were fired. When he had reached a point forty yards or so from the top of the pali, a face suddenly emerged from an opening between two boulders just above him. The eyes were friendly and reassuring. The muzzle of a rifle was withdrawn. In a few moments Father Damien stood beside Nicua and his wife. They were huddled in each other's arms, their rifle stacked against the rocks. The woman was young. As yet she showed none of the effects of the disease.

The priest pleaded with the couple to follow him back to the village. He warned them that it would be suicide to continue to shoot it out with the police. But Nicua shook his head. They would never send his woman to Molokai. He'd rather she died on the mountainside with him.

For hours Damien talked to them. He told them that it was best for the health of the community, for Nicua's own health, that his wife be segregated. Perhaps a cure would be found by the doctors for the disease, and Danai would be returned to him.

Finally Nicua said to him with tears in his eyes, "I will bring Danai back to the village, Kamiano, but only if you will promise me that I can go with her to Molokai."

Father Damien put his arm around the native's shoulder. "They don't send well men there, Nicua. You cannot expose yourself to the danger."

"Where Danai goes, I go, Kamiano. And when she passes into final peace, I must be there to close her eyes. I love Danai, and I want to continue to share my bed with her."

The rock-bound greenery of the pali had turned purple in the twilight. One area of the distant sky was crimson in the reflection of the active crater which bubbled and seethed with lava.

"You shall go to Molokai, Nicua," said Father Damien quietly, "if I have any influence at all with the authorities."

The three of them descended the mountainside. Father

Damien made good his promise. The authorities permitted Nicua to accompany his wife on her exile.

Henceforth, the priest's thoughts were never far from the leper colony. He recalled Captain Geerkin's observation that the population had been decimated by diseases imported from the outside. Leprosy had not been known in Hawaii until foreign traders had brought it to her shores. And the more he pondered this, the more the Belgian priest felt a deep, personal guilt for the sins committed by others.

A few months after the lepers were shipped from Kohala, Damien attended the dedication ceremonies of a new church on the island of Maui. Missionaries from all the islands took part in the dedication. And when it was over, Bishop Maigret (he had recently been promoted to the office of Bishop) addressed the company, assessing the results of their missionary efforts. He discussed the islands one by one. When he came to Molokai, his voice saddened.

"The conditions there are almost indescribable. The government wishes to have as little as possible to do with the lepers. They are sent, not as patients, for no doctor or nurse has volunteered to care for them, but as colonists. Can you imagine? Colonists! These people whose limbs are decomposing are expected to farm the land and fend for themselves so that the government will be relieved of the cost of supporting them. Naturally the plan has failed to work. Periodically, the government ships food out by steamer. Those who are still able to walk about steal it from the dying. Most of the diseased die of pneumonia or some other ailment even before the leprosy has run its course.

"Leprosy in certain stages acts as a powerful aphrodisiac. Several lepers have escaped from Molokai and reported scenes of sexual orgies that defy description. Women who are too ill to provide themselves with food and clothing on their own offer themselves to men who will provide these necessities. The more active lepers spend their time distilling and distributing a drink from the ti shrub which is more potent than absinthe. The whole community is intoxicated from one week to the next."

He paused for his words to take effect. Then he added, "If ever an act of kindness were needed today, these lepers certainly have first call on it. It is true that missionaries have gone periodically to the colony for brief stays. However, there is need for a permanent mission out there without delay. According to recent regulations by the Board of Health, short visits will no longer be permitted. The next missionary who goes to Molokai will have to remain there for the rest of his life."

Bishop Maigret regarded his audience with an expression that said plainly, "Although I have the authority to do so, I cannot find the heart to ask any one of you to make this sacrifice."

But four priests were instantly on their feet. All were men in good health; not one was over thirty-five. Each prayed that he would be the one chosen. Then Father Damien, who was one of the four, spoke up.

"My Lord, my three friends have only just arrived. They are new at the work. But I have had nine years of experience working with the natives. I am the logical choice."

And so it was decided. Without ceremony, without oratorical flourish, he was selected to go.

One hour after the decision was made, Father Damien, accompanied by the bishop, took a ship for Honolulu. There he found a steamer about to sail with fifty lepers for the colony on Molokai, fifty miles to the east. The priest and the bishop, who accompanied him to the colony for the final farewell, transferred to the steamer. Before nightfall, they were on their journey.

It was a brilliant evening in May. The two churchmen sat on the upper deck, each absorbed in his own thoughts. Father Damien watched the sea turn to a pale, unearthly green under the moon.

"Unclean! Unclean!" whispered the water as it slapped against the hold of the ship. Since Biblical days this had been men's warning cry at the approach of a leper.

Father Damien's thoughts went back centuries. He pictured the knocking on a door at midnight, the entrance of a priest into the house of a man discovered to be a leper, the sprinkling of holy water, the solemn procession to the church. He visualized the Requiem Mass conducted for the ailing one, who crouched under a black canopy near the altar; the weeping of his family as though he were already a corpse; then the trip to the cemetery. He saw the leper kneeling by a freshly dug grave; the priest throwing a handful of earth over him. He heard the last pronouncement: "Final prayers have been said over you. Your wife's and children's ties to you are dissolved. In the eyes of the law you are already dead. Here is a basket, a cowl, a walking stick with a rattle to warn people of your approach. At your sound men shall make the sign of the cross and drive you away with stones."

Damien pictured in his mind the lazarettos, built by courageous monks several centuries later, when epidemics of leprosy reached grim proportions in Europe. He saw the

faces of the lepers peep through barred holes in the chancel
wall of the churchyard while the Mass was being conducted
within. Through these grottoes they received communion.
The indefatigable labors of the Church were a great factor
in reducing the incidence of the disease in Europe.

As the steamer neared Molokai, the priest and his superior
continued to sit in silence. Once, however, the bishop
glanced at the priest and said, "You know, Father, there is
no act of courage worthy of the name that isn't approached
by a man with a feeling of fear."

Damien nodded and looked into the darkness.

An hour before sunrise, the vessel dropped anchor off
Molokai. The sea pounded against the shore, buffeting the
lifeboat in which the priest and Bishop Maigret were rowed
to land. All lepers who could walk had assembled on the
beach to meet the new arrivals. They stood huddled in the
fitful glare of lanterns. The bishop gave his blessings to
the group.

"Until now, my children, you have been left alone without
steady care. But this shall no longer be. I have brought you
one who will be a father to you. He loves you so much that
for your welfare he does not hesitate to become one of you,
to live and die with you."

Then the bishop boarded the lifeboat and was rowed
back to the steamer, leaving Damien alone with his company.

Molokai was long and shaped like a willow leaf. Once it
had been actively volcanic. And the leper settlements—there
were two of them a few miles apart—were sunk into the huge
crater at the north end. Behind them rose slopes two thousand
feet high, which hemmed the diseased into a virtual prison

whose front bars were the sea. Beyond the pali the vegetation burgeoned in lavish disorder. The spiked flowers of wild coarse ginger grew promiscuously alongside starshaped orange blossoms; the white poppy bloomed beside the gaudy hibiscus. Stubby mesquite, ki, and peach trees crowded one another for breathing space over areas of sunburned plain. The island foliage was growth gone feverish to the point of malignancy—fitting surroundings for the inhabitants.

As daylight arrived, Damien took stock of his new neighbors. Of the two thousand lepers that had originally been sent to Molokai, eight hundred were alive. As he made the rounds, he met lepers in every stage of the disease. The skin of some merely showed loss of color. Others had red splotches that appeared as smears on glossy skin. But many were in a more advanced stage of decomposition. Their skin had bunched together, especially about the forehead and eyes, leaving deep wrinkles in the displaced areas and giving the face a leonine appearance. The flesh was a mass of tubercles. One could not only see but smell these lepers.

He came on lepers whose fingers had dropped off while eating or talking to a friend. In other instances they had become absorbed into the body itself. He met lepers in a still more advanced stage, with ulcerous noses, eyes on the verge of blindness, eyelids and muscles of the face paralyzed, eyelashes and eyebrows missing. Their voices were hoarse due to diseased larynxes. And even these weren't the worse cases. Damien saw lepers whose pores oozed stinking black pus. He met men, women, and children whom the disease had driven insane. Some laughed hysterically; others regarded him with the peaceful stare of idiots. These were the people with whom this priest of thirty-three had thrown in his lot

He had been on Molokai only a few hours when he was called upon to administer Extreme Unction to a dying man. The leper had been converted to Catholicism before he was sent to Molokai, and he had remained faithful even without the guidance of a priest. He lay paralyzed, holding a prayer book in a hand that was a mass of sores.

As Father Damien entered the hut, the odor was so fetid he was forced to rush outside for air to avoid retching. And then he returned to his patient. The rites of the Last Sacrament required that he rub holy oil with his own hands into the tubercles. Calmly and with the feeling that he was merely a spectator, not the participant, he annointed the eyes, then the nose and the ears. When he turned to the feet, he received a shock. They appeared to be moving, although the patient had lost all control over them. Then he realized with horror that the worms were already crawling over the flesh and eating it.

Deaths were too common to warrant any particular observance by those who were living on borrowed time. This latest corpse, as in the case of the previous twelve hundred, was disposed of with the least possible disturbance in the shortest possible time. The body was wrapped in straw and carried on the shoulders of four lepers to a cemetery where the graves were hastily dug ditches, barely adequate to receive the dead.

When Damien had finished reading the burial service and had retired to rest under a pandanus tree, he received another disagreeable surprise. An elderly woman leper approached him with a bowl of *poi,* the native's favorite food,

and invited him to eat. She was certain the young *Kahuna*
must be hungry after the exertions of the morning. He accepted the food prepared by the diseased hands. He realized
that if he showed any revulsion, he would lose his influence
over these people. When he had finished eating and had lit
his pipe for a smoke, a young leper came over and asked,
"*Pule, Kahuna,* may I puff on your pipe?"

The priest handed it to him.

Father Damien's given name was Joseph. His family name
was De Veuster. And it was with prophetic insight that, on
joining the Order of the Sacred Heart, he had taken the
name of St. Damien, the celebrated physician of the fifth
century.

After he recovered from his initial disturbance at conditions on Molokai, he set about to improve them. With a
smattering of knowledge he had picked up from a medical
book, he removed the gangrenous limbs of lepers. Fortunately, no anaesthetic was necessary; the lepers had no
feeling in their diseased extremities. He laid the patients
on a bare plank and applied a knife to the putrid flesh, using
only soap and water as a disinfectant. Daily he changed
bandages and washed sores.

He transformed the burial ground into a relatively re-
spectable place, digging graves at least six feet deep and
building wooden coffins. He made over a thousand of these
himself during his stay on the island.

One of the most serious problems was the lack of an
adequate water supply. The nearest source was a creek
several miles from the settlement, but since four out of five
of the lepers were too ill to walk, they were compelled to
beg for water from their less disabled neighbors, and many

continually suffered from thirst. And there never was enough water to spare for such luxuries as bathing the body, washing sores, cleaning the huts. Father Damien reasoned that there must be mountain streams in the center of the island from which a more adequate water supply could be obtained. He made several exploratory trips and finally discovered a natural reservoir of ice-cold water.

The priest wrote to the Board of Health in Honolulu asking that piping be sent to Molokai. The Board was not receptive to requests involving an expenditure of money for lepers. The idea had been to send them off to die as inexpensively as possible. But Damien stubbornly bombarded the Board with letters until a ship was grudgingly dispatched with the piping.

However, this was only half a victory. No engineers were sent to lay the pipes. Father Damien assembled a few of the less disabled lepers on the beach where the crew was unloading the cargo. The sailors good-naturedly helped to haul the pipes into position with their block-and-tackle equipment. Father Damien drew up the blueprints himself, and he supervised the laying of the water system. Within a few weeks, the mountain water was pouring from faucets within reach of every hut.

Father Damien next petitioned the Board of Health for lumber with which to build new homes for the lepers. The majority were living in flimsy thatched huts, and they suffered dreadfully from the rain and the wind. But the Board of Health refused to spend the necessary money. After several fruitless letters, the priest boarded a vessel for Honolulu to plead his case personally.

When he presented himself at the Board of Health, he

was immediately recognized as the priest who had given the authorities so much trouble and he received the "freeze" treatment. Suddenly every official he asked to see had important conferences to attend to, and could not spare even a few minutes for him. But Father Damien stuck to his guns. He refused to leave his chair in the waiting room until finally, just before closing time, the president of the Board, to get rid of him, summoned him into his office. He told Father Damien that he had been sent to Molokai as a priest, not as a politician. He warned him to stick to the business of prayer, and leave the matter of housing to the government.

And then, rising from his desk, he delivered a final rebuke. "You have violated the quarantine by coming here. No member of the leper settlement is permitted to leave Molokai."

The priest answered quietly, "I am not diseased."

"That makes no difference. You are in contact with lepers. If you leave the island again, you will be thrown into jail!"

For a few moments Father Damien studied this Hawaiian official in the smart blue jacket and sporty flannels, whose ruddy face exuded good health and fine living. Then he replied.

"There isn't a healthy man in Honolulu who tomorrow may not become a leper. This applies to the president of the Board of Health. If the day ever comes, sir, when you are shipped to Molokai, I will labor with all my strength to provide *you* with a decent shelter against the rain."

He paused. "But whether you arrive among us or not, I will continue to speak out until the conscience of the entire world is awakened to the tragic conditions on Molokai."

Nature itself settled the issue of housing. Shortly after

Father Damien's return to the colony, a wind of hurricane proportions swept over the island and destroyed practically all the shelters. The authorities were compelled to take action. In addition to government aid, money was raised by private subscription and a shipload of tools, shingles, timber for flooring, and other construction material arrived in Molokai. An entirely new community of neat white cottages, raised on trestles above the damp ground, came into existence.

Father Damien supervised the building of the houses. He cleared land for gardens, and encouraged the stronger lepers to plant vegetables and flowers for themselves and for their weaker neighbors. Gradually the settlement acquired aspects of beauty, and its inhabitants regained some of the joys of the living.

Father Damien continued to wrest concessions from the Board of Health. Each new request was resisted stoutly, then reluctantly acceded to. He obtained larger food rations for the colony and of better quality. Each leper was allotted five pounds of fresh beef, *poi*, and biscuits weekly. He obtained medical supplies, built a hospital, and recruited the more physically able lepers as nurses. He continued to act as the doctor. Each leper was given six dollars a year for clothing. A large general store was established at which the colonists could buy canned fruit and other delicacies.

The lepers lived continually under the shadow of death— an event that took place daily in the colony. To cushion for them the fear of dying, Father Damien shrewdly turned funerals into occasions of color and festivity. He organized lepers into rival burial associations, dressing the members in colorful jackets girdled with brilliant sashes. Each group

tried to outdo the other in the verve with which it played
the flutes, thrummed the guitars, and beat the drums as it
escorted the body on its final journey. And each of the
living hoped that he would be given the same bright send-
off. Had not the *Kahuna* convinced them that their affliction
was only temporary, and that they would enter the Kingdom
of Eternal Life enjoying as fine health as other men?

Father Damien provided other diversions. He trained a
choir in community singing. Every clear evening after supper the group gave a concert, presenting Hawaiian love
songs and the music of Mozart and Bach. True, a Bach
chorale sounded rather pathetic coming from a chorus of
diseased larynxes and accompanied on the harmonium by
musicians who had only two fingers. Nevertheless, the concerts were a great success.

Despite his loneliness, twelve years passed quickly for
Father Damien. He had come to Molokai at thirty-three. At
forty-five he was still physically vigorous. His frame had, if
anything, grown even more muscular. He had cultivated a
beard, pitch black except for the graying fringes, which increased the virility of his appearance. His eyes were his only
physical liability. They had grown progressively weaker in
the glare of the tropical sun.

In the course of these years the quarantine on his movements was relaxed. He made occasional trips to see the
bishop in Honolulu, and received infrequent visitors. But
for the most part he remained a voluntary prisoner on the
island. His friends in Honolulu remarked half in jest, half in
earnest that he had long since ceased to look or act like a
white man. He had adopted Kanaka food tastes and physical habits. He had even begun to think like a native. And

as Father Damien, in his forty-fifth year, continued on his daily rounds of the hospital and leper huts, smoking his pipe and reading his breviary by lamplight, he received an indication that he had become one with his people in a way more profound and terrible than anyone had realized.

One Sunday in June he summoned his parishioners to early morning Mass. It was a torrid day. Waves of heat almost suffocated the men, women, and children as they gathered for prayer.

"*Introibo ad altare Dei,*" intoned the priest. He performed the mystic ceremony of the word made flesh, and then he offered communion.

When he finished, his chausable was wringing wet. He advanced toward his congregation to begin the sermon. He gripped the railing. In the past he had always addressed his congregation, "My brethren." Today he said in a matter-of-fact tone, "*We* lepers."

This was his way of informing them that he had contracted their disease. Faces looked at him in astonishment, unbelief, compassion.

"*We* lepers," he repeated, and entered into his sermon.

He had first become aware of his disease a few months before. One morning while shaving, he had upset a kettle of boiling water on his bare foot. He looked down at the scarlet flesh, horrified. He hadn't felt the slightest pain. He knew that insensitivity of the flesh was one of the first symptoms of leprosy.

He said nothing about it, but continued with his work. A few weeks later, a discoloration appeared on his arm, and then another. He dug his nail into the skin, then pierced it with a needle, and finally with the sharp blade of a knife. There was no feeling.

Shortly thereafter, Dr. Arning, a German specialist, arrived at Molokai for a visit. Father Damien met the physician at the beach, but when Arning put out his hand, he refused to shake it. Later, while they were walking to his hut, Father Damien explained to the doctor why he had not taken his hand. Arning gave him a careful physical examination and subjected him to tests. When he finished, he washed his hands slowly in disinfectant and lit a cigarette.

"Father Damien, I'm afraid you've made the right diagnosis. It seems to be leprosy."

The priest took out his pipe, filled it with tobacco, and puffed away. "I can't say the news has exactly shocked me, doctor. I've been expecting it for years."

At first, not to alarm his bishop, Father Damien made no mention of his illness in his reports. But the news reached his superior nevertheless, and he was summoned at once to Honolulu.

"I cannot come," wrote the priest, finally admitting his disease. "There are signs of leprosy on my left cheek and ear, and my eyebrows are about to fall. I shall soon be quite disfigured . . . but I am calm and resigned and very happy in the midst of my people."

Yet the bishop would not be put off. A new treatment involving massages and injections had been developed by a Japanese physician, and the bishop insisted that Father Damien enter the hospital in Honolulu to try it. When he arrived at the hospital, the Franciscan nuns who were on duty as nurses fought to hold back their tears. The Mother Superior swept out, whitewashed, and aired a special room for him; she hung her own crucifix on the wall. Each sister contributed some prized possession, quiltwork, holy pictures, embroidery, a hand-woven rug, to make his surroundings more homey. This was one of the few times in twenty-one years that the priest rested on a comfortable mattress between linen sheets.

But sitting passively for hours during the daily medical bath and lying on his back was more than this man of boundless energy could stand—especially when there was so much yet to be done on Molokai. After two weeks of hospitalization, he reached for his clothes and demanded to be sent back to the colony. When the doctors warned him that his only hope of arresting the disease lay in the continuance of treatments, he retorted, "I would not have my health restored at the price of having to leave Molokai and abandon my work there."

So back he went to the island, where he continued to make his daily rounds of the sick.

For twenty-one years the priest had carried on his work in almost total obscurity. Now that he had become a leper, editors found him sensational copy. The Honolulu papers featured the story of his illness. It was wired all over the globe. Overnight, millions of people became acquainted with him and with the tragedy of the Hawaiian lepers.

Father Damien's father was dead, but his eighty-two-year-old mother still lived. The priest had concealed his illness from her, but reports of it finally reached Tremoloo. The morning after receiving the news, the old lady passed away, clasping a rosary, her eyes upon a photograph of her son.

Now, four good Samaritans, inspired by the Damien story, converged on Molokai from different parts of the world to carry on his work. One was Father Lambert Conrady, who came from Oregon where he had been a missionary to the Indians; another was Father Wendelin Moeller, a member of the order to which Father Damien belonged. The third was a layman, Brother James, a barrel-chested Irishman from Australia; the fourth, another lay brother, Joseph Dutton. He had been an officer in the Union Army during the Civil War. A roisterer with the ladies, he had given up his fast-paced life of hard drinking and amorous intrigues to enter a Trappist monastery under the rule of perpetual silence. But after a brief stay, he left the monastery to seek a life of active service. Molokai presented the ideal opportunity.

In addition to these four men, Mother Marianne and two Franciscan sisters from the Honolulu hospital settled on Molokai. The nuns were quartered away from the settlement, beyond the pali. And the men who assisted Father Damien took every precaution to avoid infection. There was no necessity for these newcomers to expose themselves as dangerously as Father Damien had done when, as the only man on the island for twelve years, he had nursed close to sixteen hundred lepers.

Now at last the conscience of the world had been aroused. And men acted. An Anglican clergyman, H. H. Chapman, raised a fund for Molokai from people of all faiths. A wealthy Honolulu banker donated money to build a children's home in the colony. Now doctors arrived at Molokai with the latest medical equipment. Earlier, in Norway, Armauer Hansen, the scientist, had succeeded in isolating the bacillus of leprosy. And a preparation of Chaulmoogra oil was developed which retarded and in some cases even arrested the disease.

But for Father Damien himself, this came too late.

During the four years of life that remained, he was on his feet all but the final two months. In all weather—enervating hot spells, ravaging rain and squalls, sudden, penetrating cona winds—he continued to visit the huts of lepers. His face had turned black under his broad straw hat. His cassock fitted grotesquely over his stooped, disintegrating frame.

When the British artist, Edward Clifford, paid a two weeks' visit to Molokai, he insisted on painting the priest's portrait. For he saw only the peace that radiated from the diseased flesh. While Clifford worked at his easel, Father Damien stepped quietly behind him and looked at the canvas.

"What an ugly face! I have not seen myself in years. I had no idea the disease had made such progress. We have no demand for looking glasses here, you know."

One eye had already gone blind, and he was rapidly losing sight in the other. The disease had attacked his larynx too, causing him to speak in a whisper. Yet he continued to live cheerfully, carving out wooden dolls for the young girls, boats for the boys. He built articles of furniture which he distributed to needy lepers. He knelt in the sunshine by the peach trees while the Angelus rang. He fed the pigeons that alighted on his shoulder.

He hadn't any inkling of the honors that would be heaped on him after he passed on; of the columns of praise in newspapers, the mass meetings, the subscriptions raised by hospitals in his name for the study of leprosy, the monuments erected to him. He couldn't have foreseen that forty-six years after his passing, his body would be lifted from its island grave, escorted to Belgium to be met by the King himself, and reburied in his native land. Or that the Church would begin the traditional investigation that might eventually raise him to sainthood.

And he could not have foretold the ridiculous attacks that would be made on him in a letter by the Reverend H. H. Hyde, a Honolulu minister, who accused him of being coarse, headstrong, and bigoted, and of having sexual relations with women. No, nor could he have envisaged the classic reply written by Robert Louis Stevenson who chanced to come across Hyde's letter. "The man who tried to do what Damien did, is my father . . . and the father of all who love goodness; and he was your father, too, if God has given you the grace to see it."

The days throbbed with life in the weeks before Father Damien's death. The pali flamed in speckled greens above the coral banks. The priest sat in front of his house from morning until evening, puffing on his pipe and reminiscing. The past had become poignantly alive for him.

"Brother James," he said to his lay assistant, "you would have smiled to see how shiny my mother kept her pots and pans. She hung them so neatly on the wall, always in identical order and with as much reverence as if they were images of the Holy Virgin. I can still see them reflected in the glint of the sun as it spilled on the sandstone floor in that cheerful little kitchen."

And sometimes his thoughts would return to the seminary at Louvain where he had passed his novitiate. *Vos, Vobiscum, Vobis* . . . Night after night he had sat hunched over the Latin grammar, studying the tongue of St. Jerome, St. Augustine, St. Thomas Aquinas. He had not been blessed with a facility for book learning. Only his unconquerable tenacity had seen him through that trying period.

And his thoughts went back to other days, the period, for instance, of his brief sojourn in Paris, just before he sailed for Honolulu. He saw once again the carriages thronging the boulevards along which he took his afternoon walks, and the ice-skating parties in the Bois Boulogne. Even now he felt a tingle of excitement as he skimmed in memory over the ice of his own River Lak, past the hoary hills and meadows of Belgium, as the wind whipped snow against his cheeks. This had been his favorite exercise in the days when he had not completely broken his ties to that other world.

"Father"—Brother James interrupted his thoughts—"have you any regrets at all for coming here?"

The priest was silent for a few moments. Then he answered. "Regrets? How many men do you know who have been as happy doing their jobs as I have been doing mine?"

He paused. "Brother James, you must bury me under the pandanus tree that sheltered me before I built my first home here." He spoke with vigor, with assurance. "I am looking forward to this Easter with particular excitement."

"Yes, Father?"

"I expect to celebrate it with God."

3

Miracle Doctor of Labrador

WILFRED T. GRENFELL

~~~~~~

DURING THE NIGHT the wind brought in fog with its moist hint of rain. The seas swelled heavily, threatening to burst the solid crust of ice, as an abnormal pressure of steam explodes a boiler. Dr. Wilfred Thomason Grenfell awoke early in the village where he had spent the night and felt the wet wind in his nostrils. He looked out over the harbor, observed how the tides were already smashing the ice into floating pans, and noticed the open water a half-mile off-shore.

He shook his head. If the wind should veer suddenly and the rain come, there was no telling what trouble he would face. Yet his trip was urgent; a patient with a diseased thighbone needed him. He sipped his cocoa. Then he drew on his sealskin boots, laced his trousers up to his armpits, and adjusted the hood that fitted snugly over his chin, ears, and forehead. If his luck held out, he would reach his patient's village that evening.

Only two weeks before, he had operated on the man in his hospital at St. Anthony and had sent him home believing

51

him to be on the road to recovery. But poisoned matter had accumulated in the leg, and only yesterday he had received word that the convalescent was in a critical condition again. An amputation would be necessary.

Now, the doctor shook hands with his native host who had provided him with his overnight lodging, leaped onto his sled, and shouted "Oo-ist" to the huskies. A nervous quiver of the traces and the dogs were off to a sprint that settled gradually into a trot as the weight of the sled began to be felt. It was the morning after Easter, 1908. Spring in Labrador was still weeks away.

Grenfell had driven only a half-dozen miles when the first rain of the season began to fall. Thousands of drops nicked the frozen ground like the steel edges of a razor, shaving the ice perilously thin. The doctor cupped his hand over his eyes. He could eliminate several miles from his trip by striking directly across the bay, instead of following the shoreline. He tightened the reins. At the signal, the dogs veered out across the ice. When they were less than a quarter of a mile from the opposite shore, the wind, which had been blowing easterly and keeping the packed ice together, shifted suddenly. The doctor was horrified to find that the footing under him was disintegrating into slob. Everywhere he looked, the ice was falling apart.

He shouted to his dogs to sprint for shore only a few hundred yards away, but they balked. Remembering that a man had recently been drowned when he became entangled in the harnesses of his dogs on the broken ice, Grenfell freed the team, keeping only the traces of the leader wound around his wrist. Within moments he was churning about in open water. Looking for something adrift, he noticed that his lead dog had scrambled onto a hump of packed snow several yards to the front. He hauled himself along the traces which joined him to the animal, and when the husky slipped out of his harness, he gripped the reins of a second dog and pulled himself onto the packed snow.

The floe was speedily drifting to the sea. The odds were one in a thousand that anybody would be on the lookout for him. And even if he were observed, the chances were slim that a boat could thread its way safely through the field of dangerously moving floes to rescue him. If he were to last the night without freezing, he needed the skins of his dogs. With a knife he had salvaged he put an end to the lives of three of them. Then, covered by the skins and snuggling up for warmth beside the largest of the huskies who was still alive, he fell asleep.

He awakened at sunrise, the words of an old hymn running through his head. He laid out his wooden matches to dry. Suddenly he thought he observed the flash of an oar. But his eyeglasses had been lost. He was partly snow-blind, and he distrusted his vision. However, within minutes, the lines of a boat's hull came into view. He could make out the waving of hands. And then a shout, "Don't get excited! Stay where you are!" Soon a fisherman leaped onto the pan, followed by several others. Not a word was said, but the expression on their faces told vividly of the tension they had undergone.

Late the previous afternoon, four of the fishermen had been out on the headland cutting up seals, and one of them had noticed something amiss on the ice field. He brought a friend who owned a powerful telescope to the headland. Through the lens, a man could plainly be discerned adrift on a pan. Since miles of hurtling ice lay between the marooned man and the shore, it was apparent to those who volunteered for the rescue that they were taking their lives in their hands. Nevertheless, no one backed down. All night, attempts were made to launch a boat, and not until dawn was this successfully done.

For days after the rescue, people along the coast shook their heads and marveled that the packed snow had held together as long as it had on Grenfell's trip to sea. The doctor himself, in the hallway of his home at St. Anthony, placed a plaque to celebrate his escape.

TO THE MEMORY OF

THREE NOBLE DOGS

MOODY

WATCH

SPY

WHOSE LIVES WERE GIVEN

FOR MINE ON THE ICE

APRIL 21ST, 1908

This near-tragedy was merely one episode in a lifetime of risks. Grenfell could no more resist adventure than his ancestor Sir Richard Grenville, that amiable sea rover who, three centuries before, had trained the guns of his frigate on fifteen ships of a Spanish convoy, exchanging broadsides for fifteen consecutive hours before finally surrendering. The doctor could no more stay away from a good "dog fight" than his grandfather who had campaigned in the great Sepoy Rebellion, or his uncle who had taken part in the defense of Lucknow. Grenfell's cousin was Charles Kingsley, the preacher-novelist who had translated his enthusiasm for

ships and sailors into that classic yarn, *Westward, Ho!* And
Grenfell felt the same keen reverence for the sea.

His boyhood was steeped in reminders of the struggle for
survival. At his birthplace on the Sands of Dee, near Bristol,
the heads of tigers and leopards shot in the jungles of Bengal looked down from the walls. Through his window he saw
the terns and curlews and sandpipers flighting to the big
salt marshes, the black-and-white oyster catchers hovering
over mussel patches. And he hunted these from dawn to
evening with his gun. When he arrived at Marlborough Public School in Wiltshire to prepare for college, he was so
eager to use his fists that his classmates, with the characteristic frankness of youth, nicknamed him "The Beast."

Young Grenfell dined with three hundred other boys in
a manorial dining room and washed down his favorite suet
pudding, "bollies," with a "swipe of beer" in a blue china
mug. All the boys, even the youngest, were permitted the
beverage freely. He imported sausages from the "Tuck
Shop," wore a velvet football cap with tassels (the equiva-
lent of a letter in sports), put soap in his lids to get excused
from classes for "eye strain," and barely made chapel in the
morning, struggling into his waistcoat as he prepared for
prayers.

One day there came to Marlborough a schoolboy who was
different from Grenfell and his fellows. He was frail, sensitive, effeminate. He abhorred school athletics. He had never
been away from home before. Dominated by his mother and
five sisters, he didn't know how to get along with boys. But
he had a marvelous aptitude for chemistry and mathematics.
He was frequently so absorbed in performing an experiment
or working out an equation that he neglected to brush his

hair, or press his pants, or wash his face. The boys nicknamed him "Mad G" (G was the first initial of his surname).
They hooted at him, played tricks on him, made his life
miserable.

Grenfell, though he was one of the "regular fellows," was
nevertheless fascinated by "Mad G." He was attracted by
the boy's brilliance in the sciences to which he himself was
drawn. Defying the contempt of his friends, he invited "Mad
G" to his room nightly and listened to the little fellow speak
eagerly of the blueprints he was drawing for a self-steering
torpedo or a machine "absolutely guaranteed" to fly. At such
moments the lad's pallid face assumed a radiance and power
that was striking.

One morning, as "Mad G" stepped from the classroom, a
lump of coal hurled by one of his tormentors struck him on
the scalp. Grenfell, who was only a few steps away, hurried
him off to the infirmary.

The doctor examined the wound. "How did it happen,
boy?"

"I fell on the gravel, sir."

The doctor wasn't deceived by the explanation, but realizing that this was an affair of honor, he declined to inquire
further.

Young Grenfell received permission to move "Mad G's"
desk over to his corner of the classroom and took him completely under his charge. And, since none of the boys
wished to argue with the two-fisted descendant of Sir Richard Grenville, the persecution of "Mad G" ceased.

The experience had a stunning emotional impact on Grenfell. Without any preparation, he had become involved in
a profound human tragedy—the tragedy of the non-con-

formist. The lad who had lived by his gun on the Sands of Dee now passionately identified himself with the one who *received* the wounds.

When Grenfell was seventeen, his father, an Episcopalian minister and a classical scholar who for years had been administering a school for boys in Parkgate, grew weary of his educational duties and accepted the chaplaincy of the London Hospital. Young Grenfell entered the university associated with the hospital for the study of medicine. And his education in human suffering continued.

The hospital was the largest in England, and serviced the poorest districts of the capital. Its nine hundred beds were occupied by alcoholics, street-walkers, dope addicts, sneak thieves from Billingsgate Market to Tillbury Docks and along the riverfront from Petticoat Lane to Radcliffe Highway. This was a world of tension, frustration, squalor. Its leading celebrity was Jack the Ripper who was making headlines prowling through its alleys and butchering prostitutes.

At the end of his second year, Grenfell walked the wards with a stethoscope, assisting noted physicians and surgeons in their ministrations to the derelicts. Few of these patients had any incentive to recover; many were being nursed to health only to face the gallows. A number of the ailments were self-inflicted. But in most instances, a perverse destiny refused to let these would-be suicides die.

Here was a typical case recorded by Grenfell: "Patient, male; age forty-five; domestic trouble; fired a revolver into his mouth. Finding no phenomena develop, fired a second chamber into right ear. Still no symptoms worthy of notice. Patient threw away pistol. He was taken to an observation ward. Both bullets had lodged in the thick part of his skull doing no damage." A few days afterwards, Grenfell made a further entry. "Patient today tried to cut his throat with a dinner knife which he had hidden in his bed. Patient met with no success."

Frequently, when a patient left the ward for the prisoner's dock, Grenfell went along to give medical evidence. This was the way he earned spare money for his books and medical equipment.

From boyhood he had accepted God instinctively, unquestionably, as one accepts parents, brothers, and sisters. But not until he had become acquainted with the misery of the London slums did Grenfell realize fully his deep emotional need for God and, even more, his urge to interpret Him actively to other men. He became convinced that the world needed not so much the theorist in religion as the reformer, the builder, the man who rolled up his sleeves and helped out in the emergencies of daily living.

"We are needed to make the world better," he wrote. "We are not robots in an aimless drama. . . . We are knights on a field of honor. To love one's neighbor as oneself . . . is every bit as much a law of life as fresh air is to the body."

He was particularly fond of referring to the example of old Nehemiah, the Governor of Judea, who refused to waste time gossiping on the plains of Ono when he had God's city to build. "There is every whit as much a piece of that wall to be built by you and me today as there was by that splendid old Nehemiah in his day. When there are enough bits left unbuilt, enough gaps in the line, the nation without the protection of the wall is carried into captivity as surely as

was Israel. . . ." Herein lay the whole meaning of human
life. *"It will not be built if I do not build it!"*

The young physician received his own great opportunity
to "build" five years after receiving his medical degree. In
1891, Lord Southborough, chairman of the Board of Missions to Deep Sea Fishermen of the North Sea and the Coast
of Ireland, returned from a trip to North America. The doctor was invited before the council by a friend.

"See here, Grenfell, you've sailed boats as a hobby all
your life. Furthermore, you've had medical experience working with the under-privileged. Lord Southborough informs
us that there's a great need for a physician to help out the
fishing folk in Labrador. Would you like to look into this?"

"Where on earth is Labrador?"

Grenfell's query was not meant to be flippant. Anyone
opening an atlas in 1891 could have found an area lying
between Newfoundland and Canada marked "Labrador."
But no geographer bothered to give any details about the
country. Not one Britisher in a thousand, not even the post
office, had had any information concerning it.

One historian declared, "God made the world in five
days, made Labrador on the sixth, and spent the seventh
throwing stones at it."

Labrador was one of nature's refrigerators. Nine months
of the year its valleys, rivers, mountains, the very sea around
it were frozen solid. Even during the summer months the
ground remained frozen from a depth of five to seven feet
below the surface. What passed for "soil" was in many
places solid rock below two feet. Every summer, twenty
thousand fishermen from Newfoundland, Nova Scotia, and
points as far south as Gloucester and Boston brought their

families to Labrador, lodged them in huts near the fishing grounds, and cast their nets for cod, salmon, and herring that migrated in abundance to its banks. But with the first appearance of icicles on deck the great fleets withdrew, leaving the native population of four thousand to endure the winter alone. These "Liveyeres," as they were called, were a melancholy folk. Suicides among them were not uncommon. One out of every four died of tuberculosis. They were chronically in debt and on the verge of starvation. The poverty and hopelessness of their lives were reflected in the very names they gave their villages: "Run-By-Chance," "Port Disappointment."

"Labrador," said an early explorer, "is the land God awarded to Cain."

"Yes, Grenfell," suggested members of the mission board, "why don't you pay a visit and look into the conditions of the Liveyeres? Maybe there's a job for you."

The suggestion appealed to Grenfell. From the day he had launched his first boat from the Sands of Dee, he had passed his most exuberant hours at the helm. Over the past five years since receiving his degree, he had spent much of his spare time cruising among the fishing fleets of the North Sea, rendering medical service wherever needed. He had come to love these strong, simple-hearted fisherfolk. And now, in Labrador, there was a whole colony of them, cut adrift from civilization.

In the spring of 1892, Grenfell fitted out a boat sheathed with greenheart against the ice and rigged her as a ketch with large sail forward for running in high seas. The boat was no larger than the *Matthew* which had carried John Cabot on his pioneer voyage to Newfoundland four hundred years before. Although Grenfell possessed a master mariner's license for which years of experience as a navigator had qualified him, he signed up a skipper who had already crossed the Atlantic, and these two, accompanied by a cook, embarked from Yarmouth the second week in June. Taking the same route Cabot had followed, they traversed the seventeen hundred miles to St. John's, Newfoundland, weaving through fog banks and bucking headwinds, in seventeen days. After resting and replenishing their provisions, they sailed north for Labrador, reaching St. Anthony, the capital, on August 4.

As soon as word got around that a physician had arrived, families of English, Canadians, Irish, Russians, Scandinavians, Eskimos, and Algonquin Indians who constituted the national and racial groups of the country streamed into St. Anthony. Many of them, born and raised on the Labrador coast, had never seen a doctor or a dentist.

Grenfell discovered that Lord Southborough's report on their living standards had not been exaggerated. Purely from a medical standpoint, the situation was beyond belief. He discovered men and women blinded with cataracts that could have been cured if properly treated in time. He found rickets, beri-beri, and almost every other disease caused by malnutrition in a most virulent form. He came upon a man incapacitated for years by an ingrown toe nail that could have been eliminated in minutes. One young lad came to him suffering from a necrosis of his entire lower jaw, due to a neglected toothache. The terrible sight of his lopsided face haunted Grenfell for forty years afterwards. He dug out the tooth from the bone imbedding it, and gave the lad immediate relief. He discovered a high percentage of digestive disorders and scurvy, due to ignorance of the most elementary principles of diet.

One husband came up to him and declared anxiously: "I wish you'd see my wife. She be terrible bad and be turning black all over."

When Grenfell arrived at the hut, he found the woman coughing up blood. Her body was spotted with livid discolorations. Grenfell recognized the symptoms of scurvy. A few yards from her house was a field rich with wild parsley and dandelions that would have made her suffering unnecessary had she been educated to their use in her diet.

Before the summer was over, the twenty-eight-year-old physician had made up his mind to spend his life in this "magnified icebox" that jutted out into the North Atlantic.

"The conviction that these fisherfolk needed what I had to give, and that it would not be given if I refused the challenge, was as plain as daylight. . . . The greatest life ever lived was no smaller for having been staged among fishermen."

Having made up his mind to stay in Labrador instead of opening up a private practice in Mayfair, Grenfell returned to England for medical equipment and a staunch little steamer he could turn into a floating hospital. The population of Labrador was scattered in villages along a seven-hundred-mile coast, and the only means of access in summer was by water. He acquired a little steam tender, forty-five feet long and eight feet in beam, and christened her the *Princess May*. She was so light that a liner scooped her puppy-like out of the water and dropped her into the hold for shipment to North America. And to add to the indignity, the funnel of the little vessel was lost among the other baggage.

Seasoned skippers in Labrador shook their heads skeptically when they learned that Grenfell planned to carry on his medical practice in this baby launch. Was the doctor a madman?

Even today, when the Labrador waters have been painstakingly charted and a number of lighthouses serve warning of shoals, only captains possessing a lifelong acquaintance with this coast risk taking a vessel into its winds and tides. But in 1893, when the young doctor proposed to run the *Princess May* from Belle Isle all the way up to Cape Chidley at the northernmost tip of Labrador, the waters had not even been charted. The seas along this jagged shore were peppered with hundreds of rocky islands that had not been marked on any map. Some of them loomed up suddenly, turning the route into a mariner's graveyard. The coast was thick with fog that frequently lasted for ten days at a time, during which the visibility was no more than fifty feet. This provided hardly enough seaway for the boat to respond to the helm. Furthermore, icebergs a quarter of a mile long were adrift in these subarctic waters. The squalls, especially in August, were severe. Not a single lighthouse had yet been erected to guide a vessel in her torturous course amid suddenly projecting cliffs and boiling surf.

On all sides, as Grenfell prepared the *Princess May* for embarkation from St. Anthony, he heard experienced sea dogs comment, "He'll never make it. Why, the ice will crack that tub like a nut!"

Their predictions were almost realized at the outset. The doctor and his cook and engineer had gone only five miles from port when the engineer suddenly called out, "By God, we're filling with water!"

Grenfell made an immediate inspection of the hull and found where the vessel had sprung a leak.

"Well, luckily, we're not far out. We'd better turn back," advised the engineer.

"No," said the doctor. "Do you think I want to be the laughingstock of every sea captain along the coast? We'll plug it up and go on!"

He whittled out a plug and drove it into the opening in the hull. Within a few minutes the ship was tight and dry again.

The *Princess May* crept cautiously along the coast while Grenfell, at the helm, acquainted himself with every fjord and inlet. On the second day, as they were feeling their way through a dense fog bank, a beetling cliff seamed with deposits of black traprock suddenly jutted out in front of the boat.

"Reverse engines!" Grenfell shouted to the engineer, at the same time shoving the tiller hard over. The launch swerved sharply, barely in time to avert piling up on the rocks. A few yards more and the *Princess May* would have been splintered like a matchbox.

Checking later, they discovered the reason for the vessel's being off course. The worker who had installed the compass had used iron screws. The presence of this amount of iron was sufficient to deflect the needle from magnetic north.

Future voyages followed the risky pattern of this one. Whenever Grenfell sailed from St. Anthony, he didn't know with what emergency he would suddenly be faced, what plans he would have to improvise at a moment's notice for self-preservation. Since the *Princess May* was a wood burner and there was little space aboard for bulky cord wood, it was impossible to carry fuel for lengthy trips. Fortunately, there was a harbor every few miles along the coast. Once, however, they ran out of firewood and Grenfell had to chop up the cabin ceiling and burn it in order to reach the nearest port. On another occasion the *Princess May* was frozen fast in an ice field for eleven straight days. Twice he had to dynamite her loose from the ice.

But far from depressing the young doctor, these voyages exhilarated him. "I love the call of the sea. It's in my blood. The tang of the air . . . the fantastic midnight dances of the November aurora . . . make one forget the worries of the daily round."

As soon as he was able, Grenfell acquired a larger, more powerful steamer, the *Strathcona*. He equipped her with bunks for patients and installed an X-ray machine. He operated just under the hatchway, while the vessel pitched in heaving seas. By his side was a basin for blood.

He performed by the light that came from a swinging kerosene lamp. Much of the time the light was blocked off by the heads of patients who crowded around to see the operation. Once, when an Eskimo woman resisted being put to sleep with an anesthetic, several of her friends had to sit on her to keep her down. On another occasion, a native holding the lamp fainted at the sight of blood, and the room was plunged into darkness.

Sometimes Grenfell found men rolling on the floor, driven almost insane by snow blindness. He relieved the terrible pain with cocaine. A number of patients came in with painfully swollen forearms poisoned by offal that had collected under the skin while cleaning cod. Grenfell lanced these "water welts" and let out the pus. He operated on a young man whose eye-globe had been ruptured by a gun exploding, and he saved the sight of the other eye.

At one port, a man accidentally shot in the hand was carried aboard the *Strathcona*. To stop the bleeding, he had plunged the hand into a bag of flour and tied it up. The arm was poisoned to the elbow. Grenfell performed an immediate amputation, grafted a bone that gave him a flipper like a seal's, in addition to which he was able to oppose one index finger and "nip a line" when he fished. The doctor supplied part of his own skin for the grafting.

Some of the operations were performed under even more difficult conditions than those prevailing on the *Strathcona*. At times the doctor found himself in a hut far inland, with practically no equipment. On some occasions he amputated limbs with a pocketknife while the natives drenched the room with perchloride of mercury.

He had to contend with many native superstitions. Mothers blew sugar into the eyes of babies to "cure" them of ophthalmia. Patients put the fin bones of haddock around their necks to ward off rheumatism; or they tied green worsted around their wrists as an "infallible cure" for hemorrhage. The ignorance he encountered was beyond belief. One woman for whom he prescribed liniment for her knees swallowed it for a stomach ache, arguing that a pain was a pain anywhere. Another patient finished a whole bottle of medicine at a gulp, convinced that if one teaspoonful helped, a bottleful would do even more good. A husband, when told that his wife needed an amputation, remarked casually, "Well, she won't miss the use of her arm anyway. She's an old lady." The woman was thirty-five!

Not all reasons for visiting the doctor were medical. One lumbering youth asked to speak to Grenfell privately. "I wants to get married."

"I can't help you in that. Won't the girls around here have you?"

"It's not that, Doctor. I fancies a girl up north, but I'm shipped to a man down here for the season, and I can't get away. Since you be taking a trip north, won't you just kind a' propose to the girl for me and bring her with you when you gets along this way again?"

Reports of Grenfell's work reached Newfoundland rapidly. Within a year after his arrival, the governor of Newfoundland called a meeting of wealthy, socially minded merchants to solicit funds for the building of two hospitals. Grenfell selected for the sites Battle Harbor, in the south, and Indian Harbor, two hundred miles north. He led fishermen volunteers into the woods to cut timber. The foundation for the kitchens were dug through six feet of snow.

The hospital at Battle Harbor provided eight beds for men, eight for women. Eventually the doctor installed an electrical system run by a kerosene motor for the latest treatment and X-ray work. The second hospital was ready soon after the first. A doctor and nurse volunteered for each hospital as Grenfell's assistants, and, in time, were joined by medical students and several additional nurses.

But Grenfell had an even larger vision of medical service— that of preventing disease at its roots through the betterment of social conditions. At heart he was a social reformer. The Liveyeres were virtual paupers, due largely to the system of barter that prevailed. They turned in their entire catch of fish and furs to the merchants and traders from Canada and Newfoundland in return for food and clothing. Over the years, most of the fishermen had fallen deeply into debt and were being doled out supplies. Some, having exhausted their credit, were unable to purchase even the barest necessities of life.

Grenfell felt that the solution lay in a system of stores owned by the fishermen themselves and financed by community subscription. Each member would have a stake in management, and all goods would be purchased for cash, not credit.

But when he called together the citizens at Red River Bay, where he felt that a store should be established, he found that the cash savings of all seventeen resident families totaled only eighty-five dollars. He had to dig into his own pocket to buy the initial stock for them. He also put a thousand dollars into a store at Flower's Cove.

Unfortunately, the Liveyeres made tragic blunders in the process of gaining business experience. One co-operative at St. John's quickly ran up a debt to merchants of twenty-five thousand dollars. The manager at St. Anthony gave credit to everybody who asked for it until he showed a loss of twelve thousand dollars. Since none of the stores had been incorporated, the doctor was held personally liable for the debts. He cashed every available asset, sold his personal property, liquidated investments, and with the help of a friend managed to reduce the liability.

In the long run his faith in the fishermen was vindicated. The co-operatives survived their early financial troubles and proved a godsend to the people.

In the course of making his rounds, the doctor found many children orphaned by the death of parents from tuberculosis and other diseases common to the locale. He took them back to St. Anthony where he established a home for them, the entrance to which carried the inscription "Suffer Little Children to Come unto Me."

As a means of combating scurvy, rickets, and beri-beri, nutritional diseases endemic on the coast, he turned his attention to growing food on which the Liveyeres could depend when the fishing was poor or the traps empty. Although the ground in Labrador remained frozen until July, and seeds planted then would not germinate in time for vegetables to grow, Grenfell met this challenge characteristically. "We'll make the season for growing longer!"

He imported greenhouses from the United States. And when the summer arrived, he had plantlets three months old ready to go into the ground. In the fall he picked cabbages weighing eighteen pounds and distributed them to the Liveyeres.

Upon experimentation, Grenfell discovered that peat mixed with the bones and offal of cod, together with seaweed and kelp, formed a valuable manure, and that soil from which peat was removed became good pastureland. He grew alfalfa, perennial artichokes, and even pumpkins.

A professor at the Massachusetts State College of Agriculture, hearing of his work, came to Labrador and demonstrated methods for destroying insects. Within a short time, gardens on the coast under scientific cultivation increased their productivity 30 per cent.

Clarence Birdseye, a young biologist, came to Labrador to work with Grenfell. Once, while fishing through the ice for rock cod in weather far below zero, Birdseye noticed that the cod which froze instantly on contact with the outer air jumped about again when thawed out in the kitchen. This discovery led him eventually to perfect a process for preserving meats, fish, and vegetables indefinitely by instantaneous freezing. Birdseye founded the frozen food industry.

In addition to Grenfell's other duties, the Newfoundland Government, which since 1927 had exercised territorial jurisdiction over the eastern part of Labrador, appointed him an unpaid justice of the peace. He accepted this additional duty good-naturedly, holding court on the deck of the *Strathcona*, or wherever else he happened to be. Most of the offenses were minor. And punishments were equally mild. The petty thief worked out his sentence by cleaning out the jail, keeping it well supplied with wood and water, performing some task of social benefit during the work hours, and then locking himself up punctually for the night. Frequently the judge, bailiff, and prisoner chatted away amiably as they worked together on a job.

Once, when the *Strathcona* was on its annual medical tour, a young carpenter of sixteen came aboard. Grenfell looked him over. He seemed healthy enough.

"What do you want?"

"A little learning, Doctor."

For some time Grenfell had been planning to sow the seeds of industrialization in this backward country by sending Liveyere students on scholarships to foreign universities for professional and technological training. This ambitious lad was the first to be selected. He entered the Pratt Institute in Brooklyn. Other hand-picked young men and women were subsequently enrolled in universities in the United

States, Canada, and England, and after receiving their degrees returned to Labrador to serve as teachers, nurses, engineers, electricians, dieticians, cabinet makers, dressmakers,
stenographers.

In 1927, when Labrador's fireproof, concrete-reinforced
hospital was erected at St. Anthony with central heating,
modern plumbing, and electric lights, Grenfell didn't have
to send for outside specialists. The man who supervised
the construction was the ex-carpenter who thirty years before had come to the doctor "for learning."

In 1909 Grenfell, hitherto a confirmed bachelor, amazed
his friends by bringing a wife home to Labrador. While returning to North America on the liner *Mauretania* after a
brief trip to Europe, he had met a charming dark-haired
young woman. The ship was due to dock in a few days, and
there was no time to lose, so he had asked the stranger to
marry him.

She was taken aback. "But you don't even know my
name!"

"It doesn't matter. I know what it is *going* to be!"

By the time the ship reached port, Elizabeth MacClana-
han had become Grenfell's fiancée.

He accompanied her to her home in Lake Forest, Michigan, where he met her father, a Tennessean who had fought
in the Civil War under Lee and Braxton Bragg. In the
autumn they were married. The aristocratic Southern belle
abandoned her life of comfort, her rounds of party-going
and gay living for the rigors of the North country. She spent
the rest of her life as her husband's helper.

As the doctor's plans became increasingly ambitious, he
took time from his duties to lecture in the United States

and Canada. In this way he raised sorely needed funds for the Grenfell Mission—the international organization formed by interested people in his name to provide the financial sinews for the development of Labrador. The story of Labrador was a dramatic, even a sensational one. It attracted tremendous audiences. Grenfell, whose own instincts were for action, not oratory, gracefully bore the ordeal of one-night stands, the lavish attentions of a new host in each new city, and a thousand handshakes. Nonetheless, he was incorrigibly absent-minded. Once, a passenger, recognizing him on a train, came over and asked, "What do you think of Toledo?"

"I don't know," answered the doctor politely. "I've never been there."

"But you spent two nights as a guest in my house!" said the other.

On another occasion, he was in a hurry to make a train. He strode up to the wicket gate, reviewing in his mind a lecture he had to deliver shortly. A hand was thrust toward him. Believing it to belong to another of his innumerable well-wishers, he shook it mechanically, mumbled thanks— and hurried through. A roar of laughter from bystanders and a hasty pursuit brought him back to reality. His "admirer" was the ticket collector.

Once, after mentioning that the Eskimo colony in Labrador had never seen a lamb or sheep, and that in discussing the meaning of the "Lamb of God," he had been obliged to substitute the concept of a white seal, an elderly woman among his listeners promptly mailed him a woolly toy lamb with a little note pinned to one leg, "Sent in order that the heathen may know better."

The Eskimo's ignorance of the gospel resulted in amusing incidents. In the days before Grenfell, when a Moravian missionary visited an elderly Eskimo lady and asked, "Do you know that Jesus died for you?" the lady is reported to have replied, "No, sir. Is he dead, sir? We'uns don't ofen git news down here."

The story of Grenfell's achievements in Labrador gripped the imagination of people everywhere. A tragically backward country was being transformed from semi-wilderness into a civilized, up-to-date community through the efforts of a physician who quite simply and literally followed the precepts of Christ. This was a revolutionary approach, so full of common sense as to have been overlooked by many "practical" reformers since the Crucifixion.

Grenfell had turned the capital city, St. Anthony—named after the patron saint of fishermen—into a vigorous, socially productive community, the symbol of his countrywide achievements. From a dock in St. Anthony's harbor ran rails on which handcars carried goods to all parts of the settlement. One line led to the hospital, where a visitor might observe lung patients sunning themselves on the veranda. Another led to the home for orphans. Still another led to the Seaman's Institute, and another to a thriving quarter which included a modern laundry, a machine and carpenter's shop, and an industrial school where women, under Grenfell's encouragement, developed their natural aptitude for rug-making and basketry, and men their skill in ivory work, into a profitable business that found markets all over the world.

The doctor's house stood on a hill overlooking the town and harbor. In his living room was a huge "picture window" through which one was almost tempted to step into the outdoors. On the walls hung the antlers of reindeer, fishing rods, a rifle, snowshoes. On a table stood a bowl of blue lobelias imported from South Africa and blooming in the subarctic. In summer, the hillside was luxuriant with pink fireweed, purple monkhood, blue lupins.

In this home so expressive of his personality, the doctor spent his few precious hours of relaxation, smoking a briar pipe, reading his favorite authors—Kipling, Twain, Kingsley —annotating with pithy, trenchant comments the text of his Bible. Visitors felt instantly at ease in the company of this unassuming host whose gray eyes were kind, whose mouth seemed forever on the verge of a smile. Grenfell was amazingly well preserved. Even in his seventies he retained the build, the youthful, springy step of an athlete.

During a typical winter Grenfell spent only three Sundays at home. The rest of the time he was out driving his dogsled on a round of calls. His medical assistants took charge of the hospitals.

Picture him traveling to a sickbed, detaching the dogs and lifting the sled himself over a ridge, stumbling over tree stumps hidden by the snow, the perspiration of his body turning to ice. More than once he passes men frozen to death upright in the drifts. Once he comes across a diary written by a trapper in his own blood. On one occasion, when he arrives at a sickbed, the host hands him a pipe to smoke. It clatters to the ground. Before it reaches his mouth the doctor is asleep in his chair with exhaustion.

At times he is so tired that he drops off to sleep in a snowbank. Protected by a sleeping bag, by the light drift which blows in and forms a blanket, and by the flames of a pinewood fire, he rests comfortably and awakens refreshed.

And then, when the ice is broken and the villages can be reached by sea, he works with his crew to scrape the rust from the hulk of the *Strathcona,* tightens or replaces the bolts, overhauls the engine, and casts off from St. Anthony on his way to care for nine hundred patients on his annual trip.

Atop his mainmast flies a blue pennant reading: "God is love," and his helm is inscribed: "Jesus saith, 'Follow me and I will make you fishers of men.'"

He grips the helm for hours, his eyes sparkling with the sheer joy of living. Beside him, paws on the rail, stands his black and white mongrel Fritz, sniffing at the spray. On the starboard side pass serried peaks of red granite, scarred with torn, twisted strata, fantastically carved boulders pale with ice, sudden, leaping fjords, and overhead the northern lights, thought by the Eskimos to be dead spirits at play.

Nights, he anchors in a cove, and awakens several times to check the weather. He dives into the water for an early morning dip and is at the wheel before the sun has risen. After a strenuous day's work, he sits up frequently till midnight, reading a favorite volume.

Most of his own books and articles on his activities in Labrador he writes in longhand, sitting on a pile of firewood abroad his ship, inhaling the pungent smell of fir blazing in the firebox, or listening to the scurrying of mice foretelling a blow.

After every storm, while en route to patients, he patroled reefs and rocky islands, searching for stranded vessels, and he towed them to port, carrying shipwrecked crews south to the mail boat.

Once he came on a group who were beyond help. According to notes that he found, the party had become lost. Their food exhausted, they drew lots to see who should be eaten by the others. The lot fell to a woman. Her brother offered himself in her place. When Grenfell came on them the following spring, he found several bodies lying under a frozen sail. Between the fingers of one was a piece of flesh torn from another.

He discovered new cod banks for trawlers. He navigated his vessel where no preacher ever went before, to marry, christen, and bury, in his role as spiritual counselor. With the aid of experts he charted the seaboard and surrounding terrain for the safety of the fishermen and geographers. He climbed peaks three thousand feet high with surveying instruments, accompanied by his friend Noel Odell, the famous climber of Mt. Everest. He flew in a plane with a cameraman who took aerial pictures of timberland, fjords, and salmon rivers where men had not ventured on foot.

During his forty-two years in Labrador he was honored by the world. He was knighted, received the only medical degree Oxford ever bestowed, was made a Companion of the Order of St. Michael and St. George by Edward VII, and elected Rector of St. Andrew's, the oldest university in Scotland. He received from the Royal Scottish Geographical Society the Livingstone Gold Medal as the spiritual successor of the famous missionary-explorer. Yet despite these tributes, Grenfell drew, at his own request, a salary of only fifteen hundred dollars a year from his mission.

He had paid his first visit to Labrador at the age of twenty-seven to "look into" conditions. He stayed until the age of sixty-nine. Then, at last, this old Viking admitted he was tired. "I'm getting too old to drive a dog team, and I'm afraid I must take it easy until the time comes to cash in my checks."

As a matter of fact, he had developed a serious heart ailment, and his physicians urged him to leave the country he had made so uniquely his own. In 1934, with his wife, he retired to Charlotte, Vermont.

On December 9, 1938, Lady Grenfell passed away. For thirty-three years this "First Lady" of Labrador had worked patiently and painstakingly for the Liveyeres. It was she who inspired and carried out to the smallest detail the child welfare and group educational projects, and a variety of other social services that so effectively supplemented her husband's activities.

He had written of their life together: "Now that the final goal seems not so far away, we are holding hands closer than ever, confident that the final experience will be easier to face. . . . When these worn out bodily machines of ours shall be discarded, on the other side we shall work again in new fields together."

Since it had been Lady Grenfell's wish to rest in Labrador, the widower of seventy-four accompanied the remains to St. Anthony. Thirteen months later—on October 10, 1940—he died and was buried beside her.

But the miracle in Labardor continued. True, there was a new medical superintendent of the mission, Doctor S. E. Curtis. Yet the heart and soul of it was still the indomitable doctor from the Sands of Dee. He had, by an act of brotherhood, set up a chain reaction all over the world. During Grenfell's last years of service, and after his death, men and women left their offices, colleges, farms, shops, laboratories, and hospitals, and flocked to Labrador. Professors and car-

penters, engineers and army officers, librarians and debu-
tantes, surgeons and architects—more than fourteen hundred
people in all—put aside their personal affairs summers and
went north without pay to construct roads, erect dams, build
wharves, tend the sick, and teach the young. They battled
mosquitoes in the dense undergrowth—a professor of higher
mathematics at Princeton and a well-known publisher from
New York, a member of the French Legion of Honor by the
side of a famous athlete, the sons of millionaires together
with day laborers—unloading coal from ships, painting
houses, erecting schoolhouses, building reservoirs.

Some of the volunteers remained through the winter. One
nurse who had stayed several years told Grenfell that she
was returning to the States to earn enough money to volunteer again.

A schoolteacher ran a tea shop in the States in her spare
time and with the profits managed to spend eight years in
Labrador, helping to educate the children. A young medical
student came north on the proceeds from the sales of pup-
pies bred by his spaniel. A carpenter traveled all the way
from Kentucky at his own expense to teach the women how
to make looms and weaving equipment. Grenfell warned all
applicants that the work would be hard and the circumstances of life trying, that the food was not too good and
the journey north apt to be terribly fatiguing. And still they
applied in such numbers that many had to be turned away.

There were martyrs, also, to this experiment in human
fellowship. One volunteer, Varick Frissell, came out to make
a film depicting the hardships of life in Labrador. He was
aboard a sealing steamer in the ice fields taking the final
shots when the ship's boiler exploded. The wailing of his

large Newfoundland was heard by a search party above the
roaring of flames. Neither dog nor master was ever again
seen.

However, the story of sacrifice most vivid in the doctor's
own mind took place several years before his retirement.

Early one spring, a serious epidemic of influenza broke
out on the coast. The tiny village of Hebron was wiped out.
At Okkak, only one-quarter of the population of two hundred and sixty-seven survived. The number of Eskimos along
the coast was cut in half. The situation had gotten completely out of control. Grenfell was working day and night
with his assistants caring for the patients who poured into
the hospital at St. Anthony when word reached him that a
little village to the south had been particularly hard hit and
that medical help was needed immediately. But neither
Grenfell nor his fellow doctors could spare themselves for
the trip.

A young nurse stepped forward. "I'll go."

"It's a long, dangerous trip for a woman to make," cau-
tioned Grenfell.

"I am ready for it."

The doctor silently blessed her. The huskies were hitched
to the team. The girl slipped into her kossack, tightened the
fur hood around her face, and started off.

Overhead the skies turned gray, and the wind whipped up
squalls of snow as the sled moved forward with the motion
of a huge caterpillar adapting itself to the uneven terrain. It
required steady nerves for a girl to travel alone, night and
day, with a team of dogs whose breed had been known to
turn suddenly upon a driver and tear him to pieces. But the
nurse refused to brood over this possibility. She carried an

axe, chopped ice for water, sometimes boiled snow. The air was so chill that she found lumps of ice in the middle of her pork even after it had been cooked over a fire. At times, the tide rolled over frozen ground underfoot, and she found herself waist deep in chilling water. Icicles formed over the fur of the huskies, and they had to rub the coating from their eyes to see the track ahead. During the final lap, the wind reached gale strength and blew her savagely across the ice. Only the snowdrifts acting as a brake kept her from smashing up and being killed.

When she arrived in the village, she permitted herself one night's sound sleep and then made the rounds of the sick. In time she had the epidemic under control. She began to think of returning to St. Anthony.

Then, one evening just before midnight, a man stumbled into her lodgings. His eyes were wide open in a paralysis of horror—as if he couldn't believe what was happening to him. His stomach was ripped open up to his chest. His intestines had spilled out into his hands—white, fat, bloody. This man, in a delirium of fever brought on by the flu, had leaped from his bed, grabbed his fish-splitting knife, and had ripped himself open.

The nurse helped the patient to bed. He was hemorrhaging. An operation was necessary, but the nurse had never performed surgery in her life. Grenfell was many miles away. Since her arrival, the ice had broken up, making travel by dog sled impossible. And it would take days for a launch to pick its way through the floating pans.

The nurse wired Grenfell at St. Anthony. The answer came back:

"There's only one thing to do, my girl, operate yourself.

May God be with you!" Then followed brief instructions telling her how to proceed.

The nurse called on a priest who happened to be in the village on business.

"Father, you must assist me in an operation."

"But I've never even been present at one!"

"Well, Father, we'll just have to learn together."

The priest nodded. "All right. But first let me administer the Last Sacrament." He dipped a pellet of cotton in holy oil, made the sign of the cross over the patient's eyelids, nose, mouth, hands. The nurse produced a bottle of chloroform from her maternity bag. Following her directions, the priest administered the anaesthetic. The nurse bathed out the abdominal cavity and rearranged the intestines to the best of her ability. Then, with sterilized needle and thread, she sewed up the wound.

One afternoon six weeks later, a small trapboat made its way through the ice floes into the harbor of St. Anthony. It had been converted into a floating convalescent home. A tent had been erected on deck and through it poked a little home-built funnel. Out of it stepped the nurse followed by her patient who was already on the way to full recovery. "I'll be fishing again for my family in the fall," the man reported to Grenfell.

The plucky nurse had truly acted in the spirit of the Labrador doctor who once said, "It is . . . deeds of love—not words however touching—that never fade from the soul."

4

"Goddess" in the Burmese Jungle

ANN JUDSON

〰〰〰〰〰〰〰〰〰〰〰〰〰〰〰〰〰〰〰〰

"But this is the most quixotic venture I've ever heard of,"
exclaimed William Carey, as he put down his cup of tea and
looked at the two young people before him. "You have practically no funds. You're ten thousand miles from your families, among a people whose language you can't even speak—
and to top it off, you've just gotten married!"

He said the last as if marriage were the final straw.

The young man had copper-colored eyes and receding
black hair that was already silvered at the temples. "It's not
as insane a desire as it seems, Brother Carey. True, I was
offered the pulpit of the largest church in Boston when I
graduated. Ann would have made a splendid wife socially
for a Boston minister." He put his arm around his bride. "But
America has enough competent clergymen. We feel that
we'll be happier out here."

"Happy!" exclaimed Carey. "Do you know what missionaries in the Orient have been going through?

"Let's take a typical country, Burma." He reeled off the record. "Two Englishmen of enormous energy went out there to set up a mission. They abandoned the job as hopeless. A Portuguese priest—a native convert—was denounced by his own nephew. He was seized by the Burmese authorities and beaten with an iron maul from the soles of his feet to his chest; when he went insane, he was turned loose in the jungle. My own son, Felix, went out there and was forced to take refuge for fifty days on a British frigate. Only after marrying a native woman was he allowed to return. Today Felix is more oriental than Western."

He paused. "And if by some miracle you escape the anger of the natives, there's the British East India Company to contend with. These traders hate missionaries because they're afraid that the introduction of Western ideas will lead the natives to rise against colonial rule. The company wields tremendous political power, and it will hound you out of all territories under its jurisdiction."

The couple heard these facts in silence. William Carey knew what he was speaking about. He had come out to India as a missionary from England nineteen years before. Today he was prematurely old, broken in health. His mission had survived because he had the backing of important members of Parliament who protected him from the East India Company. The Judsons had no such support.

The woman spoke up. She was richly dark in complexion, with brilliant, brown eyes that looked at one penetratingly above a whimsical smile. "I am not surprised at what you say. When Adoniram proposed to me and told me he planned to take me out here, my friends advised me to turn him down. Mr. Kimball, the father of one of my school chums, said he'd tie his daughter to a bedpost before he'd let her marry a missionary!" She smiled. "But somehow, Asia seems an awfully small price to pay for Mr. Judson."

William Carey took both of their hands. "So you are determined to risk it, despite all I've told you." He added softly, "I'm terribly, terribly happy. I had hoped I couldn't unnerve you!"

He poured another cup of tea. "You can remain here at the mission as long as you like—or at least until the East India Company makes trouble. Of course, you may eventually want to set up your own Baptist mission in another area. But stay here until you get a bit used to the ways of the Orient."

That evening as they were retiring for the night, Ann said to her husband, "Well, Don, India's a long, long way from Massachusetts. I'm afraid we're going to be rather lonesome."

"Nancy," he replied—that was his name for her—"wherever you are, you'll never be without friends. I wouldn't be surprised if you have the wealthiest nabobs at your feet." He added whimsically, "I just can't understand, dear, why you picked a chap like me—a fellow possessed with the wanderlust, and the need to deliver a message."

"Don't be silly. My prospects weren't *that* good. Thank heavens," she added soberly, "we at least have Sam and Harriet Newell with us."

There had been five volunteer missionaires to begin with—five graduates of Andover Seminary in Massachusetts who had offered themselves as the first American Protestants to bring Christianity to the Orient. And three young brides had volunteered to share the adventure with their men.

We are concerned with two of these couples.

One cold wintry day in Salem, in February, 1812, the Judsons and the Newells received the captain's summons to go aboard the liner *Caravan*. They had waited nervously for two weeks until a favorable wind arose. Now, tucked in furs and mufflers and bundled in with their luggage, they rode through the narrow streets of Salem in a sleigh, past the Old Tabernacle Church where only a few days before Sam and Adoniram had been ordained for the ministry as their women looked on fondly—Ann a bride of a few days, Harriet to be married shortly.

And now after a tedious five months' sea voyage cooped up in a tiny cabin and having to jump rope on deck for their daily exercise, they had finally arrived in Calcutta. This capital of British India was a wonder and a revelation to a girl from New England. Ann rode with Adoniram through the squalid streets in a palanquin carried by four trotting natives, past the homes of opulent Englishmen furnished half in European, half in Asiatic style. At many street corners, coolies gambled with dice on chalked-out squares, and idol-makers swarmed around the carriage with their charms and images, crying, *"Baba ko waste, Sahib*—Buy for the children, Master!" In the foreign quarter, pale-faced Armenian women with expressive black eyes under tiara-shaped caps looked curiously at the Americans, and civil officials before the government buildings touched their foreheads and bowed. And coldly aloof from everyone but their own class strode the Brahmins, pausing now and then to extend a lordly blessing. Their skin was the color of weak coffee; the palms of their hands were as white as any European's. "You can always tell the Brahmins by their swagger," Adoniram remarked to Ann, "and the assurance with which they blow their noses through their fingers."

At William Carey's invitation, the Judsons remained for several months at the mission in Serampore, just outside Calcutta. Since Harriet was expecting a child, and a permanent home had become desirable, the Newells left for the Isle of France in the Indian Ocean, where Samuel Newell hoped to serve the British garrison and the native population. At their departure, the Judsons' final ties with America were severed.

Four months after their arrival in India, the crisis was upon them. They received an order from officials of the East India Company to leave India immediately: "We'll have no traffic with American missionaires." Within hours, Ann and Adoniram's names were published on the passenger list of a ship bound for England!

The Judsons were in a dilemma. If they yielded, Adoniram's career as a missionary was finished. There was only one thing to do—to leave for a country in the Orient out of reach of the East India Company, and to do it before they would be forcibly put aboard the British vessel.

Through friends, Adoniram learned that a ship, the *Creole*, was about to leave for the Isle of France where the Newells had gone. The captain was willing to "look the other way" if the Judsons came aboard secretly. Late at night they drove to the docks, through city gates that were opened by friendly native officials. Early next morning, the *Creole* proceeded down the Hooghly River toward the Bay of Bengal. But the East India Company learned of their flight and sent a boat which overtook the *Creole*. The Judsons were ordered ashore. However, after some parleying, they were permitted

to continue on the *Creole* providing they promised never
again to enter the territory of the East India Company.

After a stormy passage they arrived at Port Louis, on the
Isle of France. There they received a shock. Harriet Newell
was dead. She had given birth to her baby at sea, unattended
by a physician. The child had died, and Harriet, becoming
seriously ill, had passed away shortly after the ship docked.
She was the first American missionary to lose her life in the
Orient.

The prospect of remaining at Port Louis—so closely associated with Harriet's death—was distasteful to Ann. There
were islands that provided an even more fertile field for
missionary work. Prince of Wales Island, for instance, in the
Strait of Malacca, was populated with Chinese, Malayans,
and Siamese, many of whom were receptive to Western
teachings. Accordingly, after resting a few months at Port
Louis, the Judsons set sail, this time for Madras where they
planned to wait for a vessel to the Straits.

But when they arrived at Madras, an Indian port within
the jurisdiction of the East India Company, they were reported to the company officials. Adoniram learned that de-
portation orders would soon be forthcoming from the
government in Calcutta. There wasn't time to wait for passage to Malacca. If they wished to remain in the Orient,
they had better take the first vessel out of Madras. To com-
plicate matters further, Ann was about due to give birth to
a child.

Although the police kept a watch on Adoniram, he managed to slip away to the docks at night and make discreet
inquiries among the sailors. For several evenings he dogged
the waterfront. Finally, he came upon a seaman whose small

eyes peered from under a tightly fitting skullcap. Yes, his vessel was clearing port in a day and the captain would take the Judsons aboard if they met his price for the passage. And where was the vessel bound?

"Burma, Sahib."

If the sailor had said, "Hell, Sahib," the answer couldn't have stunned Adoniram any the more. Instantly he recalled William Carey's story of his son in Burma and of the tortures of the Portuguese priest. Of all the countries in the Orient, Burma was the one most definitely to be avoided by a missionary. But when he reported his information to Ann, she replied, "Well, Don, if it's Burma or home—let it be Burma."

Their first sight of Rangoon was hardly calculated to revive their spirits which were at a low ebb because of the sudden death of the child born to Ann during the voyage. The city was nothing but a swampy settlement of shacks. A few streets were paved with brick, but most were muddy trails. Chickens, dogs, and crows feasted on the garbage and animal dung that lay in steaming piles under the houses. These smells mingled with the miasma of the swamp were enough to sicken the stomach.

Tigers roamed through the outskirts of Rangoon and sometimes made off with a pig or even a child. The natives kept their dovecotes caged on top of poles to prevent their being eaten by wildcats. Armies of white ants continually destroyed the furniture.

There was a single, well-paved highway lined with pagodas to which the Burmese brought offerings of food and flowers for the Buddha. And two miles north of the city stood the great Shwe Dagon Pagoda, its golden spires contrasting sharply with the desolate countryside.

Felix Carey, William Carey's son, had established a mission outside the city walls. When the Judsons arrived, he was away on business for the Burmese king. But his native wife offered Ann and Adoniram lodgings.

"There are about eight million Burmese," Adoniram explained to Ann. He had been reading up on the country. "Each province is governed by a Viceroy whom the people call 'The Eater.' And with very good reason. He 'eats' them out of house and home with his taxes.

"The King is the 'Lord of Life and Death' and the natives speak of him always as the 'Golden One.' Remember this, Ann, when you deal with the natives: the King never *smells* a rose. Instead, 'the perfume of the rose has been privileged to reach the Golden Nose.' Next to him, the highest rank in Burma is held by a white elephant. He is stabled in splendor near the palace. When he goes for a walk he is fanned by attendants. Foreign ambassadors are presented to him and shower him with presents. One of the King's proudest titles is 'Lord of the White Elephant.'

"You and I will probably not be molested until we attempt to reach the people with our ideas," he added. "Then we had better watch out!"

It was precisely to teach, however, that the Judsons had come. But first they had to learn the language. And this was not an easy matter. No Burmese dictionary or grammar existed. Native books were written with a stylus on palm leaves in one continuous line without punctuation. Adoniram hired a native teacher, but the Burmese balked when he discovered he was expected to instruct Ann as well. It was unheard of for a man of his standing to teach "so inferior" a being as a woman! However, under Adoniram's prodding, he yielded.

The teacher didn't speak English, and the only means of communication at first was for Adoniram to point to various objects to which the teacher gave the Burmese word.

While her husband grappled with the intricacies of grammar, Ann acquired a speaking vocabulary through her dealings with shopkeepers and domestics in the course of her daily housekeeping. When she decided to pay a visit to the Vice-Reine, the chief wife of the provincial ruler, she possessed an adequate enough vocabulary to make herself understood.

Adoniram, realizing that it was essential to establish friendly relations with the government, had already visited the Viceroy. But that official had elaborately snubbed him.

"Let me get acquainted with his wife," suggested Ann. "White men are no curiosity here. But the Vice-Reine won't be able to resist looking *me* over."

And so she put on her best dress and a charming bonnet and paid a social call at the palace. When she arrived, the Vice-Reine had not yet risen. But the lesser wives were already about, and they gathered around Ann, admiring her dress and gloves and bonnet with expressions of delight.

At length, His Excellency's senior wife put in her appearance. Her face was a pale yellow, heavily dusted with sandlewood powder. She was dressed in a scarlet gown and smoked a silver pipe. While the lesser wives crouched in respectful silence, the Vice-Reine welcomed Ann warmly and led her to a mat, seating herself beside her. One of the women approached with a bouquet of hibiscus, and the Vice-Reine tucked the flowers in Ann's hair.

"We are glad to have you with us, American Teacher. Tell me, are you the chief of Maung Judson's wives?"

"I am the only one," replied Ann. "In America a man can have only one wife legally."

"They must be very lonely, those American women," replied the Vice-Reine between puffs on her pipe.

At her command, musicians played on harps, and a featured performer, seated within a circular frame of bells, energetically pounded out an oriental rhapsody.

When Ann took her leave, the bevy of lesser wives made their salaams. The Vice-Reine escorted Ann to the door and insisted that she come again "to tell me more about American wives."

The Vice-Reine became one of Ann's staunchest friends. Shortly after Ann's visit, she invited the Judsons on a picnic in the country. A richly attired elephant appeared at the mission and conveyed them to the palace. Here they were joined by the Vice-Reine and a procession of courtiers on elephants followed by two hundred foot soldiers carrying spears. As the company moved ponderously along country trails, the beasts trampled over small trees, shrubbery, roots—everything that stood in their way. The food was served on exquisite lace tablecloths under banyan trees while performers played the kettledrums and danced.

After six months, the Judsons moved from the mission into the city to come into closer contact with the people, and at the same time to receive the protection of the city walls from assassins who terrorized the countryside.

The Baptist Mission Board in America contributed to their financial support. They continued their study of the language. Adoniram steeped himself in Burmese folklore and started work on a Burmese-English dictionary and a grammar. His efforts made the learning of Burmese relatively easy for those who came after him. His grammar, published after twenty years of labor, was hailed as a momentous contribution to linguistics. But, as with all pioneer excursions into language, his progress was exasperatingly slow. After two and a half years of study, he said to Ann, "I just now begin to see my way forward. I've got to be able to handle the language so skillfully that I can challenge the most intricate ideas of the Buddhist teachers. I've got to be able to *think* in Burmese."

He worked so indefatigably that his eyes gave out. Reading print caused him agony. But after several months' rest, he resumed his studies. Six years after their arrival in Rangoon, he announced to his wife:

"I'm ready to teach—and to defend my ideas." A playful smile touched his lips. "We're going to have a little schoolroom, my dear, but not the little red schoolroom of New England. When in Burma do as the Burmans. We'll build a Buddhist *zayat* on the Great Road of the Pagodas!"

Ann looked at him in amazement. In every Burmese village there were small wayside huts where natives gathered to smoke and chat, travelers to sleep, and Buddhist monks to preach to their followers. Many of these *zayats* were erected with elaborate roofs and carvings.

Adoniram had visited several *zayats* and had sat on a mat with a congregation of worshipers—the men on one side, the women on another—all of whom held flowers to their foreheads and closed their eyes in ecstasy as a monk spoke to them of the highest happiness the soul could attain—oblivion.

"We'll reach the Burmese in their own dress, Ann, with

the story of Jesus and the American way of life!" And
Adoniram leased land along the highway to the Great Shwe
Dagon and, with the help of native labor, built a *zayat*. It
was a simple one by Burmese standards. There were three
rooms. The first was really an open veranda looking out onto
the thoroughfare; the second was a classroom for men and
boys; the rear room was a classroom for women.

In early April, six years after his arrival in Burma, Adoniram took a seat on the veranda, and Ann stationed herself
in her classroom. Both anxiously awaited the results of this
experiment. For some time now they had been teaching
neighbors privately, and so for the opening there were fifteen Burmese students sitting at the writing table, a charcoal
blackboard in front of each on which to write the English
alphabet. To passersby, Adoniram addressed the words of
Isaiah. ". . . Everyone that thirsteth, come ye to the waters,
and he that hath no money, come ye and eat!"

The highway was thronged with Burmese. Women—their
teeth and the edges of their eyelids blackened with betel
juice—winked or made jeering remarks to the preacher on
their way to the bazaar. Moslems in brilliant turbans with
flashing, arrogant eyes heckled Adoniram. Some threw
stones. Wealthy businessmen listened with curiosity while
their servants shielded them from the sun with umbrellas
and held out gilded spittoons to catch the cheroot juice.
Beggars entered the *zayat* to rest their feet but would have
none of the teachings. The tinkling of pagoda bells, and an
occasional gong struck by a worshiper in the distance mingled strangely with the white teacher's exhortations from
the Bible.

One day, a Buddhist monk, shuffling along in his yellow

robe with his begging bowl, entered the *zayat* and sat at
the feet of the American teacher.

"Oh, Wise One," he said, looking up with a sardonic expression, "what blasphemous things are you teaching in the
language of my fathers?"

The Buddhist monks were a proud, subtle lot, in whom
the refined ethics of Buddha had degenerated into a doctrine
of Oriental passivity. Believing that the present life was
merely one of a series of reincarnations determined by the
deeds of the previous life, they strained the gnats from the
water they drank and carried a brush with which they carefully swept everything they sat on, lest they crush insects
who might well be their deceased relatives. Their reverence
for all living things, however, did not move them to lift a
finger for the masses of Burmese oppressed by their government, many of whom lived under rags on poles and fed on a
diet of lizards and snakes.

Adoniram entered the dispute with zest. "I preach the
message of Jesus who promised Eternal Life even to the
leper."

"There is no eternal life," mumbled the monk, "only a
series of miserable existences in one form or another until
the soul has amassed sufficient good deeds to enter *neikban*
—the state of eternal extinction. The only sensible thing to
look forward to is a final release from the endless turning
of the wheel of life, the pains of birth, the misery of death."

"We may disagree about the future," returned Adoniram.
"But surely you cannot deny the facts of the present. Your
religion has brought your people only misery. When a fire
breaks out among them, they are too superstitious to take
steps to put it out. They have no medicine, no physicians to

cope with epidemics of cholera and smallpox. You, their spiritual leaders, spend your lives speculating about fate while your people die through ignorance.

"Wasn't it Buddha," Adoniram continued, "who taught that when a human being is wounded by an arrow, he doesn't stop to discover facts about the person who discharged it? He removes the arrow!"

Discussions such as this never failed to attract crowds into the *zayat*, for the Burmese had a zest for debate. Some of the onlookers returned day after day to ask questions of the American teacher, and a few became his ardent disciples.

In the meantime, Ann patiently initiated the women and children into the mysteries of geography. Her facts astonished the natives who had thought of the world as a giant mountain around which clustered several hundred islands, the most civilized of which was Burma.

"Ma Judson, you are a very, very good woman," exclaimed one pupil. "You have attained such merit in this life that I am sure fate will decree you are born into the next existence as a man."

Even before the erection of the *zayat*, Adoniram had been concerned with devising picturesque ways of interpreting the teachings of Jesus to the natives. One day he received word about several Christian converts living in Chittagong, a city on the northwestern coast of Arakan. These natives had been baptized by an English missionary. "I'd like to bring at least one of them to Rangoon. He'll help me to reach the natives here," Adoniram told Ann.

Adoniram estimated that he would be gone for three months on the trip. But Ann would have companionship during his absence. George Hough, a missionary, and his wife had arrived from America to join forces with the Judsons. Hough had brought a printing press from Serampore, and his training in printing combined with Adoniram's knowledge of Burmese resulted in the turning out of pamphlets on Christianity at a lively rate.

But despite the presence of the Houghs, Ann was terribly lonely. She had recently lost her second child. They had been overjoyed at the coming of this second baby and had named him Roger Williams in memory of the great pioneer missionary. But the infant died of a tropical ailment.

"Don," she said on the morning of her husband's departure, "I don't think a woman ever needed a man as much as I do you now. Come back quickly!"

She watched the boat as it disappeared down the Irrawaddy River, then returned to her teaching. For three months she waited anxiously for her husband's return. Then, early one morning, a ship arrived. But Adoniram was not among the passengers. "I have sad news for you, Mrs. Judson," declared the captain. "The ship your husband sailed on didn't reach Chittagong."

Shortly afterwards, Ann received a letter from friends in Bengal confirming the captain's report. Adoniram had not arrived at the Arakan port. The young wife, frantic with anxiety, paced the harbor daily. Had the ship been blown off course? Was her husband safe in another port? Had the vessel gone down at sea?

Political events in Rangoon added to her alarm. There were rumors that the British, exasperated by Burmese violations of the Indian border, were about to declare war, and that the excitable Burmese king was preparing in retaliation to imprison all foreigners. The friendly Vice-Reine and her husband had been recalled to another city, and the new Viceroy was hostile. Mr. Hough, the American missionary, had suddenly been haled before a police court "to give an account of himself." For two days he was examined in a threatening fashion, forced to answer endless questions about himself and his family. Then, with the coming of the rainy season, an epidemic of cholera broke out. All day long the natives beat the death drums and set up a hideous wail to drive off evil spirits. At the government's order, cannons were fired from the roof tops. But the deaths increased.

Mr. Hough felt that he should leave Rangoon with his wife and Mrs. Judson while there was still time. He was convinced that the British were on the verge of bombarding Rangoon. No ships had entered the harbor in recent months. Those already in port had lifted anchor and stealthily made their departure. A single vessel remained. It, too, was preparing to sail for Bengal.

Ann was unwilling to leave Rangoon, the one place where her husband was sure to find her if he were still alive.

"But even if he is alive," Mr. Hough pointed out, "he will never be able to reach you through a war blockade. You will be cut off from him, and your life will be in continual jeopardy."

Ann yielded to these arguments, gathered the few articles that could be conveniently transported, and, with the Houghs, boarded the vessel in the harbor. She wanted to take along Adoniram's Burmese teacher so that she could continue her language studies, but he refused to leave his country because of the possibility of war.

As the ship proceeded down the river, Ann's misgivings about leaving grew. Then, as they were about to enter the open sea, the ship unexpectedly put into a harbor; an inspection by the captain had revealed the need for emergency repairs. "We'll be here for a day or so," he announced.

Ann sent for her baggage. "I'm going back to Rangoon."

She had made up her mind. And this time she would not be budged. The Burmese were her people, ravaged by cholera, faced with the prospect of bombardment. Her duty was to remain with them, to suffer with them if need be. She would not surrender the mission.

The Houghs were aghast. "You can't go back alone! You will be the only white woman in the city."

Nevertheless, she negotiated with a native boatsman to take her back to Rangoon. And late that evening she re-entered the city.

The native students and domestics connected with the mission received her with joy. "Ma Judson, you have come back to us!"

"Yes," said Ann, as she assembled her class and set up the blackboards. "Now let us continue with our lessons."

War did not come. British vessels re-entered the harbor one by one. The epidemic of cholera ended. And one month after Ann's return, natives brought news that a ship had arrived in the harbor and Maung Judson himself was aboard.

In a short while, Ann was in Adoniram's arms. His ship had run into tricky winds and had been buffeted helplessly back and forth in the Bay of Bengal for weeks before making port at Masulipatam, north of Madras. Abandoning his attempts to reach Chittagong, he made a three-hundred-mile trip by sedan chair to Madras, where he booked passage for Rangoon, arriving there seven months after leaving it.

"My trip has been a failure, Nancy. But you have saved

the mission. I'm sure if you had quit it, the government would have confiscated the property and our work have been finished. I always suspected I had married the most courageous woman in all the United States. Now I know it!"

Six years after arriving in Burma, the Judsons baptized their first native convert, Maung Nau. He was a man of thirty-five, without a family, employed by a lumber merchant. The second convert, Maung Tha Hla, was an intelligent, well-educated fellow. And so was the third, Maung Bya. Several women entered the fold. The government's penalty for the adoption of Christianity by a Burmese was severe; the convert faced persecution and possible death. Several of them had been baptized at night to avoid being spied upon by their neighbors, many of whom were paid informers. One convert, who held an important post in the government, was reported to the viceroy and accused of heresy. He had to hide for his life.

The Judsons were threatened with physical harm. Once, while riding to the mineral tank beyond the Shwe Dagon Pagoda where he took his daily bath, Adoniram was confronted by a ranking Buddhist churchman who warned that if he didn't cease his teachings, he would be beaten up. Adoniram decided to go to Ava, the royal capital, and try to interest the "Golden One" himself in the teachings of Christ. At the very least he hoped to persuade him to adopt a policy of religious toleration.

The old King had died, or, in the phrase of the court, had "gone up to amuse himself in the Celestial Regions." His grandson had claimed the throne after murdering one uncle and imprisoning another. When Adoniram arrived at the palace and presented a gilt-bound edition of the Bible to the "Lord of Life and of Death," he glanced at it briefly and tossed it contemptuously to the ground. "In regard to your petition," the interpreter declared, "His Majesty gives no order. In regard to your sacred books, His Majesty has no use for them. Take them away!"

Adoniram returned to Rangoon filled with forebodings. "We'll have to leave Burma, Nancy—at least temporarily—until this wave of persecution blows over." Within the last few years the British East India Company had relaxed its restrictions on missionaries. "Perhaps we can set up in Arakan."

Several days later, Ann assembled her pupils and entered Adoniram's study. "I have spoken to them about our leaving. Listen to what they say."

Each had broken off ties with his friends, in some cases even with his family. All had risked their very lives to adopt Christianity. "Teacher," said Maung Bya, "since I have heard that you are going away, I can neither eat nor sleep. There aren't enough of us here to carry on by ourselves. Stay at least until there are eight or ten disciples. Then if you leave the country, we won't be completely lost."

"Yes," agreed another. "Then the religion will spread of itself. Even the King will not be able to stop it."

So the Judsons remained. And, surprisingly, relations with the government took a sudden turn for the better. Doctor Jonathan Price, an eye specialist from New England, arrived in Rangoon. He was a skillful surgeon, and he achieved quick fame removing cataracts from the eyes of the natives.

News of his success reached the "Golden Ears" in Ava, and he was summoned to the palace. Adoniram went along as interpreter. The King was delighted with Price's bag of "magic" instruments and his surgical skill. No doubt this Yankee wizard would be able to prolong his life. He added Price to his palace entourage, and in a superabundance of good spirits invited Adoniram to take up permanent residence in Ava.

This was exactly the opportunity the Judsons had been waiting for. Leaving the mission in Rangoon in the hands of the Houghs, who had returned to the city, and a second missionary couple from America, the Wades, they set out for Ava in high humor. For six weeks they sailed up the Irrawaddy, during which time Ann kept house, not only for Adoniram but for the ten oarsmen who navigated the boat, the Hindu laundryman, and the guard who kept watch over the guns that had been provided against river pirates.

They passed forests of teakwood and mangrove and huge dye vats drying in the sun. They skirted gleaming fields of rice paddy and the pagoda ruins of dead cities, to which a forlorn monkey or a riotously colored peacock brought the only life. They came upon villages so flooded by rain that children fished from bamboo houses raised on stilts, and old men paddled through the streets to borrow a cheroot from a neighbor.

Upon arriving in Ava, Ann opened a school for girls, teaching them to read and sew. Doctor Price remained their warm friend. He continued to operate on the ailing poor.

One Sunday afternoon while the Judsons were visiting Doctor Price, and Adoniram had just finished conducting prayers, a friend brought them astounding news. "The British Army is invading Burma. Rangoon has been bombarded and captured. A full-scale war is on!"

The war that had been threatening to materialize for years had finally broken out.

For years, refugees from the tyranny of the Burmese kings had sought sanctuary in Chittagong which was under British rule. The Burmese government finally sent an ultimatum ordering the British to return these refugees and threatening to seize Chittagong if the demand were not met. When at last it became evident that the Burmese were actually gathering an army for an invasion, the British General Sir Archibald Campbell beat the "Golden One" to the punch. At the head of three thousand British soldiers and two thousand native sepoys, he suddenly crossed the Irrawaddy from Arakan and marched on Rangoon, encountering only scattered resistance.

When the news reached Ava, the capital was thrown into a frenzy. Natives were snatched from the streets and impressed into the King's army. Pagoda gongs rang mournfully. Shopkeepers closed their businesses and sat by the roadside wailing *"Aime!"*

Within three days, Maha Bandula, the King's general, raised an army of ten thousand Burmese to march on Rangoon. The Judsons, from the windows of their house, watched the columns parade by. Hordes of white elephants carried high-ranking officers under a blaze of umbrellas, followed by court astrologers in silver-studded robes, capering madly and loudly prophesying victory. Dancing girls trooped abreast of spearmen in flaming red caps and green jackets. Carts crammed with Chinese, Indian, and Siamese captives rumbled through the streets. They were the expendables in battle. In a pompous farewell, General Bandula stated that victory over the British was certain and exhibited golden fetters in which the British General Sir Archibald Campbell would be carried captive to the feet of the king.

A few weeks later, while the Judsons were having dinner, the door was forced open and a police official strode into the room followed by a dozen assistants.

"Maung Judson, you are summoned by the King!"

This was the form used when a man was to be put under arrest.

Adoniram was accused of spying for the British. The sudden capture of Rangoon by the British could only mean that plans of the city had been sent them from the inside. The government knew that Adoniram had been corresponding with English friends in India for years. What was more natural than that he had given them military information upon which to base an attack? Furthermore, they came upon evidence that, in their minds, clinched the case against him. It had been Adoniram's habit to cash at a bank in Bengal the salary checks sent him by the Mission Board in America. The Burmese knew nothing about checking accounts. The fact that Adoniram drew money on a British bank was evidence enough that he was in the pay of the British government.

Besides the Judsons, there were seven foreigners living in Ava at the time of Adoniram's arrest. Doctor Price was one. The others were Gouger, a young British merchant; Rodgers, a former British naval officer who had been in the service of the Burmese court for forty years; Laird, a Scotsman, the lumber agent for the king's brother. A Greek leper, an Armenian, and a Spanish collector of the "Golden One's" customs completed the group.

All but the Spaniard, Lanciego, were now rounded up and thrown into jail. Lanciego was seized several months later, when sufficient evidence had been collected against him. The prison, called by the Burmese "Let-ma-yoon"—"Hand, shrink not"—had no windows. The only air came through the crevices in the woven bamboo floor. In addition to the whites, there were fifty native prisoners. The floor was strewn with betel juice, human feces, and the remains of rotting animals; and this, mingled with the sweat of unwashed convicts, caused a stench that was almost too much to bear. The temperature exceeded 100 degrees, day and night. The white prisoners were strung on bamboo poles so that their feet were raised into the air while their shoulders rested on the floor. Each night the feet were hoisted just high enough to cause terrible agony without destroying life, and each morning they were lowered to within a foot of the ground to permit the blood to circulate again. Some of the native prisoners lay in chains; others were fastened in stocks.

The jailor was an ugly man with betel-stained teeth, nicknamed "Father" by his assistants. He was a connoisseur of methods of torture. "I make sure," he was fond of saying, "when I have wrung a rag dry that another twist will not bring a drop."

With the arrest of Adoniram, Ann found herself completely alone in a city hysterically aroused against foreigners. Yet she kept a cool head. One fact stood out. Her husband and the other white men would in all probability be put to death unless she could hit upon a way to save them.

She now found herself placed under twenty-four-hour military guard. She accepted her confinement without any show of fear. When a magistrate arrived to confiscate her property, she treated him with such adroitness that she was permitted to keep Adoniram's books, her supply of medicine, and her work table.

Eventually, the house guard was relaxed. She was allowed to visit her husband. Her first meeting with him was a terrible shock. Released by the jailor from the bamboo pole, this man who was normally so fastidious about his appearance now looked like a wild animal and was crawling with vermin. It was only with a supreme effort that Ann kept up her courage in his presence.

Prisoners were not furnished food by the government; they ate whatever their families managed to smuggle in. Ann, with her gift for making friends, thawed out the hostility of the prison guards to such an extent that she was able to send food through daily. At first she also sent letters to Adoniram, secretly, through a laborer who worked in the prison grounds. But one morning the man was seized by the authorities with one of Ann's messages and he was put in the stocks. Thereafter, she hid her letters inside cakes she baked for her husband, or rolled them into the fish and rice.

For ten years Adoniram had been at work on a Burmese translation of the New Testament. This was the fruition of his exhaustive study in the language. At the time of his arrest, however, the manuscript was still unfinished. Only minutes before the authorities came to search the mission, Ann had buried it in the garden. But she was afraid to keep it concealed there permanently, realizing that the damp earth would ruin it. Then she had an idea. At first it seemed fantastic, but on careful analysis it impressed her with being sound.

Each of the prisoners was allowed a pillow for sleeping. Suppose, she reasoned, she were to sew the manuscript into a lumpy, old pillow and send it to the jail for Adoniram, informing him privately of the ruse. The New Testament would then be out of the reach of the authorities who might at any time order a new search of the mission. Furthermore, the officials would not be likely to look for anything valuable right under their very noses—in the prison itself. The very obviousness of the hiding place would in all probability protect it—and not even the greediest jailor would be apt to steal an old bundle of rags. There was this additional point: the presence of the gospel would provide Adoniram with a tremendous spiritual uplift in his loneliness. And so, Ann concealed the manuscript in a pillow and sent it into the prison.

As the weeks lengthened into months, the suspense concerning her husband's ultimate fate was terrible for Ann to endure. She stubbornly refused to admit to herself that Adoniram faced execution. In her efforts to obtain the release not only of her husband but of the other foreigners, Ann petitioned high court officials, even members of the royal family. She visited the wife of Bandula, the absent general, in the hope that this lady might have influence with the government. But each individual she approached shrugged his shoulders and declared that the prisoners' fate was not up to him and he could give no assurance concerning their welfare. Daily she plied the jailors with gifts to extract favors for the men. She obtained their release from the bamboo pole torture. She gained permission to send in extra food, to distribute clothes, books. Nights she walked home alone from the jail many blocks through unlit streets and dropped wearily into her rocking chair to ponder a new scheme for freeing them. In the midst of her great anxiety, she gave birth to a baby girl, unattended by a physician.

Meanwhile, the prisoners expected to be executed at any moment. Doctor Price, who had managed to hang on to his penknife, got a piece of bamboo from a jailor and carved out a set of crude figures that passed for chessmen. Judson and Gouger found an old buffalo hide, held it up to an oil lamp, and burned patches into it to represent a board. For hours they played chess. Price performed a miracle with his penknife. One of the jailors had a tumor on his eyelid, and Price removed it with his stump-blade.

On one occasion, a hundred sepoys captured by Bandula's army were marched in. To provide additional fetters for the sepoys, the white prisoners were manacled by two's. Young Gouger was chained to the Greek leper Constantine. For twelve hours, the windowless prison, only thirty feet by forty, was packed solid with flesh. Each man was wringing wet. The breathing came short and rasping and was punctuated by cries for water and air. Even the jailors were alarmed, and opened the wicket door to let in enough air to keep the inmates alive. The following morning the sepoys were removed.

Each day was welcomed by the wailing of the Burmese convicts chanting the *Pali* prayer. At three every afternoon, an ominous silence settled over the jail. A gong sounded in the prison yard. The executioner strode in, walked over to a native prisoner, and disappeared with him. Those so honored never returned.

One morning a native woman covered with smallpox was brought into prison. The white inmates puffed furiously on

pipes lit by a well-meaning jailor in a desperate—and un-
scientific—effort to ward off the deadly germs with smoke.
A few days later the woman was removed. Fortunately, no
one caught the disease.

There were pathetic little annoyances, too. Doctor Price,
seized with bad dreams, poked his knees violently into
Adoniram's back, causing him sleepless nights.

Tensely the white men would discuss the prospects of the
opposing armies. They speculated as to whether the British
would arrive in time to free them. They strained their ears
to hear the sound of guns fired from the palace. One gun
signalized an inconclusive battle; two, a Burmese victory;
three, a defeat.

In the meantime Ann left no stone unturned to rescue
them from the executioner. One day at noon the governor of
the jail, who lived across the yard from the prison, looked
up from his meal in astonishment. Mrs. Judson, the American teacher, stood before him attired from head to foot as a
native woman. Her dark hair was straightened back from
her forehead and knotted with a cocoa blossom. Her deep
orange-colored vest fitted casually like a kimono, revealing
a crimson silk gown that flowed to her feet.

To allay the wartime suspicions of the natives toward
aliens, Ann had shrewdly decided to be as Burmese as possible in her daily dress and habits. As a final resort, she
came to the official whose duty it would be to execute the
prisoners once the government issued the order.

"Maung Judson is not a British spy," she declared. "If you
were to come to America, you would not be thrown into
prison on any complaint whatsoever without first being
given a public hearing. You would be offered the opportu-

nity to speak up in your defense. You must persuade your
superiors to give my husband that same chance."

The governor was a fat, merry-tempered old fellow who,
like so many of his countrymen, secretly hated the tyranny
at court. He asked "Ma" Judson to tell him more about
America and he called in his wife to listen. In her effort to
win his good will Ann found herself somewhat in the position of a modern Scheherezade whose influence over the
Lord High Executioner depended on her ability to divert
him with interesting stories. Gradually she wrung concessions from him. Under her prodding he transferred the prisoners from the suffocating, odoriferous main shed into airy
little bamboo huts in the prison yard. He permitted Ann to
stay with her husband several hours daily. On one occasion
he confided to Ann that the Queen's brother had told him
several times to put the prisoners to death, but that he had
successfully stalled off the execution. "I did this only because of my regard for you, Ma Judson."

One morning the governor gave her startling information.
Under orders from his superiors, the foreigners had suddenly been moved out of the Ava prison and sent to Armarapura, a village to the south.

Ann bargained with a boatman to take her there, together
with her baby, a Burmese girl she had adopted into the
household, and her Bengali cook. After a short trip down the
Irrawaddy, they transferred to a cart for the remaining distance to the village. When she arrived there, she learned that
her husband had been transferred to Aunginble, further
south, and she continued on to this new destination.

The prisoners had been forced to undergo a "death march"
from Ava. Stripped to the waist and tied two by two, they

had been driven along the road like oxen. They had no covering to protect their heads from the broiling sun. They were barefoot. The gravel of the road worked into their blistered feet, causing them acute agony; their backs were a mass of welts from lashings.

Constantine the leper fell to the ground. He was prodded into consciousness with a spear and forced to his feet. But he died before Armarapura was reached. Adoniram went temporarily out of his mind. As he crossed a bridge over a river, he made an attempt to throw himself into it, but Laird, the Scotsman who was bound to him, held back with all his might and prevented both of them from being drowned.

Aunginble was a village in the heart of the jungle. It was the hot season of the year, and the people were suffering from a food shortage. Relieved to learn that her husband was still alive, Ann moved into a hut near the new prison. She had no furniture, only the bamboo floor to sit or lie on. When she stepped outdoors, there were pythons in the underbrush. Lizards dropped from the rafters onto the floor as she ate. Very soon after her arrival, Mary, the Burmese girl she had adopted, and who helped her care for the baby, developed pustules over her face. The smallpox! News of this spread rapidly through the village, causing a panic.

Among Ann's medicines in the mission at Ava, was a vaccine for inoculation against smallpox. In her hasty flight, she had neglected to take her store of medicines along. Now she must go back for them. Leaving the Bengali cook to care for her baby, she obtained a cart and a pair of oxen and started through the jungle alone. It was a miserable trip. The oxen stumbled through bamboo thicket and bog, passing the headless bodies of criminals strung on poles by the

"Golden One's" executioners. Pariah dogs roaming half-wild through villages snarled at their feet, and huge paddy birds wheeled disagreeably close. She was tortured by the mosquitoes bred in polluted waters and the heat that rose in clouds of steam.

When she reached the mission, Ann fell ill with a high fever. Several pupils who had learned of her coming hastened to her bedside. They were greatly concerned over her condition. "Ma Judson, you must rest. We shall take care of you."

She shook her head. "Everything will be all right, children. I must be going back. I have business to attend to." She fed herself laudanum, two drops at a time for several hours, then collected food, packed it with her medicine, and started on the return journey.

Back in Aunginble, she turned a centrally located hut into an infirmary and sent word to the villagers to queue up for their smallpox inoculations. At first the natives were suspicious of her medical intentions. Inoculation was a revolutionary procedure for them. But she persuaded a few to submit to the needle and gradually the others followed.

Among the first to be inoculated were the children, including the children of the jailors who guarded her husband. Every child who had not had the disease filed up and put out his arm. Several of them had to be carried in by their fathers, accompanied by shrieks.

"Don't be afraid," said one father to his boy. "This is 'Ma' Judson. She received her magic needle from the Great White God, Himself, during one of her visits to His village beyond the sun."

The epidemic was averted by the use of the vaccine together with the distribution of food, assuring the villagers of a properly balanced diet. A few suffered a very mild form of the smallpox but recovered quickly. Even Ann's adopted girl regained her health.

Only Ann Judson, herself, was unwell. She was very tired now. It had been a long, bitter existence for her since the day she had landed in India, a young New Englander whose chief concern previously had been with picnics along the Merrimac. A lesser woman would have long since given up. As it was, she now succumbed to spinal meningitis.

"God grant that we may live and die among the Burmese though we should never do anything else than smooth the way for others. . . . Yes, others may come and do the work better because we have opened the doors." These had been Adoniram's words to her, and they ran through her mind again and again during her lucid moments, before she wandered off into delirium. Finally the fever subsided and she slept peacefully.

One evening she felt the presence of lips on her cheek, the brushing of a hand across her face. She looked up. It took moments before her reason fully interpreted to her what her eyes reported. It was Adoniram—Adoniram himself— bending over her. The same rugged, serious face, now emaciated; the same warm and gentle eyes.

"Adoniram!"

"Darling, I am free again. Free! The war is over. The British army has forced the Burmese government to capitulate. All its political prisoners have been released. I acted as interpreter at the peace negotiations."

Indeed, the Burmese had been no match for the British. The decision had never been in doubt. But the "Golden

One" had stubbornly resisted until his armies had been thoroughly routed and the British were only forty miles from Ava.

It had been a grim ordeal for Adoniram, seventeen months of it. But when he bent over Nancy and looked into her face, he was stunned. It was hard to believe that his wife was only thirty-seven; she looked like an old woman. Attendants had shaved her hair to the scalp to keep her more comfortable during the hot weather. She wore an old nightcap, and its severe lines accentuated the hollowness of her cheeks, the drab color of her lips, the puffy skin that hung heavily under her eyes.

"Nancy, dear," he took her tenderly in his arms. "We'll have a second honeymoon on a houseboat down the Irrawaddy. Only this time we won't be headed for trouble. The British are permanently occupying a strip of territory along the southern coast, and Sir Archibald Campbell has invited me to set up a mission under his protection. From now on we'll be able to live in peace."

She smiled and her eyes were young again. She turned to Maung Ing, a convert who had recently joined her household. "Bring Mr. Judson the present we have been saving for his homecoming."

Maung Ing left the room and returned in a few moments with a manuscript which he placed in Adoniram's hands. The missionary looked at it in astonishment.

"My Burmese Bible."

It was the precious New Testament that Ann had sent into the prison at Ava and that Adoniram had been compelled to leave behind when he was abruptly transferred to Aunginble.

Briefly Ann explained how it had been salvaged. "When

they moved you to Aunginble, dear, with the governor's permission I immediately dispatched Maung Ing to the jail to retrieve your pillow. He looked for several hours before he found it. One of the guards had seized it, ripped off the matting for himself, and thrown the rolled up manuscript into a corner. Poor fellow! He hadn't any notion what he was discarding!"

The convert nodded his head and said, "God Himself protected the Bible, Maung Judson. May the beautiful words of Jesus reach my countrymen very soon and bring them peace and understanding."

To this day, Christians in Burma relate how Ann's ingenuity saved the New Testament for them.

Yes, it seemed that the Judsons would have happiness at last. Sir Archibald Campbell invited them to his headquarters and gave a dinner at which Ann was the guest of honor. The British, valuing Adoniram's knowledge of the country, offered him a government position with a tempting salary. But he told them he wished to continue as a missionary, free of entanglements.

"I wouldn't leave my present position to be a king, Nancy," he said.

The integrity of the Judsons was to be amply rewarded. Twenty-seven years after his release from prison and just before his death, Adoniram would have the satisfaction of knowing that the Christian movement in Burma had attained surprising maturity. There would be sixty-three churches under the leadership of one hundred and sixty-three missionaries, native ministers, and assistants.

Indeed, the Judsons had played a decisive role in awakening Americans to the crying need for foreign missions.

When the heartwarming story of the Burma mission became known in the United States, fellow Baptists and Americans of other denominations were electrified into taking action that had long been overdue. Rallies were held to raise mission funds, boards were established. Young men and women from all over the country volunteered to follow in the footsteps of Ann and Adoniram. The Judsons and their missionary colleagues in India had inspired and led the way for a mighty spiritual invasion by America of the Orient—one that has continued up to the present.

At the conclusion of the British-Burmese War in January, 1826, Adoniram traveled with a British party of exploration through the new British province of Tenasserim, and selected a site for a mission to be erected in Amherst, the new capital. There were indications that the natives would flock to Amherst in sizable numbers to be under British protection. Ann had high hopes of having a record class of pupils.

The British requested Adoniram to accompany, as interpreter, a civil commission to Ava to negotiate a commercial treaty. "I hate to leave you again, Nancy," he said, "so soon after your illness. And even before our new house is finished." This was to be the mission home they had always dreamed of having.

"Nonsense, Don, you must go," Ann insisted. "I'll rest easy for a change, knowing that you won't be in danger."

And so Adoniram left her once again. On this occasion she was completely relaxed and happy. Her days were spent in recruiting and teaching pupils and in supervising the construction of her new home. Several weeks after her husband's departure, she wrote him joyfully: "Today I have moved into our new house. And for the first time since we were broken up at Ava, I feel myself at home. The house is large and convenient, and if you were here I should feel quite happy."

In the classroom she told of the American constitution and the war fought for freedom. She smiled as a little boy stood up and asked, "Do you mean, Ma Judson, that in America I could grow up to become King?"

"No King dear, President. But you can become one only if you are an industrious little boy and learn to read and write so that you can understand how to serve the people. Now pick up your spelling book immediately. And no more whispering in class!"

One morning Ann failed to appear in the classroom. Maung Ing took over the instruction. His face was grave. Quickly the word passed through the mission. The great white mother was ill. She had never really recovered from her sickness at Aunginble—she had never recuperated from thirteen years of suffering and deprivation. It was a weak, pathetic little body that now met the dreadful onslaught of jungle fever—a body that had nothing left to spare.

For sixteen days she struggled desperately to stay alive. Most of the time she was delirious, but occasionally she opened her eyes and cried out impatiently for her husband. "The teacher is long in coming. Where is he?" And once she murmured to Maung Ing who attended her day and night, "I am not afraid of death, but I am afraid that I shall not be able to bear these terrible pains much longer." The last forty-eight hours she lay on her side without moving, facing the wall, her head resting on an arm. From time to time she uttered exclamations of agony in Burmese. Then, finally, her stubborn spirit yielded. She was at peace. They buried her in the mission garden beside the Hopia—the tree of hope—in the month of October, 1826. She was thirty-seven.

Her final words were spoken to Maung Ing. "Tell the teacher why I couldn't write to him. Tell him all that you see. Take care of my little girl and my house until he returns."

For he would return to her; of that she was certain—as surely as the sun over Burma pours its heat on the fields of gleaming rice paddy and the rain drenches the forests of Pyingado trees. He would return as surely as they both *believed.*

5

Pioneer on the Zambezi

DAVID LIVINGSTONE

&&&&&&&&&&&&&&&&&&&&&&&&&&&&&&&&&&&&&&&&&&&&&&&&&&&&&

ONE AFTERNOON when the thermometer registered 134 degrees and insects died after only ten seconds' exposure to the sun, David Livingstone came upon a lion in the African jungle. Aiming carefully, the explorer fired two shots into the animal. The tail of the beast stiffened, and he sprang at the man, his huge paw catching him by the shoulder. Together they fell to the ground.

"The shock produced a stupor similar to that which seems to be felt by a mouse after the first grip of the cat," wrote Livingstone afterwards. "It caused a sensation of dreaminess in which there was no sense of pain, or feeling of terror, though I was quite conscious of all that was happening."

Livingstone was saved from death by a diversionary attack of his followers. Nevertheless, the lion's assault crippled him permanently. Besides crunching the bone of his arm into splinters, eleven of the lion's teeth had sunk into his bicep. Thereafter he couldn't hold a rifle steady with his left arm. He had to use a specially built telescope stand which, when screwed into a tree, gave him a steady sight.

When he was asked what had been his thoughts under the lion's paw, he replied, "I was wondering what part of me he'd eat first!"

Livingstone's entire life was spent, in a sense, under the lion's paw. Adversity continually seemed to have him on his back. And yet, time and again, he managed to rise to his feet and strike out through the jungle.

Born in poverty in Blantyre, Scotland, he entered a cotton mill at nine, working twelve hours a day to help keep his family alive. He made friends with the operator of a spinning jenny. The machine had a ledge on which a book could be placed at eye level. The boy received his friend's permission to place a Latin grammar on the jenny. All day long as he carried messages, he made it a point to pass the book and read a sentence, a paragraph, a page. And as he continued on his errand, he turned over in his mind what he had read. Books on geography, history, mathematics followed the Latin primer onto the ledge. A whole library of information was acquired on the run—and never forgotten.

Nights when the boy returned from the mill, he put his arm around his mother who was herself exhausted from her household duties. "If ye'll close fast the door, Mother, I'll scrub the floor." A lad didn't admit publicly to doing a woman's chore.

Livingstone won promotions in the mill. At nineteen he was earning enough money to attend medical classes in Glasgow at night. Not only had he organized his time, but his mind as well. There was no wasted motion to his life. He already knew what he wanted to be—a missionary doctor.

Looking around for fields of activity, he met in London Doctor Robert Moffat, an African missionary, who was home after thirty years of service in Bechuanaland. "Africa is the field for the young missionary today," Moffat declared. "But you can't sit down contentedly. You mustn't choose an old comfortable settlement. You must push on to the north. My son, on a clear morning I have seen the smoke of a thousand villages no white man has ever reached. There is your field!"

This was Livingstone's field—no doubt of it. But he almost failed to make the grade as a minister. He was a poor public speaker. Shortly before the final examination, he was asked to deliver a guest sermon. When he stood up to speak, every last syllable of his carefully prepared sermon vanished from his mind. "Friends, I have forgotten what I had to say," he blurted out. He threw up his hands and rushed from church.

The London Mission Board debated his fitness for service. But good sense finally prevailed. Livingstone was given another opportunity to deliver a sermon and this time he acquitted himself.

Four days before he was ordained, he received his medical degree from the College of Physicians and Surgeons in Glasgow, and two weeks later he set sail for Africa, in December, 1840.

Arriving in Capetown, South Africa, he traveled by wagon seven hundred miles north to Kuruman in Bechuanaland where the mission of Robert Moffat, the man who had inspired him to come to Africa, was located. For two years, Livingstone used this mission as his base, taking frequent trips through the countryside to acquaint himself with native life. At Kuruman he fell in love with Robert Moffat's daughter, Mary, and made her his wife. Shortly afterwards, the couple moved to Mabotsa, two hundred miles to the north, where Livingstone established his first independent mission.

Within the next few years he made two moves further north, into the territory of the Bakwains. He studied this tribe, acquiring their language, familiarizing himself with their ways of thinking, listening to their tales around the campfire. He acted as their doctor, taught them farming, and developed a system of irrigation. He was immensely attracted to these people, and to other tribes he visited. "I never yet knew anyone who dealt with them in a Christian manner who ever regretted it."

Many of the natives were musically gifted; some were experts in wood carving. Most had their folk legends, their native histories, their poets and bards. But they were not a happy people. There was a disease eating away at them like a cancer—a disease brought by the Portuguese and Boer traders. The Europeans on the coast made continual raids on native villages, kidnaping men, women, and children and selling them into slavery.

From the moment he arrived in Africa, Livingstone had heard stories about this trade. He had heard how natives were shipped to the markets of Turkey, Arabia, Iran, where women were sold into harems and men were turned into eunuchs for kings, and how cargoes of human beings were delivered to Cuba and the West Indies for the great sugar plantations. He learned of instances when the Africans were packed so closely together that epidemics of disease swept the ship, annihilating the masters as well as the slaves.

Livingstone heard how sick natives were drowned to provide additional room for the living, how entire human cargoes were thrown overboard when a customs vessel gave chase, how on the march from plundered village to the boat, those too weak to continue were beheaded.

At first Livingstone refused to credit these stories. He couldn't believe that Europeans who professed to be Christians were guilty of these crimes. But on journeys into the interior he came on villages that had been raided. What he saw scandalized him. Whole areas were in ruins. Women roamed the fields collecting insects, wild fruits, and whatever else could be eaten, the crops having been destroyed. Children lay listlessly in their huts dying of starvation. The bodies of suicides floated past Livingstone's canoe.

Livingstone's anger mounted when some of his fellow missionaries shrugged their shoulders and said that nothing could be done to stop the raids. Great Britain, they pointed out, needed the alliance of the Portuguese Government in her diplomatic maneuverings for world supremacy. Intervention against the traders, the majority of whom were Portuguese, would be detrimental to her interests.

Livingstone realized that his efforts as a missionary were worthless so long as the trade existed. What was the use of devoting one's life to Christianizing a tribe when at any moment it might be sold into slavery at gun point? Years of painstaking labor could be nullified in a single hour. Everywhere he went, natives came to him in sorrow. Many of them had been on the move for years to keep beyond reach of the raiders. "We are tired of flight," they said. "Give us rest and sleep!"

And so Livingstone looked beyond the problems of his own little Bakwain village to the plight of Africa as a whole. And he was inspired with an idea. The only way to abolish the slave trade, he realized, was to introduce into Africa a morally proper and, at the same time, profitable commerce. He had seen with his own eyes that Central Africa, far from being the bleak, arid wasteland of popular belief, was in fact teeming with natural resources that made her one of the wealthiest areas on earth. The ivory trade alone would reap a fortune.

But to open up the resources of Africa to Europe it was necessary to find routes from the coast into the very heart of the continent. Here was a project for an explorer—for the sake, not only of trade, but of justice to the natives. And Livingstone decided that he would undertake the necessary expedition.

As a matter of fact, he had already acquired some experience in exploration. In the course of several trips across the Kalahari Desert in South Africa to bring the gospel to the tribe of the Makolo, he had discovered Lake Ngami and had established the course of the Zambezi River in a part of the continent where it had not been known to exist.

His plans for carrying out the project were simple and practical. He would set out from his furthest penetration into the interior—the village of Linyante, some fifteen hundred miles north of Capetown—and proceed westward along the Zambezi River until he arrived at the Atlantic coast. He believed this would be the shortest practicable route by which Europeans could reach the resources of the heartland.

His supplies consisted of a few pounds of coffee, tea, and sugar; several spare shirts, trousers, and shoes to be worn when he reached civilization. He carried a Bible, a sleeping tent, two compasses, and a thermometer. In addition, he took along beads for trading with the natives and a magic lantern for their entertainment. And that was virtually his only equipment for a journey of several thousand miles through unexplored jungle, the end of which no man could foretell. He selected twenty-seven natives to accompany him, and he distributed three muskets among them. But the men were such poor shots that Livingstone was in danger whenever they took aim. He sent his wife and children to England before departing on this trip.

No sooner had the party started out from Linyante than it encountered all the harrowing, strength-sapping conditions of the jungle. The heat was terrible. The boiling miasma from the swamps fogged the sight, and the travelers were knocked off their oxen by the sudden outthrust of branches. The baggage grew mouldy, and the guns rusted despite continual oiling. Swarms of the tsetse fly killed the oxen with their bites, threatening to exterminate the party's means of transportation. The grass cut like a razor, causing numerous wounds. When a wagon axle broke, it could not be repaired, for the timber at hand was too spongy to take the axe. Food ran short, and they were forced to eat locusts. The rains turned the ground into a bog, and when Livingstone lay down at night, he prayed that they would not be washed away in a flood. Then, when the rains let up, the men were consumed with thirst. "No one knows the value of water until he is deprived of it," the explorer wrote in his journal. "I have drunk water swarming with insects, thick with mud, putrid from other mixtures, and no stinted draughts of it either."

Weakened by hunger and thirst and the constant exposure to moisture, Livingstone suffered attacks of African fever. During a seizure he lost all sense of time and place. He could not read his instruments accurately. He forgot the days of the week, the names of his companions. And with it all came a deadly, terrible depression, an overwhelming desire to die. Livingstone suffered no fewer than twenty-seven attacks of fever during the trip.

But during his lucid moments, he recorded painstakingly in his journal the flora and the fauna of the country through which he passed, the social organization and customs of the tribes he met. His journal became a treasure house for the zoologist, the botanist, the geographer.

When the party reached territory that had felt the impact of the slave trader, the natives were no longer friendly, unspoiled children of nature. Unable to differentiate between this missionary and the Portuguese and Boers who had stolen their wives and children, they confronted Livingstone with open hostility and duplicity. They demanded that he pay them "a man, an ox, a gun or a tusk" as the price for going through their territory. They held him up at river crossings, threatening violence. They furnished him guides who vanished as soon as they received their wages.

And daily, Livingstone's physical condition grew worse. His fever had brought on acute dysentery, and he was compelled to leave his ox every few minutes to relieve himself. He spent all night gulping water, unable to sleep. Yet he continued on.

Six months after departing from Linyante, he reached the settlement of Loanda on the Atlantic coast—in Portuguese West Africa. When he sat down for his first civilized meal in a white settlement, he tore into the food like a madman. And even then the needs of his stomach were not satisfied. Only the presence of others at the table, he afterwards con-

fessed, prevented him from pocketing the leftovers so that
he could eat them in private.

His native companions who had lived all their lives in the
jungle were amazed by their first sight of the sea. "We
marched along with Father Livingstone, believing that what
our ancestors had always told us was true, that the world
has no end. But all at once the world said to us, 'I am finished and there is an end of me!'"

Shortly after Livingstone's arrival, a British cruiser docked.
Her commander offered to take him back to England. The
invitation was a tempting one. Livingstone's health was
ruined. Yet he refused to go. The arduous journey westward
had convinced him that he had by no means found the practical route for commerce. This ailing man actually made up
his mind now to *retrace his steps* back to Linyante, and
then strike out again, eastward to the Indian Ocean. He projected a journey *twice* the length of his recent terrible one
because he believed he had failed in his mission!

He permitted himself a four months' rest at Loanda. And
then he started back to Linyante with his companions. His
rate of progress was about two miles an hour. The rains
turned the streams into torrents. Entire valleys were broken
up into floating islands of earth. Livingstone could travel
only one day in three; the rest of the time he remained en-
camped on ground he had to pile into mounds above the
water level. He lived on manioc roots and meal purchased
en route from the natives. By the time he reached Linyante,
he had suffered thirty-three additional attacks of African
fever, followed by a siege of rheumatic fever that left him
partially deaf. But he completed the journey, bringing home

safely every man he had led out of Linyante with him two years before.

And then, when he had regained his strength, he resumed with his native followers the odyssey he had set his heart on —this time moving eastward toward the Indian Ocean. Experience had taught him to take certain precautions that made the trip easier. He no longer walked in the hot sun soaked to the skin. As soon as it began to rain, he called a halt, lit a fire, and remained camped until the downpour was over. This time he carried flour and baked his own bread instead of depending on the unpalatable food of the natives on the way.

Just a few days out of Linyante, along the Zambezi River, Livingstone discovered one of the world's great natural wonders—a roaring mass of water more than a mile wide that suddenly plunged three hundred feet into a narrow rocky channel, sending up a spray like great clouds of smoke. The natives called this caldron of shooting water the "Falls of Sounding Smoke." Livingstone named it Victoria Falls in honor of the Queen of England.

To investigate the Falls as closely as possible, he paddled his canoe to the very head of the rapids—a risky maneuver because of the swiftly moving current—and landed on an island in midstream, just above the plunging waters. On a second visit to the Falls, he lay with his head over a projecting ledge and lowered a line, to the end of which was fastened a weight wrapped in calico cloth, to measure the depth of the drop.

He navigated the final stage of his trip down the Zambezi by canoe, emerging on the eastern coast of Africa at Quelimane. The voyage convinced him that the eastward route was the most practicable one to the interior.

And now he sailed for England to report on his explorations. This lank explorer with the furrowed, melancholy face, curt in speech and gesture, received a tremendous welcome. He had constructed a map of the interior of Africa, revealing its physical relief features with uncanny, scientific accuracy. Where to the popular mind there had been only a wasteland, he demonstrated that a world existed. London, Edinburgh, Glasgow vied with one another to honor Livingstone. Prince Albert invited him to an interview; the Royal Geographic Society awarded him a gold medal; the leading universities in England and Scotland conferred degrees. At the request of a publisher, he wrote a book on his missionary travels which became a best seller.

But Livingstone was disturbed by the quality of his reception. He was being honored solely as an explorer. In the tumult of popular acclaim, the words of the missionary went unheeded. "The end of the geographical feat is only the beginning of the enterprise." Few cared to examine the motives that had led him to his great physical discoveries—the desire to end the trade in human beings. The subject closest to his heart, the mainspring of his activities, was overlooked in favor of his secondary achievements.

However, when the government urged him to return to Africa and continue his explorations, offering to appoint him consul at Quelimane, he accepted eagerly He felt that this appointment with the influence it carried would bring him closer to the realization of his own plans. And since he now represented the government, he resigned from the London Mission Society. He did this not because he had become any less the missionary, but because he had enlarged the scope of his crusade.

And so, at the age of forty-five, he returned to Africa in 1858, this time with an official party of scientists. His master plan was to push forward until he reached Lake Nyasa, a strategically situated waterway in the path of the slave trade. He felt that a vessel patrolling the lake would deter the slave traders, who used the waterway as a crossing.

He brought along a small steam vessel from England that could be disassembled for overland travel and then reassembled on the bank of the lake. However, shortly after he launched her in the waters of the Zambezi and started on the voyage to Lake Nyasa, Livingstone realized that he had been sold a leaky tub. At the end of each day's sail, he had to dock her on a sandbar to insure that she wouldn't sink while all hands were sleeping. When her engines were banked for the night, it was necessary to stoke them for hours to get her moving again. And when she finally worked up steam, her speed was so slow the canoes of the natives could overtake her. In disgust, Livingstone christened her the *Asthmatic*. Eventually she had to be abandoned, and he returned to the coast to obtain a new vessel.

As Livingstone, after this temporary setback, went forward with his plans, he was stunned by a sudden, overwhelming tragedy. His wife, Mary, fell ill of African fever and died within a week. A coffin was constructed out of mahogany trees, and she was buried on the bank of the Zambezi River he had so painstakingly explored. All her married life she had been a patient, uncomplaining partner of this active, uncompromising man. Apart from a trip to England, she had kept up a home for her children at her father's mission in Bechuanaland. And now she had died at her husband's side in the jungle. Livingstone in his sorrow took comfort in one passionate belief. Mary had given her life to the civilizing of Africa. He prayed that he, too, would die along the Zambezi, the mighty symbol of his odyssey.

On he traveled toward Lake Nyasa. Forty miles from the lake, he reached the limit of water travel. He and his party took the vessel to pieces and started the herculean task of constructing a road through the wilderness for the transportation of the parts.

And then one day a messenger brought word from Lord John Russell, Prime Minister of Great Britain, that he was dismissed from his post of consul and recalled home. The Portuguese traders, resentful of Livingstone's efforts to throttle their business, had protested to their government. This government had, in turn, lodged a protest with the British Foreign Office. The British, deeply committed in a struggle with the other great European powers for the partition of Africa, regarded Livingstone as a pawn to be brushed off the chessboard of international politics when he became too troublesome. That they were playing with a man's heart was of no account.

There was nothing for Livingstone to do but comply. His government salary was cut off. Furthermore, he had invested the bulk of his personal savings in the expedition, and he was left penniless. The only possible way for him to continue his work in Africa, even for a short time, would be to sell the one asset that remained—his vessel. But the only customers for it in this part of the country were the Portuguese, who would put the boat into the slave trade. Rather than sell it for such a purpose, Livingstone vowed he would send it to the bottom of the sea.

And then this missionary who time and again had risked his life for an ideal decided upon an incredible plan. He would take his vessel to Bombay, the nearest port where a suitable sale could be made. Livingstone knew next to nothing about sea navigation, yet he now prepared to set out on a voyage of twenty-five hundred miles across the Indian Ocean! He had no mechanic to repair the engines in case of accident. The monsoon season was perilously close and if he were caught in it, the chances for survival were slim. His crew consisted of ten African natives who had never before been out of the jungle, and three Europeans—a sailor, a carpenter, and an engineer.

Livingstone set sail at the end of April. Two of the three Europeans immediately fell ill, and Livingstone had to remain at the wheel continuously until he had trained the Africans to steer. These courageous natives stayed by the helm and manned the ship in weather that would have tried the soul of an experienced sailor. During the entire voyage, only one of the ten took to bed with seasickness. After forty-five anxious days, the *Lady Nyasa* made port, her sails torn to tatters. The affair had a tragically ironic ending for Livingstone. He sold the boat and put the money into a Bombay bank. It failed, leaving him without a cent.

But before this reverse occurred, Livingstone was back in England. He had come home to try once more to awaken his countrymen to the need for a free Africa. In a house that had once been Lord Byron's, he wrote a second book, an account of his explorations along the Zambezi and its tributaries. He lectured, preached, appeared before the

House of Commons. He buttonholed people of every class with his arguments. When Lord Russell, who had so recently recalled him, in an expression of remorse sent a representative to his home to ask how the government might suitably reward him for his services, he replied, "If you stop the Portuguese slave traffic, you will gratify me beyond measure."

The Royal Geographic Society came forward with an offer to replenish his finances for a new African trip, and this tireless crusader who was nearing sixty accepted with an enthusiasm that neither bitter experience, nor betrayal, nor official stupidity had been able to dull. There was still much work to do. "The sweat of one's brow is no . . . curse when one works for God."

Having failed to persuade the British Government to place a patrol vessel on Lake Nyasa, Livingstone now decided an alternative plan. He would open up the wilderness *north* of Nyasaland, beyond reach of the Portuguese, to lawful commerce. And so he returned to the steaming lowlands along the Zambezi, where insects rose from the water like mist, to rocky twisting trails through the forests, past tangled stinging creepers that seemed poised by instinct to inflict injuries on the passersby. He returned to the regions of the raiders where natives hurled stones at him, where the rustle of the dense vegetation meant the thrusting of a spear, where weapons hurled by unseen assailants missed him by a foot or grazed his back before striking upright in the ground. He returned to the agonizing pains of hunger, to hallucinations of banquet chambers heaped with the richest viands. His dreams of food were so vivid, in fact,

that mornings when he awakened, his pillow was drenched
with saliva.

But he was sustained in his hardships by another, more
sober vision—the dream of a united, civilized Africa opened
to commerce and to the colonization that would inevitably
accompany it. He thought of the millions of underprivileged
people in Europe struggling to stay alive. Here before him,
once the jungle was cleared and human life was no longer
at the mercy of the elements, were stretches of country that
could provide opportunity and a new lease on life for Europe's emigrants. At the same time, he deplored the desire of
the great European Powers to carve up Africa for their own
exploitation. "Let the pathway into the interior be free for
all; and instead of . . . forts . . . let real colonies be made."

Circumstances made his path more difficult than ever.
When he once again reached Lake Nyasa, he was confronted by a revolt of his native companions. The men he
had taken along on this trip were not the sturdy loyal tribesmen of his past adventures. They had supposed that Lake
Nyasa would be the limit of the trip, but when they learned
that Livingstone planned to strike still further north through
country unknown even to them, they grew panicky. All but
five turned and fled. Livingstone was lenient in his judg-
ment of them. "They were tired of tramping. And so am I!"
Nevertheless, he continued forward with the five.

The leaders of the deserters were cunning. Realizing they
would have to account for their flight, they reported to the
colonial officials in Zanzibar that the Livingstone party had
been attacked by tribesmen, the missionary murdered, and
the rest of them put to route. The lie was a detailed and
very plausible one. They even reported the number of bul-

lets that had been fired into Livingstone—with rifles presumably supplied by the Portuguese.

News of the missionary's death was flashed around the world. England was stunned. The Geographical Society sent out an expedition to investigate. A search party followed Livingstone's trail as far as Lake Nyasa. There it lost the traces, but after a detailed questioning of the natives, the investigators announced that the report of his death was a fabrication. Nevertheless, no clues to the missionary's whereabouts were found. And millions persisted in their belief that he was dead.

Other rumors were spread by irresponsible tongues. It was reported that Livingstone had disappeared deliberately in order to become the husband of an African village queen, that he had grown rich trading with the natives, that he was planning a continental uprising of the tribes.

In the meantime, the missionary, ignorant of these canards or of the deep alarm felt by his friends about him, made a record penetration northward, into the lonely, practically inaccessible regions of Lake Tanganyika. For three years no word was received from him. While millions anxiously awaited news, Livingstone went about his business quietly, making new discoveries, climbing unmapped mountains, struggling through unexplored forests, using his own body to measure the width of uncharted streams, jotting down every detail in that marvelous journal of his to the last inch of space. Having run out of blank paper, he used the pages of old newspapers, writing over the faded print with an ink he had extracted from berries.

He now suffered a bitter stroke of fortune. Two native followers deserted him, carrying off his medicine chest. He was deprived of the medication vitally needed to combat his attacks of fever or any other ailment. "I felt as if I had now received the sentence of death."

A few days later, while changing his clothes, he was stunned to observe how emaciated he had become. To boost his spirits, he roasted a little grain and pretended it was coffee.

His feet had become ulcerated. Whenever he took a step, black blood oozed from the open sores. The pain at night prevented sleep. "I have three ulcers and no medicine," he wrote in his journal. For close to three months he was confined to a hut, unable to move. His appearance had, by now, undergone a striking change. He had lost most of his teeth, partially as a result of biting away on the hard green maize that had been his only solid food for months. "I have such an awful mouth!" he wrote some time later to his daughter Agnes. "If you expect a kiss from me, you must take it through a speaking trumpet."

But there was even worse luck ahead. He had arranged for one of his associates to go ahead and meet him at the village of Ujiji, on the shore of Lake Tanganyika, with the supplies of beads and calico with which he paid off his native guides and bought his passage through tribal territory. When Livingstone reached Ujiji, he found that the man to whom he had entrusted these supplies had sold them and deserted with the profits, leaving him stranded. This was the final straw. "I feel in my destitution as if I am the man who went down from Jerusalem to Jericho, and fell among thieves; but I could not hope for . . . a good Samaritan to come by."

However, help was actually at hand. On the fifth morning

after Livingstone arrived at Ujiji, a native ran up to him, exclaiming, "A white man is approaching the village with a large company!"

Livingstone stepped from his tent and saw in the distance the American flag. His eyes widened as the extent and equipment of the caravan disclosed itself. Every kind of luxury—a portable bathtub, tablecloths, silverware, cases of champagne, goblets, a silver teapot, Persian rugs—had been transported through the jungle by an army of men and mules as if at the command of an Oriental potentate. "This traveler is not at his wits' end like me," observed Livingstone wryly.

The leader of the caravan who stepped up to shake the missionary's hand was Henry Morton Stanley. He was an American newspaper correspondent, and he had been sent on an assignment to find Livingstone. The project that brought Stanley to the village of Ujiji had been formulated three years earlier in a Paris hotel room by James Gordon Bennett, owner of the *New York Herald*, at a time when the air was filled with rumors of the missionary's murder. Bennett, who had a keen eye for publicity and an understandable passion for boosting the *Herald's* circulation, had called in his top foreign correspondent, Stanley, and directed him to launch a search for Livingstone in Central Africa.

But before organizing the search, Stanley was told to take care of other business in the Near East. He was to report to *Herald* readers on the ceremonies accompanying the opening of the Suez Canal, travel up the Nile, write a book on Egypt for tourists, cover politics in Constantinople, and visit the Crimean battlefields. Accordingly, it was close to three years before Stanley started out on his search for the missionary. Bennett has been severely criticized for placing dollars above humanitarianism; nevertheless, an expedition financed by him did bring relief to Livingstone, belated though it was. And no one found the explorer sooner.

Stanley, in the winter of 1871, organized a party of a hundred and ninety-two people and twenty-seven mules to move into the interior in five different sections. After an eight months' search, during which he experienced no little hardship on his own, Stanley came upon the missionary on the shores of Lake Tanganyika. In a book he wrote subsequently, the American recorded with purple trimmings his feelings when he entered Ujiji and learned from the natives that his search was ended. "What would I not have given for a bit of friendly wilderness where, unseen, I might vent my joy in some mad freaks such as idiotically biting my hand . . . in order to allay those exciting feelings that were well-nigh uncontrollable. But . . . I did that which I thought was most dignified. I pushed back the crowds, and passing from the rear, walked down a living avenue of people, until I came in front of the semicircle of Arabs, in the front of which stood the white man with the gray beard. . . . I would have run to him; only I was a coward in the presence of such a mob; . . . I walked deliberately to him, took off my hat, and said: 'Dr. Livingstone, I presume?' "

This narrative of the meeting has passed into the popular folklore.

Livingstone perked up considerably at the coming of the American newspaperman. He ate four hearty meals a day on a clean tablecloth, drank out of a goblet, bathed in the portable bathtub, brewed tea in a silver pot. Stanley brought him letters from his children, and Livingstone's face grew radiant at the sight of the handwriting. The newspaperman filled him in on events of the outside world in the last three years—the election of Grant to the American Presidency, the completion of the Transcontinental Railway, the Franco-Prussian War.

Stanley had fought in the Confederate Navy in the War between the States. An excellent raconteur, he proved to be a stimulating companion. He remained with Livingstone for four months, during which time they explored Lake Tanganyika together. The American put the inevitable question to the doctor: Was he coming back to England?

Livingstone shook his head. He would remain here and continue his exploration. "I would like very much to go home and see my children. But I cannot . . . abandon the task I have undertaken."

In England they were awaiting him with a pension and further national honors. But he had no desire to return to a civilization that had not really understood him. Mary's grave was in Africa; here he would die. Stanley used every argument to persuade Livingstone to change his mind, but the explorer remained adamant.

Finally, the American, profoundly disappointed, for he had become deeply attached to the doctor, made preparations to leave alone. From his own caravan he transferred to Livingstone tools, weapons, beads, wire, and cloth. In turn he received the doctor's journal of his latest explorations for delivery to England. The correspondent took back with him a vivid recollection of the elderly physician in his gray tweed trousers, his red-sleeved waistcoat, and weather-soiled, peaked hat banded in gold, standing gaunt and erect as he waved goodbye. Stanley was the last white man to see him alive.

Livingstone insisted upon remaining in Africa because his mission had by now developed into more than a question of combating the slave traders or of finding the watershed of Africa west of Lake Tanganyika; it had developed into an impassioned investigation to place the moral struggle in Africa in its historic setting.

His thoughts went ever more deeply now into the religious past. He recalled the trials and abuses of another great adventurer in the wilderness—yes, in Africa itself; the pioneer who had led a people to freedom over a mighty sea. The Old Testament had stated that Moses had come into inner Ethiopia with Merr, his foster mother, and had founded the city of Meroe. That would be in the general area in which Livingstone now found himself. "I dream of discovering some monumental relics of Meroe, of confirming, bevond all doubt, the truth of the scriptural history, of translating the moral grandeur of the past into the Africa of the present. Then the toil and hardships, the hunger and pain I have endured, the irritable ulcers, would only be discipline."

In addition to searching for Meroe, Livingstone attempted to locate also the semi-legendary fountains of the Nile mentioned in Ptolemy's ancient geography. As in the case of many men not far from death, the past had become more real than the present, because the present was too terrible to bear. Livingstone had indeed stepped out of time.

In retracing the footsteps of the past, he struck out southwest of Lake Tanganyika with fifty-seven natives to Lake Bangweolo, which he had earlier discovered, and made a sweep of its shore. His followers, accustomed though they were to the climate, complained of inflamed feet caused by the radiation of heat from the burning soil. Then followed the inevitable rains, turning the rivers into inland seas. The vast waters of Lake Bangweolo expanded as much as thirty and forty miles beyond the shores. In some sections the natives had to carry the ailing Livingstone over a flooded stream through water up to their mouths. Never in all his travels had the missionary seen anything like these rains. "It is not all pleasure this exploration," he remarked sardonically.

Daily he jotted down in his journal the distance the party had covered. But he was too exhausted to write more. He was now carried by the natives in a litter, for he was past walking or riding an ox. And the swinging of the litter caused him such agony that before long he could not go forward for more than an hour or two out of the twenty-four. But when he was placed down on the street of a new village, and his men set about to erect shelter, he would beckon to the natives to approach and question them in a whisper about the topography of the region. Had they heard of the city of Moses? Did they know of a hill on which four rivers had their source—the fountains of the Nile? They shook their heads pityingly. The white man was having evil dreams.

Even on mornings when his followers were convinced he could go no further, he would insist on proceeding. They would take down a side of his wattle hut, bring the litter to his bed, lift him gently on it, and resume the march.

Then one day they came to the village of the chieftain Chitambo. Livingstone lay in a drizzling rain while his hut was being built, and the villagers gathered around him, as usual, in silence and awe. At last the shelter was finished. He was carried inside and put to bed. Early the next morning several of his followers went to his quarters to awaken him. They found the hut in darkness. They lit candles and approached his bed on tiptoe. But they drew back respectfully when they saw the missionary on his knees, his head buried in his hands.

But one of the natives whispered, "Before I went to sleep last night I looked in and the master was kneeling just as he is now."

The group timidly drew nearer. One man touched his cheek. It was cold. David Livingstone was dead.

For thirty thousand miles he had wandered through the African heartland. And yet, in some ways, his journey home was the most remarkable of all. His followers, after debating what to do with the body, decided that they would carry it to the British authorities at Zanzibar, a journey of a thousand miles. They removed the heart and intestines and buried them in a tin box. Then they embalmed the body in a preparation of salt and brandy, exposing it for fourteen days to the sun. They wrapped it mummy-like in calico with the knees bent inward for convenience in travel.

The natives were exhausted from their own sufferings. On the third day of their journey homeward, half of their number collapsed. The cortege had to halt for a month to gather strength. Because the tribes that lay along the route had a superstitious dread of dead bodies, the party had to use every stratagem to gain passage through tribal territory. Encountering particularly stubborn opposition in one village, they announced to the chief that they would turn back with the body. Secretly they made up a bundle of sticks in the shape of a corpse. Six of them carried it away, taking care to attract attention to their withdrawal. The others, unobserved, packed the body in with a bale of goods and passed through the village successfully. When night came, the decoys joined the main party.

Over mountains and swollen rivers, through marsh and arid plateau, they made their way toward the coast, retracing the steps Livingstone had taken. One after another they dropped out, unable to keep up the pace. But five indomitable souls remained with their burden until Bogamoio, Zanzibar, was reached. Only then did they surrender it to the British consul.

When the body arrived in England, even those who had known the man for years couldn't believe that these emaciated remains belonged to Livingstone. But surgeons made an examination and found the break in the bone of the left arm where the explorer had been crunched by a lion.

And now perhaps the greatest irony of all befell Livingstone. The man who had not been listened to in life was buried in Westminster Abbey with the pageantry usually reserved for kings. And when men looked upon the wasted little body and realized all it had given for an ideal, a great feeling of shame came over them, and they promised that his work would go on.

And so it has. Eleven years after Livingstone's death, the European powers met and pledged themselves to suppress the traffic in human beings. "Livingstonia," a religious, educational, and industrial settlement, was established for missionaries to carry on his work in Nyasaland, where he had suffered his greatest defeats Within a generation, roads and steamers were taking the casual traveler into what today is the Belgian Congo, the region of his deepest penetration. Locomotives roared past his first mission settlement in Bechuanaland; a telegram was sent to Edinburgh in less than three hours from the wilderness where Livingstone had been lost for three years.

Courage is rarely forgotten. And the man from Blantyre lives on for the very spirit that moved him to declare, "Nothing earthly will make me give up my work . . . I encourage myself in the Lord my God, and go forward."

6

Explorer of the Mississippi

JACQUES MARQUETTE

THREE HUNDRED years ago, the Indians who roved through the American middlewest brought stories to the traders, trappers, and missionaries of a mighty river whose banks were a mile apart, whose waters, when flooded, rose to such a height that only the tops of trees could be seen. The whereabouts of this fabulous river—the Indians called it the "Messipi"—became a favorite topic of the day. Where was its source? Into what body of water did it flow? For all its vastness, it remained as elusive as Ponce de Leon's Fountain of Youth. In 1541, one man, the Spaniard Hernando De Soto, had actually stumbled upon the lower banks of the "Messipi." But he died before he could trace its course. His body was buried by his men beneath the current.

For the next hundred years the "Messipi" eluded the attempts of numerous explorers to find it. It remained for a man of an entirely different stamp to achieve the triumph. He was Jacques Marquette, a thirty-six-year-old missionary who belonged to the Society of Jesus. He had come to the American wilderness neither for gold, furs, nor diplomatic honors. Like our other crusaders for god, Marquette made his magnificent practical contribution—one that opened up the heart of America to civilization—while on an errand of the spirit.

Born of a leading family in Laon, France, Marquette was fair-skinned, gentle, an aristocrat to his fingertips. As a boy, he aspired to be a chevalier in the tradition of his ancestors who had helped free Europe from the armies of Attila, the Hun.

As he grew up and looked around for fields in which to exercise his talents, his attention was drawn to a group of his countrymen who were living dangerously in the American wilderness.

The first Jesuit missionaries had arrived in North America at the beginning of the seventeenth century. Within fifty years, operating out of Quebec, they had penetrated into the wilderness south of the Great Lakes, encountering, among the Indians, adventures as marvelous as any conceived by Scott or Dumas. They were scientists, diplomats, and explorers, as well as priests. They observed minutely the flora and fauna of their environment, prepared summaries of the tides and currents, drew a map of Lake Superior that was, according to the historian Francis Parkman, "a monument of enterprise."

They knew how easily a man could freeze to death in the gloomy birch forests; how quickly the snow could bury him. They learned how to exist alone far from their base of supplies; how to build shelters, sleds, and canoes; how to live the life of an Indian, as disdainful of physical hardship as the savage himself. They were scalped, imprisoned, tortured —and worshiped—by the unpredictable red man. And they accepted the bad and the good with equal indifference. By their mercy and their epic suffering, they won the respect and even the love of the Indians and smoothed the way for the fur trapper, the trader, the hustling man of commerce. The Colonial French Empire was reared on the graves of the martyred priests.

Every year the Jesuits sent a report of their labors to Paris. People of all classes were deeply touched. The nobility donated money; the convents sent prayer books; the nursing orders enlisted recruits for the missions. And no Frenchman was stirred more profoundly than young Jacques Marquette. This, he decided, was the life he was meant for. At seventeen he entered the Society of Jesus and spent twelve years in preparatory studies. Then, at the age of twenty-nine, he was assigned to teach among the American Indians.

In 1666, he arrived in Quebec, the capital of New France. The city rose gloomily above the St. Lawrence River. One narrow path led from the pebbly beach where traders and shippers had erected a row of warehouses to the rocky heights on which the schools, churches, and other public buildings were grouped. Only a few hundred people lived in the capital. In fact the entire white population of New France, from Newfoundland to Lake Superior—including fishermen, traders, settlers, and missionaries—numbered only ten thousand people. Quebec had a *joi de vivre* that defied her bleak surroundings. During the severest part of the winter, the inhabitants, with typical Gallic exuberance, staged ballets in an unheated, frozen warehouse while the flutes and violins played the latest tunes from Paris.

Within three weeks of his arrival in Quebec, Marquette was sent to Three Rivers, a mission on the northern bank of the St. Lawrence River for "on the spot" training. Two years later he was sent to one of the furthest outposts of French influence—the settlement at Sault Ste. Marie among the Ottawa Indians; and the following year, to the Hurons at Chequamegon Bay to conduct a mission entirely on his own.

His final instructions before setting out were indicative of the grim life that awaited him. "Unless you are temperamentally able to love the Indian like a brother, you might as well go back to France. There will be no earthly reward for you in this life."

And then his superior general added this advice: "When you are traveling with the Indians, never make them wait for you. If your broad-brimmed hat annoys them, take it off and wear your night cap. Fasten up the skirts of your cassock, so that you will not carry water or sand into the canoe. Wear no shoes or stockings. You may put them on in crossing portages. Do not volunteer to paddle, unless you are prepared to do so all day. Do not lend an Indian any part of your clothing, unless you have made up your mind to do without it for the rest of the trip. Do not ask the Indians too many questions. Take along a flint and steel to light their pipes and kindle their fires at night. Try to eat the food as the Indians cook it, bad and dirty though it is. You will get used to it. It will do no harm to play with the children, flatter the old people, speak kindly of the departed relatives. And God be with you!"

A chief stumbling block for missionaries was the Indian languages. Some of the most learned Jesuits gave up trying to learn them and returned to France in despair. But the young aristocrat from Laon was a born linguist. In the course of his career, he was to learn how to speak six Indian dialects fluently.

From the outset, Marquette encountered adventure. To reach the Hurons at Chequamegon Bay, for instance, he paddled a canoe four hundred miles over Lake Superior, through waters so treacherous at times that even today large steamers often run into trouble.

The Hurons were experiencing hard times. They were a shadow of the once mighty tribe that had ruled the Great Lakes. Reduced in numbers by war and famine, living in constant terror of the warlike Iroquois to the east, they were only too happy to welcome French missionaries and to gain the friendship of the powerful French nation.

"Greetings, Blackrobe," the sachems declared at Marquette's coming. "Never has the sun seemed so fair, or the corn so ripe, or the fishes so abundant in the streams, as today when you arrive among us."

Few white men were able to endure life in an Indian village. But Marquette entered into it without complaint. He lived in a windowless cabin so filled with acrid smoke that frequently he had to lie down and hug the floor for air. His eyes were constantly inflamed. He ate without any outward indication of revulsion the Indian meal that "tasted like the glue used for papering the walls of houses." He endured the crawling vermin, screaming children, snarling dogs, the constant quarrels of his savage neighbors. As he sat in his cabin in the dead of winter translating Christian prayers into the language of the Hurons, his ink froze and his fingers grew numb. The drinking water in his flask turned to solid ice. Sometimes, to get away from the foul air, he went into the forest and read his breviary shivering by moonlight.

He accompanied the braves on long journeys over the snow, trudging wearily under his share of equipment as the dogs led the way through the drifts. And when the warm weather came, he traveled with them many miles by canoe, suffering almost unbearable fatigue.

Marquette discovered that the Indians had no word for God in their language. But they were eager to hear about the Great White Spirit. They believed that birds, beasts, and reptiles had ears to overhear human speech, that lakes and rivers and waterfalls were living beings. Once, when the missionary asked an elderly savage about a dream he had had, the Indian replied:

"I cannot talk now. It is spring. The streams are flowing, the animals are awake. They will overhear me and do me harm. Wait until the winter when everything is asleep, and I shall tell you."

When Marquette explained about God and eternal life, one sachem asked anxiously, "But will I be able to smoke my pipe in your paradise? I cannot do without tobacco."

Marquette's chief opponents were the medicine men, whose influence was threatened by his teachings. They pointed to the breviary in which he was absorbed by the hour. "The Blackrobe is mumbling incantations to destroy our corn and bring us famine!" If the harvest were poor, or the winter unusually severe, they demanded his life.

The missionary warded off harm by matching the tricks of the medicine men with "magic" of his own. He had brought along a magnifying glass with him, and he astonished the Indians by turning a flea into a monster under the lens. He showed them a handmill which ground their corn. But their chief delight was a clock. The entire village sat for hours around him in tense silence waiting for it to strike. The Indians believed it was an animal. "What does it eat?" they asked. When the last stroke sounded for the hour, the missionary would cry, "Stop!" And to the astonishment of the audience, the clock remained still.

For two years Marquette lived among the Hurons at Chequamegon Bay, preaching, baptizing, ministering to the sick. When, as the result of an inter-tribal quarrel, the Sioux Indians to the west went on the warpath and threatened to annihilate the Hurons, the missionary helped the Hurons to emigrate hurriedly to Michillimackinac Island in Lake Michigan, out of reach of the Sioux warriors. During the five-hundred-mile trip by canoe, he kept up their morale; and when they debarked at Michillimackinac, he shared in the labor of constructing a new village.

"I am very happy here," he wrote. He looked forward to spending the remainder of his life among these Indians, and dying in the wilderness, as Saint Francis Xavier, the man he most admired, had done.

But now events suddenly conspired to thrust the priest from a life of honorable obscurity into the headlines of history.

From time to time Marquette as well as other missionaires had received reports from the Indians about the great "Messipi" River that flowed through fertile lands where the snow rarely fell and where two crops of maize were harvested yearly. The Spaniards had named it the "*Rio del Espiritu Santo,*"—the "River of the Holy Ghost"—and had estimated that it ran south of the Great Lakes. But whether it flowed into the Gulf of Mexico or into the Pacific, no European knew. The fact was that no white man had as yet explored its source. For years the nations of Europe, aware of the strategic importance of the "Messipi," had vied with one another to be the first to navigate it.

In June, 1672, France took a decisive step. A minister of Louis XIV wrote to Jean Talon, director of financial policies in New France, authorizing him to launch a new exploration. If this were successful, it would unlock the American west to French commerce and make possible the erection of a barrier of colonies that would seal the English off on the Atlantic coast. "His Majesty desires you to give this your immediate attention," wrote the minister from Versailles.

Jean Talon recommended to Count de Frontenac, governor of New France, that Louis de Joliet be the leader of the expedition. Joliet was the son of a wagon maker, in the service of a fur company. Tall, blue-eyed, bronzed by many suns in the wilderness, a hunter, trader, and explorer, Joliet had traveled widely among the savages and was an expert in Indian dialects. He was a flesh-and-blood realization of Natty Bumppo, the hero of Cooper's *Leatherstocking Tales*.

The authorities decided to appoint a second man to head the expedition—a spiritual leader with the ability to gain the good will of the Indians encountered on the way. When Father Dablon, superior general of the Jesuits in New France, was asked to recommend a missionary, he answered without hesitation, "The best man for the job is Père Marquette."

This was a logical selection. Although Marquette had been in the New World only six years, he was already hailed by his associates for his magnificent achievements among the Hurons and Ottawas. Furthermore, he was a specialist in Indian tongues. And he had demonstrated striking ability to endure physical hardships.

Joliet was sent to Michillimackinac to inform Marquette of the decision. He traveled by canoe down the Ottawa River in the crisp autumn of 1672, and arrived at the mission just as ice was forming over land and lake.

The priest was astonished and thrilled. "What an opportunity this will provide for my missionary work! Why, I'll be able to contact tribes no white man knows the existence of!"

The preparations for the trip were extensive. Nothing was left to chance. All the information about the great river compiled since the days of De Soto was evaluated. Half-breed trappers who had spent years in the western country, Indians resting at the mission en route to their tribes were called in and questioned at length. The leaders traced a huge map estimating the course of the river, based on the various reports. For this journey that would carry them several thousand miles through unexplored country, they took along five French Canadian woodsmen and two canoes. The canoes were light but strong, built of birchbark and ribs of spruce and cedar splint covered with yellow pine pitch. Four men could carry them over the portage paths. In smooth water they could be paddled at five miles an hour. Into these canoes the men packed rifles, ammunition, extra clothing, sails to take advantage of favorable winds, equipment for the making of maps, gifts for the Indians to be met on the way. They stocked up on smoked meat and Indian corn as their basic foods.

On every side they received warnings. The Indians were especially gloomy in their prophecies. "Even if you succeed in reaching the river," one chief declared, "we have heard that the heat that rises from its banks will shrivel your flesh. The river is filled with monsters who will overturn your canoes. And if you escape these dangers, you will be put to death by hostile tribes."

On the 17th of May, 1673, when the ice had broken up at Michillimackinac, the party was ready to set out. Blackrobes and trappers, Huron and Ottawa Indians lined the shore of Lake Michigan. Joliet, nattily dressed in a blanket coat and vivid blue sash, and Marquette, in his black robe and wide-brimmed hat, said their goodbyes and joined the Canadian woodsmen who were already kneeling by the paddles. Just before they rounded Point Barbe, each man gave a glance backward, and Joliet tipped his puddingbag cap to the on-lookers.

They passed the frowning stone of the Point. Then they were swept up by the current that surged through the Strait of Mackinac and spun along the northern shore of Lake Michigan, entering a body of water from whose slimy bed rose vapors that fused with the odor of a salt spring into such a stench that the French called it "Putrid Bay." Sudden squalls of wind churned the waters. The air held a lingering nip. Paddling as they knelt on birchbark rushes, they pro-ceeded into Green Bay through the "Door of Death," so called because of the crosswinds and currents that had sent many craft to the bottom of its waters.

The shores of Green Bay bristled with tamarack and pine whose pungency sweetened the air. From time to time they sponged their faces in the cool, invigorating waters at their elbow. In passing through the Fox River, they entered water so shallow that the canoes scraped on the bedrock and the men continually had to carry their craft into deeper water, wounding their feet as they walked. At points, the river narrowed into creeks choked with wild vegetation, making the passage tremendously difficult. At one stage they came on a series of rapids that could not be navigated.

"We will need guides to lead us overland," declared Joliet. "Otherwise we cannot get through."

Fortunately, a tribe of friendly Indians, the Mascoutens, who were well known to the Jesuits, lived in the area. The canoes were beached, and the travelers made their way to the Indian village for guides.

The chiefs were delighted to see the white men. They presented them with three guides and with reed mats to serve as beds for the rest of the voyage. The canoes were unloaded of all their equipment. Then, while several of the party carried the craft over their heads, the rest strapped the food and equipment on their shoulders, and the Indians led the way over the portage path that skirted the rapids. The canoes were put into water that had dropped a hundred and seventy feet from the head of the falls. The Indians were sent home, and the paddling was continued.

Daily, Father Marquette and his colleague made notations in their journals on the foliage and vegetation, the animals and insects they saw along the banks. They took soundings of the river, consulted their maps, and speculated as to what awaited them.

Several days after leaving the Mascoutens' village, they passed into the flooded waters of the Wisconsin River from whose banks rose bluffs three hundred feet high. The travelers threaded their way past islands, some of which were merely small sandbars; others were larger and looked like huge chunks of the Sahara Desert transplanted to North America; still others were thick with poplar saplings or lush with flowers.

On they proceeded, approaching the limits of country explored by white men, making steady progress toward the great river they were convinced lay ahead. They skirted the twisting shoals, paddled past dense forests of walnut, oak, and basswood so unlike the white pine of Lake Michigan, and finally crossed the delta of the Wisconsin into the watershed of the "Father of Waters" that today powers a thousand turbines and numerous pulp mills.

On June 17th, one month out of Michillimackinac, the seven canoeists passed at last into the "Messipi." The travelers recognized the river instantly by its broad, sweeping current, the great distance between its banks—a mile at this point. They had never before seen anything like it.

"Who can doubt this is the river!" exclaimed Joliet, his face flushed with excitement as he stood up and waved his cap in a salute to nature for providing such a miracle.

Marquette's joy—"a joy which I have no words to express"—was conveyed in a more quiet manner. He knelt in prayer and thanked God that he had been spared to witness this occasion.

Now that they had entered the "Messipi," it was necessary for them to proceed wherever it would take them. They were fascinated by the scenes that met their eyes—the great Iowa bluffs of limestone crowned with oak and birch, the shoreline indented with sodden bayous, the vast stretches of sycamore and cottonwood forests. Frequently they drew in their paddles and sailed under a smartly blowing breeze, only to have it change direction and necessitate their paddling again. At night they prepared their meals over a fire on shore, but they slept in their canoes a distance from the bank to avoid attack by animals or unfriendly Indians. Even with this precaution, they kept a sentinel constantly on the alert.

Occasionally they stumbled into swamp choked with wild oats and duckweed, or became entangled in half-submerged colonies of muskrats. Once, toward nightfall, as Marquette and Joliet were talking quietly, they were jolted as the canoe gave a sudden lurch. Only the steady nerves and quick reflexes of the canoeists kept it from turning over. A huge catfish had catapulted through the air and struck the side of the craft with the force of a boulder. Then it disappeared as quickly and mysteriously as it had come.

"*Nom de chien!*" muttered Joliet, white-lipped.

On another occasion, a fish, described by Marquette as having "the head of a tiger, a pointed snout like a wildcat's, and a black neck with beard and ears erect," leaped out of the water only yards away from the leading canoe and glared at the voyagers. It was an American tiger cat.

One day they came on a sinister sight—a sheet of rock rising perpendicularly from the water, upon which a group of half-human and half-bestial figures were painted with savage power. The eyes were blood-red above tigerish mouths. The bodies were covered with ugly scales. Their tails were so long that they passed over their heads and down between their legs.

"These monsters must have been painted by Indians," remarked Joliet. "But imagine savages risking their lives to climb to such a height!"

"No doubt they are worshiped as sacred spirits," answered

Marquette. "How horrible! At any rate, here is evidence that there are Indian tribes in the neighborhood. We should be meeting them soon."

Other voyagers who followed these pioneers down the Mississippi in later years commented on the painted monsters. But the colors gradually faded under the rains of centuries, and today there is no trace of them.

A dramatic encounter occurred when the canoeists reached the juncture of the Missouri River, called by the Indians the "Pekitanoui"—the "River of Muddy Waters." Swollen by streams and rivers for a thousand miles and bearing great masses of trees, the "Pekitanoui" hurled itself with such impact into the "Messipi" that the canoes spun around like tops. Miraculously, the paddlers managed to breast the boiling waters without capsizing.

"It was truly a terrifying experience," Marquette confessed in his journal.

Eight days after entering the "Messipi," they came for the first time upon footprints on the shore. These led inward through the brush, evidently to an Indian village. Since it was their purpose to investigate the tribes that inhabited the valley, the explorers beached their canoes.

Marquette said to the five Canadian trappers, "We have come on an errand of peace and this must be instantly evident to whomever we meet. Therefore, you men will stay behind. Monsieur Joliet and I will go forward alone."

The Canadians, protesting that this was foolhardy, asked to go along with their rifles. But Joliet agreed with the priest. "Be on guard against any surprise and keep your powder ready."

The two leaders followed the footsteps for a distance of

five miles and came upon a settlement of Indian huts. They drew close enough to hear the Indians conversing. And then they announced their presence.

Several savages stepped from the huts and scrutinized the strangers in silence. Other Indians quickly made their appearance and stood quietly in groups regarding the Frenchmen with noncommittal expressions. Finally, four elderly braves were deputized to greet the Frenchmen. Two of them carried peace pipes of red sandstone adorned with plumage. When they were a few yards away, they halted. Then one addressed Marquette.

"What do you desire, Blackrobe? From where have you come with your friend?"

Marquette was instantly relieved. He recognized the language as belonging to the Illinois tribe, branches of which the Jesuits had already had dealings with.

"My friend and I have come on an errand to explore the mouth of the Father of Rivers. We have presents for your people."

The Indians invited the Frenchmen to proceed with them to the village. Townspeople of all ages swarmed around them. Some ran a few yards ahead, then turned around and walked slowly back toward them to get a better look. This was done without a word being uttered. Even the dogs were banished—a mark of the Indians' great respect for the visitors. The Frenchmen were brought to a centrally located cabin, at the entrance to which stood a wrinkled old sachem, entirely naked, his hands outstretched to the sun as though screening his eyes from it. Around him were gathered the dignitaries of the village, eager to hear Marquette's remarks.

"I bear a message from the great pale Manitou," Mar-

quette explained. "He has made men white and red and
yellow. And He has commanded all of them to love one another."

The old sachem replied. "That sounds well. Enter our
cabins in peace."

Joliet sent back word to his Canadians to bring up the
presents. And the company sat down to the traditional feast.
The first dish was a platter of Indian meal, boiled in water
and seasoned with grease. The Indians, like all nutritionally
starved people, had an inordinate fondness for grease. They
even forced hunks of it into the mouths of infants. The hosts
insisted on stuffing mouthfuls of meal down the white men's
throats with their own dirty fingers. This was the prescribed
etiquette for feeding guests.

The next course served was fish. Blowing on choice mor-
sels to cool them off, the savages put them into the Frenchmen's mouths as one would give food to a bird. For the third
course, the hosts brought forward a freshly killed dog. Dogs
were highly valued by Indians, and it was the highest com-
pliment to serve them at a feast. However, when the guests
balked at eating this, the dish was withdrawn and an ox was
substituted, the fattest portions of which were crammed into
the guests until they were on the verge of gagging.

The Illinois were among the most civilized of Indians.
And yet they had their touch of arrogance. "Illinois" in their
language meant "the Men." All other Indians were "the
Beasts." During his stay Marquette discovered that these
Indians were incurable gamblers. They staked their canoes,
pipes, weapons—even their wives—on the throw of a die.
Experimental marriages lasting for a day, a week, or longer
were common among them. Such a union was sealed when

the suitor presented his girl with a gift of wampum. An attractive young lady sometimes contracted as many as twenty such marriages before entering into a permanent union, and she appeared at dances proudly decorated with her collection of wampum. Once her period of affairs was over, though, the squaw became a household drudge, and her hard life turned her into a sour, querulous person. Marquette was amazed at the number of homosexuals he saw. These males were dressed like squaws, did womanly chores, never married. They were permitted to accompany war parties but were forbidden to use the bow and arrow—the brave's prerogative. Instead, they carried clubs.

Marquette and Joliet passed the night in a sachem's cabin preparatory to resuming their trip at dawn. The priest had a talk with the chief, an agile-minded savage. "I have seen your cross, Blackrobe, when I have visited my cousins on the Wisconsin among whom your people have come. Will you plant a cross here in the center of town? We will decorate it with red and white skins and bows and arrows. And we will pray before it and ask the Great White Spirit to ward off famine. When, Blackrobe, will you return to teach us your prayers?"

The priest, touched by the old fellow's earnestness, promised he would revisit them or send a fellow missionary as soon as he had completed his trip.

The chief nodded his head. "That is well. Let me give you a pipe of peace to take down the river." He handed the priest his own calumet. Its stem was two feet long, decorated with eagle's feathers.

"Blackrobe, wherever you go, even your enemies will shrink from harming you when you show this pipe."

And then he added, half jokingly, yet fully meaning to flatter, "There is a warrior who guards the path to heaven. His name is Oscotarach, the Head Piercer. And he removes the brains from the heads of all men before they pass into Eternal Life. But you, Blackrobe, are the cleverest man I have ever met. I am sure you will find a way to slip into heaven with all your wits about you!"

Once again the Frenchmen embarked in their canoes and continued down the "Messipi." They came upon large herds of buffalo, an animal none of them had ever seen before. Marquette sketched the buffalo in his journal. The bottom lands seemed to be crowded with them. In many cases they were hidden by the cottonwoods and elms, betraying their presence only by bellowing. One of the Canadians shot a buffalo so tremendous that it required the strength of all seven men to remove the body.

As they passed into the lower "Messipi," clouds of mosquitoes arose from the banks and tormented them. The Indians of the area drove the insects away by sleeping on raised platforms and building fires underneath. And at night the white men, too, used fire for protection. But during the day there was little escape. They arranged their sails into a shelter, but this gave little protection, and they suffered in silence.

One afternoon when, according to their calculations, they had traveled over a thousand miles down the "Messipi," they encountered the trouble they had feared since the start. While passing a heavily wooded bank, they heard a war cry. A party of Indians slipped down to the water's edge armed with bows and arrows. So sudden was the meeting, it was impossible for the canoeists to turn back; and such gesture of

timidity would result in a volley of arrows. The Frenchmen
stopped paddling and sat rigid, their rifles across their laps.
The Indians jumped into canoes and paddled out in a large
semicircle as if to envelop them. Several plunged into the
water from the shore and started to swim toward the French.
A club was hurled through the air and barely missed Marquette's head.

Joliet motioned his men to hold their fire. While the Canadians were crack shots, they were so outnumbered by the
savages they would be overwhelmed. Father Marquette rose
to his feet. All his skill and courage in dealing with the Indians was now brought into play; the lives of his friends depended upon him. He held out his peace pipe and motioned
for the Indians to come forward. Several of the older savages
on shore entered a canoe, putting down their weapons. They
paddled a short distance and then signaled the whites to
draw near.

The Frenchmen landed and were surrounded by unsmil-
ing faces and weapons noticeably held in readiness. Marquette addressed them in one Indian tongue after another,
but received no indication they understood him. Finally he
tried the Illinois language. An ancient brave nodded his
head. While he could not speak the tongue, he understood it
well enough to act as interpreter.

This was a small warlike tribe—the Mitchigumeans—who
inhabited a few scattered settlements along the St. Francis
River. They fed the white men sagamité and fish, and conducted them to their lodgings for the night. When the sun
rose, an escort led them to a canoe in which they were carried down the river some twenty miles to a more populous

Indian village settled by the Arkansas tribe of Indians who greeted the Frenchmen with apparent friendliness.

The men were naked but for loincloths. The women couldn't afford the luxury of beads. However, they put their best foot forward for the whites, feasting them for an entire day. But the food was of poorer quality than that provided by the Mascoutens or the Illinois, and there was a scarcity of meat.

"We are surrounded on all sides by enemies," explained the chief. "They cripple our trade and keep us from hunting game. Whatever skins we obtain we are compelled to exchange for the knives and hatchets needed for our defense. You tell me, strangers, that you wish to proceed to the mouth of our great river. But I warn you to go no further. The tribes who torment us on every side will certainly annihilate you."

That night the white men stretched themselves out on their mats, anxiously awaiting the dawn. Not one of them slept. In the cabin of the chief, just a hundred yards away, a council of braves was held. "Let us put these strangers to death," argued several of the younger men. "The Great Sun Spirit has guided them into our midst for our own gain. We can well use their rifles and food."

"They are my guests," answered the chief, gravely, "I would willingly kill them in combat. . . ."

Then he shook his head decisively. "They are my guests."

As the sky grew gray with morning, he summoned the whites to his cabin. "You are not safe here. There are those who seek your life. Times are hard with us, and even good men are sometimes urged to evil. You must leave before we are tempted further."

And then, as a sign of friendship, he picked up his calumet and began to dance. He lifted the peace pipe toward the ceiling, offering a smoke to the deities who ruled his life, and then dipped it earthward with a graceful gesture. Sometimes he spread its feathers as if he wished it to fly, or he pushed it toward the faces of the Frenchmen, only to withdraw it quickly. The dance was in the spirit of a ballet. At its conclusion, he repeated softly, persuasively, "Leave us. Go home!"

The Frenchmen retired to their cabin and held earnest council. "We know for a fact we are now at 33'40°, and we have not reached the sea," declared Joliet. "We have established beyond a doubt that the 'Messipi' does not empty into the California ocean—or into the Atlantic by way of Virginia. Its mouth can only be the Gulf of Mexico. This is the information we were sent to obtain. Let us start back before the season becomes more advanced."

The Canadians agreed with him. "If we continue further downstream," one pointed out, "we are likely to be murdered by the Indians or fall into the hands of the Spaniards who control the Gulf. In either case, our journals and maps will never reach France."

Father Marquette concurred. "We've carried out our basic mission. Now I'm anxious to get back to my teaching."

And so, on July 17, 1673, at the mouth of the Arkansas River, just seven hundred miles from the Gulf of Mexico, the seven explorers started homeward. Paddling upstream against the current of the "Messipi" was a far different proposition from navigating downstream. Moreover, the travelers were by now very tired—they had already come more than sixteen hundred miles. On the trip homeward, to avoid the

swiftest water, they crossed and recrossed from bank to bank
and probed their way among islands. The shoreline was de-
ceptively studded with bayous that frequently led them
miles inland, until, at last blocked by fallen timber, they
were forced to turn back to find the true passage.

The heat of August made the mosquitoes more unbearable than ever. Camping for meals on the malarial shores
and sleeping in fogs that chilled them to the bone gradually
undermined the health of the most robust among them. But
of all the party, the physically frail Marquette suffered the
most. Slowly but surely he was leaving his strength on the
shores of the "Messipi."

Acting on the advice of the Illinois Indians whom they
revisited, they returned by way of the Illinois River instead
of the Fox-Wisconsin route by which they had approached
the "Messipi," and thus saved more than five hundred miles
on the trip. In September they reached Lake Michigan once
more and proceeded along the western shore. The three-
hundred-mile voyage through this inland sea was the stormiest of the entire trip. Strong waves whipped by sudden gales
threatened to swamp the slender canoes, already battered
and damaged by their long ordeal. In the stormiest weather,
the men beached their craft in a cove where possible, or
huddled on a narrow, spray-saturated strand, improvising
shelters of rush mats and driftwood.

"It seems," remarked Joliet, "as if the worst has been reserved for the last!"

In this slow fashion, they made their way to Green Bay.
Here, a hundred and fifty miles of paddling could be saved
by carrying the canoes over the neck of land that separated
Lake Michigan from Sturgeon Bay. The exhausted men un-

packed their supplies, lifted the canoes out of the water, and trudged with them along an old Indian portage, breathing heavily and calling on their last physical resources. When they put their canoes into the waters of Sturgeon Bay, they realized with joy that they had but a short distance to travel to the Mission of St. Francis Xavier, along the De Père Rapids of the Fox River. This was the journey's end.

At the end of September, before the first snowfall, the seven men stumbled into this mission. St. Xavier's was thrown into a fever of excitement. Missionaries and Indians gathered around the travelers as if they had returned from the dead. The four-month voyage had seemed like an eternity to those at home. And, indeed, there was cause for rejoicing. One of the most remarkable explorations on record had been accomplished by the Jesuit father, the fur trader, and their five assistants. In four months they had paddled two thousand, seven hundred and sixty-seven miles by canoe to open up the heart of the continent to colonization and give the world its first authentic knowledge of the American West.

Both Marquette and Joliet spent the winter months at St. Xavier, completing their journals, drawing their maps, and preparing reports to their superiors. With the coming of spring, Joliet set out by canoe for Montreal to present his report to Count de Frontenac. When he was eight miles from the city, a sudden wind capsized his canoe in the St. Lawrence River. Two of the three boatmen and a young Indian were drowned in the undertow. Joliet clung to a rock for four hours until a fisherman pulled him ashore.

His map, journal, and all the other records of his voyage were lost. He was stunned by this stroke of ill luck.

"I had escaped every danger," wrote the heartbroken man to the governor. "I had suffered no harm from the Indians. . . . I was nearing home, full of joy at the success of a long and difficult voyage, when suddenly a wind overturned my canoe . . . within sight of Montreal which I had left two years before. Nothing remains to me but my life, and the ardent desire to employ it in any service you may direct."

Joliet continued to be hounded by misfortune. He married the cousin of a high colonial official and was granted valuable fishing privileges together with the ownership of several islands in the St. Lawrence River. But war broke out between the French and British. Joliet's islands, estates, and fisheries were laid waste by New England troops. He died in poverty.

The loss of Joliet's records in the rapids assured Marquette of an even more important place in history than before; for the journal that he submitted to Father Dablon, the superior general, was the only surviving account of the voyage. But the Jesuit father was not interested in his position in history. Once more he gave himself up, mind and body, to his teaching. Nor had he forgotten his promise to return to the Illinois. Of all the Indians he had met, they had stirred his sympathies most deeply. And so in October, 1674, nineteen months after returning to St. Francis Xavier's, and although he was still far from well, he set out for Illinois country, traveling with a party of Indians.

The weather was bitter. Along the shore of Lake Michigan, they encountered furious snowstorms; blocks of ice threatened their passage. Marquette suffered an attack of dysentery and was put ashore at the mouth of the Chicago River, which was frozen more than a foot deep.

In a wasteland of sand dunes and bog where, a hundred

and fifty years later, the city of Chicago would be founded, the Indians erected a cabin of bark and skins. And here the missionary spent the winter. Among his other claims to notice, Marquette was Chicago's pioneer settler.

During the winter, friendly Indians brought him food and medicine. And a fur trapper, spending the season in a camp forty-five miles away, sent him corn and dried blueberries. Then, when the streams had quickened into life again, the missionary continued on his trip to the Illinois. He arrived at Kaskaskia in April.

Easter was in the air. He preached on the Resurrection before an altar of skin and saplings as the tribal elders sat around him and a thousand braves stood in an outer circle, while the women and children listened intently from the background. All dogs were banished.

"The Great White Spirit has a special place in His heart for this land of prairies, pine forests, and the Mighty Messipi. Let us not exclude Him from *our* hearts!"

He told them that he was very tired and would shortly be going to his rest. "But another missionary will be sent you to carry on my teachings."

His health was broken; the dysentery continued to sap his strength. He felt that he had not much longer to live, and so he started back by canoe with two Indians for the Mission of St. Ignace, to receive the last sacrament from a fellow priest. As the redskins skirted the eastern shore of Lake Michigan, he was unable to assist with the paddling. He lay prostrate. And when it was evident that he would not last out the trip, the Indians beached the canoe and carried him ashore in a wood of oaks. Here his grave was dug.

"I thank God," he murmured, "that I have been permitted

to die like Francis Xavier in the wilderness." He was only thirty-eight.

The following winter, a party of Kiskakon Indians hunting along the shore came upon his grave. They dug up his bones, cleaned them and exposed them to the sun, according to tribal custom, laid them in a birchbark coffin, and carried them two hundred and fifty miles to St. Ignace where they were reburied. Thirty-three years later, the chapel at St. Ignace was gutted by fire. A large trading center was established in the area, and all traces of Marquette's grave was lost. But in 1877, a missionary priest who was something of a detective rediscovered fragments of the bones, together with strips of birchbark in which they had been encased, under the site of the old log chapel.

A hundred years ago the historian Bancroft prophesied, "The people of the West will build his monument." And so they have. They have erected it out of the great civilization that has been developed from Canada to the Gulf of Mexico. With their cities, towns, schools, and farms they have paid ample tribute to the pioneer who opened up the main artery of this continent on an errand of good will.

7

Mission to Ireland

ST. PATRICK

O NE SPRING afternoon in the fifth century A.D., ominous
news spread through the town of Bannaventa Berniae in
north Briton. The word was first broadcast by bargemen to
fishermen along the waterfront who laid aside their nets and
rushed into town to relay it to charioteers on their way to
the Forum. The news reached the crowds who were attending a bullfight in the amphitheater, spread rapidly through
the quarters of the poor, and penetrated to the suburban
villas where decurions, emerging from their baths, paced
their terraces in deep anxiety.

But it was in the marketplace of Bannaventa—that pot-
pourri of shops and bazaars whose green and scarlet awnings
contrasted strikingly with the chaste marble halls of the magistrates and scribes—that the excitement reached its peak.
Here a dense crowd had gathered. And the feeling of alarm
reached the proportions of hysteria.

Voices shouted: "The Roman legions are leaving Briton!
The Emperor has recalled them for the defense of Italy!"

"What will become of us, our homes, our industries!"

Before a store window that displayed the latest silks and jewelry from the Levant stood a boy in his teens. His hair was carefully curled. He wore a white robe girded with a sash of Tyrian purple and on his finger an amethyst ring. He had the bearing of a young Roman patrician, a member of the ruling classes. It was the pleasure of this lad to mingle in crowds. He did not feel affronted when a squat Syrian shopkeeper with skin like faded papyrus gripped him by the arm and exclaimed:

"Imagine the legions leaving us in the lurch! Why, the Picts and the Irishmen will pounce on us like timber wolves! And even if this doesn't happen, I am ruined personally! I make my living from the amber I import from overseas. The instant Rome withdraws her fleet, the pirates will confiscate my cargoes. How am I to support my wife and children?"

The young man made no reply; he had nothing encouraging to say. He simply nodded his head and elbowed his way through the mob to an exit of the Forum. The streets of the town were laid out straight as an arrow at right angles to one another. It would take him only a few minutes to reach his villa.

As he walked homeward, he reviewed in the light of the news he had just heard what his tutors had taught him about the history of his country. The Roman legions had come to Briton three centuries before under the Emperor Claudius, and ever since they had safeguarded her from the barbarians to the north and west who sought to enslave her. He, Patricius Magonus Succatus, son of the wealthy decurion, Calpurnius, who owned landed estates and enjoyed great political influence, was a first-class citizen of Rome, sharing in all the comforts and privileges of Roman civilization, thanks to the continued vigilance of the Emperor's cohorts.

But even before his birth, the balance of power in the world was being threatened. For generations, ruthless new peoples in Europe—the Goths, Huns, Vandals, Teutons, Slavs —had been hammering away relentlessly at the perimeter of the Empire, threatening to wipe out civilization. Now matters had reached a crisis. The Emperor Honorius, needing every available reserve for the defense of Italy, had ordered troops home from the relatively noncritical battle areas.

And now Patricius, hurrying to his family to discuss the latest news, recalled the remarks made repeatedly by his grandfather, Potitus, a bishop, that the civilized world had brought its misery upon itself.

"How can we defend ourselves against the barbarians when we have failed to keep our own house in order! What is the most important goal in a Roman citizen's life today? To become rich, to amass luxuries! Corruption and scandal reach into the government itself. The barbarians at least have faith in their own destiny. But we have lost the power of belief!"

Two weeks after the news of its projected withdrawal, the Twentieth Legion embarked for Rome. Patricius stood in the throngs that lined the shore as centurions, scarlet plumes poised arrogantly over their eagle-crested helmets, led their troops aboard the transports to the sounding of trumpets. And along with his fellow townsmen, the lad went home profoundly disturbed.

However, in the months that followed, life went on as before. Each morning at breakfast, his father, Calpurnius, pronounced the blessing with his usual serenity while the family sat under the pear trees in the garden and dipped their rolls in wine. After the meal, Patricius retired with his tutor to the library and exposed himself to the wisdom of Horace and Seneca. Actually, Patricius was an indifferent scholar. He preferred hunting for birds' nests and fishing for salmon to studying Roman philosophers. Apart from his lessons, his life was a round of pleasure seeking. He went to the races and bet on his favorite charioteer. He diced with his companions, went duck hunting in the marshes, and attended bullfights in the Colosseum. Occasionally, in a less frivolous mood, he visited the shop of his friend Galba, the artisan, and watched him carve saints and jewel boxes from the tusks of native boars.

Summer passed into autumn and then suddenly—history does not record the actual date—the catastrophe occurred. Irish clansmen on the hunt for slaves raided the British coast.

The people of Bannaventa were aroused from their sleep, one morning before sunrise, by the trumpeting of war horns. Hordes of bearded invaders, dressed in animal skins and shouting in a wild, strange tongue, leaped from high-prowed ships and swarmed into the town. Drunk on mead and whipped to a frenzy of blood lust, they overwhelmed the men of Bannaventa, who offered only scattered resistance, and forced their way into the houses of rich and poor alike, plundering everything in sight. Taking captive men, women, and children to sell into slavery, they forced them to carry on their backs the invaders' booty. The prisoners were herded at sword's point through the surf into large curracks anchored offshore. As a parting shot, rear patrol guards, to smoke out from hiding any residents who might have eluded them, set fire to block after block of houses until Bannaventa was an inferno of flames.

By noon the raid was over. To a strident flourish of horns, ranks of sailors leaned into their oars and commenced a wailing chant as the armada set out for Ireland.

Patricius was one of the hundreds taken captive. For two days and nights he lay half-conscious on a heap of straw. Periodically, he could hear the mutterings of his fellow prisoners punctuated by the snatches of drunken song from the decks above. He wondered about his parents, his sisters, his grandfather. Had they been murdered? Or, even worse, were they lying in the hold of another ship, bound like him for captivity?

In a single morning the entire structure of his life, his position in society had been obliterated. From a Roman citizen, the son of a patrician, he had been plunged into slavery. Only now did he realize how ephemeral, indeed, were the material blessings of life.

The oars carried the fleet closer and closer to port until early the third morning, when the flaring night torches had been extinguished, a shout rose from the decks. Through flakes of mist the purple Mountains of Mourne emerged. The armada bore north along the Irish coast and landed the captives at the huge slave market of Dalaradia where they were to be auctioned off to native chieftains.

Patricius mounted the block with hundreds of his countrymen. His robe was in shreds. His hair fell in filthy bunches about his shoulders. His amethyst ring had been stolen by a sailor. But he held his head high. The words of his grandfather Potitus came into his mind above the haggling of the auctioneers:

"I tell you, lad, we've been Christians in Briton for a hundred years. But it takes suffering to make a man believe!"

Patricius was bought by a pagan chieftain, Miliucc, and assigned to watch his sheep on the slopes of Slemish Mountain in western Ireland. He resigned himself to spending his life beside the herd. And a grim existence it was to sit in the chilling rain and bitter raw wind, constantly on the lookout for wolves and robbers lurking in the forests. It was cheerless indeed to awaken from a dream at night and find, instead of the red Samian vases and tesselated floors of his bedroom in Briton, the bleak walls of a sheeling in the woods gleaming fitfully in the light of a fire he had built for protection against animals.

But there were times when the lad forgot his gloom. Guasacht and Bronach, a son and daughter of the chieftain Miliucc, brought him food from their own table. Sometimes, when the weather was too severe for the sheep to remain on the mountainside and the shepherd would drive the herd into the enclosure of Miliucc's dun, he would be smuggled by the children into their father's wickerwork house that stood behind a high earthen rampart. Peering from the kitchen, he would watch the gaudy ladies of Miliucc's clan with their crimson-colored fingernails and eyebrows dyed with berry juice, as they mingled with the equally flamboyant men whose yellow hair flowed to the waist. And sometimes, when the night wind howled outside, an aged bard would arise and to the tinkling notes of a musical branch recite a great heroic legend of the Irish past—the tale of Deirdre of the Three Sorrows, of the gallant Fienna, or of the fabulous Comac Mac Art. Enthralled by the beauty of the Gaelic tongue, Patrick—henceforth we shall call him by the Irish form of his name—studied the language until he could speak it fluently. And once young Guasacht, Miliucc's son, managed to slip Patrick into a holiday fair where fiddlers, pipers, and masked actors cavorted to the delight of the peasants.

Word reached Miliucc of his children's association with the shepherd. He whipped his son and forbade him and his sister from going near the mountainside again. But the children continued to steal out of bed at dawn and visit Patrick. Miliucc rebuked himself for allowing himself to become upset over a slave in his household. And yet there was something about this Britisher that got under one's skin—the calm assurance in his voice even though he spoke only words of submission, the serene smile, the proud look in his eye. Truly, he must be watched with double the caution exercised over the other slaves.

One night in a dream, Miliucc saw Patrick enter the dun, his face wreathed in flames. And though he, Miliucc, escaped, his children were consumed by the fire.

The following morning Miliucc summoned his shepherd. "What spell have you cast over my children?" he cried. "I have been warned in my dream that you are plotting to destroy them!"

The lad knelt. He mumbled a Christian prayer that was incomprehensible to Miliucc. The chieftain, in angry frustration, bade him leave the room. From this time onward, Patrick was under close surveillance.

For six years he lived in this fashion. Then one midnight he was awakend by a hand on his shoulder. His eyes focused on two faces in the flare of a torch. One was that of Guasacht, who had awakened him. The other belonged to a stranger. Patrick jumped to his feet, took a step backwards, but Guasacht said to him:

"Do not fear this man, Patrick. He is our friend."

The face of the other flickered in the light of the torch. "Greetings—in the name of Jesus."

Patrick was astounded and thrilled. He hadn't heard that name from anyone's lips since he had set foot in Ireland. "Who are you?"

"A Christian, Patrick. Guasacht here has led me to you."

Patrick had heard from servants in Miliucc's household that there were underground groups of Christians in Ireland who met secretly in homes and caves, much like the early Christians in Rome. Several generations before—no historian knows exactly how—these people had received the message of Christ from the outside world.

Patrick invited the newcomers to be seated. The peasant placed the torch he had been carrying on the table and sat down beside Guasacht. Then he said:

"I am Victor. I come from a poor, lonely people. Our farms have been laid waste, our sons taken from us in the continual wars waged by chieftains and kings. In our wattle huts, in the keening of the winds, we have heard the voice of One who said that all men were equally precious in the eyes of God. A number of us meet before secret altars beyond the reach of the high priests, and we offer ourselves to the service of Jesus."

He paused. "But I have not climbed Slemish in the middle of the night to give you our history."

"Why have you come?"

"To help you escape from captivity."

Guasacht, who had been sitting quietly, nodded.

"But how?"

"Two hundred miles from here there is a harbor from which ships leave regularly for the mainland of Europe. You will start for there at once, traveling through the forests and keeping off the main roads by day. We Christians are not numerous, yet we have huts from one end of Ireland to the other. Each evening you will head for the home of a Christian whose locality I will describe to you carefully. You will be given food and a bed for the night. You will make this journey through Ireland safely—in the love of Christ."

Victor sketched on the dirt floor the route Patrick was to take, explaining that the huts of the Christians were known by the crosses they placed in the window for the friendless traveler.

"Goodbye, Patrick. And good luck!"

Patrick packed his few belongings in a knapsack. Between him and the port of freedom lay vast primeval forests abounding in wild boars, wolves, even lunatics; quagmires that could swallow up a host of men without a trace; unscrupulous chieftains who impressed the unwary into service for their interminable wars.

At times Patrick measured his progress in yards as he threaded his way up mountains or ploughed waist deep through the chill waters of a bog whose hidden tree stumps slashed his feet. But each day, when darkness fell, he emerged onto the roads and came upon the hut of a Christian peasant with its cross in the window. He was welcomed as the poor the world over have always welcomed the homeless. He was given a meal of barley bread, the roots of vegetables, milk in a yew-wood cup, and invited to sleep on a pallet of straw by the fire. Each dawn his host would awaken him and, whispering "Peace be with you," send him on his way.

Sometimes when he reached the end of his strength Patrick would halt in a cave and fling himself down to rest. Then, after a brief nap, he would continue onward, struggling through swamp and river and thicket as huge kites and golden eagles wheeled over his head, and goshawks swooped down for their prey.

For twenty-one days, Patrick persevered in his flight. And then he arrived at the harbor described by Victor. Surely enough, as the peasant had said, curracks lay beached on the shore.

Patrick hid with Christians in a hut on the outskirts of town. When a crew of sailors led a herd of wolfhounds down to the shore to be loaded on one of the vessels, he followed them. The hounds were to be shipped to a port in southern Gaul where they would be sold, at a premium price, for exhibition in public games. The captain, a burly, bearded sailor with a cleft lip, was in an angry mood, for the dogs were giving his men a hard time.

Patrick walked up to the captain. "Please let me have passage aboard your vessel," he asked.

One glance at the lad's rags was enough. The captain said abruptly, "Get about your business. I'll have no riffraff aboard my ship!"

Wolfhounds had guarded Patrick's sheep on Slemish, and he pleaded, "But I'll work for my passage. I can take care of the hounds."

The captain turned his back on him. Patrick approached

several of the sailors, repeating his request first in Gaelic and then in Latin. But he was received with silence. He walked sadly back to his hut, fell to his knees, and prayed.

A knock at the door brought him to his feet. Two sailors entered; they had followed him home from the ship. "The captain has changed his mind, lad," they said. "He'll take you aboard. But be prompt. We leave at dawn."

What had caused the captain's sudden change of heart was this: His sailors had reported that the boy had spoken to them in Latin, a language they well knew from their trips to Italy. The wily old captain guessed that the destitute lad was probably a Britisher, possibly of noble birth, who had been kidnapped into slavery. If he returned him to his home, the reward from the youth's family might make him rich for life. The captain sent his sailors to follow the young man and invite him on board.

Patrick was assigned to the wolfhounds, whom he scrubbed, fed, and soothed with the melodies he had sung to his own dogs on Slemish. When the vessel was only a few hours at sea, it ran into a gale, and for three days and nights the lives of all hung in the balance.

On the fourth day, the boat was wrecked on the headlands of northern Gaul. The ship's company barely escaped with their lives. They found themselves without food and water in a territory that had been laid waste by the Vandals. Occasionally, on their way inland, they found honey and pools of brackish water; once they managed to kill several wild hogs, and the sailors crammed their bellies in a two-day feast. But Patrick's stomach rebelled against the orgy. He was content with his ration of honey.

After twenty-eight days, the party reached a populous

community. Here, they rested and made plans to continue their journey. With the loss of his ship, the captain had given up his dream of collecting a reward for Patrick's safe return, and he now advised him to make his way back to Bannaventa the best he could.

After much additional hardship, Patrick arrived on the coast of Gaul, where he worked his passage aboard a boat to Briton. With trembling heart he entered Bannaventa and rejoiced to find that, in the years he had been away, it had been entirely rebuilt. The streets thronged anew with townspeople who had moved here from various parts of Briton.

As he hurried toward the suburbs where his father's villa had stood, he passed merchants haggling over their goods, women with flamboyant coiffures walking their Spanish poodles, workers hurrying home from the tin mines, sweating in their leather jerkins, street venders hawking their cool delicious grape drinks, town guards moving about officiously, fingering the butts of cudgels hanging at their sides. A wagonload of Egyptian dancing girls rode by, bound for the great inland cities; the eyes of these languorous beauties expressed their indifference to the world around them.

When Patrick reached the suburbs, he turned a corner and before him, on the site of his father's villa, stood a magnificent new residence, raised on the ruins of the old. When he reached the terrace, aunts and cousins rushed forward to greet him.

They had shocking news. "Your father and mother and sisters were killed in the raid. But you have returned as a son!" They marveled at the radiant young man whom they had last seen as an awkward youth.

Word spread that the son of Calpurnius had returned. The most beautiful girls in town showered him with invitations to dances and parties. In a ceremony witnessed by decurions, deacons, and other high-ranking townspeople, Patrick assumed the toga of citizenship and succeeded to the privileges and rights of his powerful father. He was named a member of the legislature, and a day was appointed for him to deliver his speech of acceptance.

The night before the occasion, Patrick went to bed early. He tossed restlessly. Suddenly his room was flooded with light; wailing voices rose in an agonizing swell. A hand rested on Patrick's shoulder, and he looked into the face of Victor.

"So you have returned home, Patrick, exactly as I foretold. Now, what are you going to do with your liberty?"

"I am taking over my father's seat in the legislature."

For a few moments Victor was silent. Then he shook his head sadly. "We are calling upon you, Patrick, the people of Ireland, the folk who fed and housed you in your flight to freedom. We ask you now for your payment—a share in your liberty."

"But what can I do to help? There are thousands of you. How can I change your world?"

"It can be done when there is faith. It *must* be done when one is selected by God."

"What do you mean?"

"God has chosen you to deliver our nation from bondage!"

And then, in an instant, Victor vanished. The room was dark and silent again. The only sound came from the wind as it sifted through the branches of the trees outside the window. Patrick sat up suddenly in his bed. He was profoundly disturbed and puzzled. Had he dreamed this? Had Victor actually visited him through the agency of God?

The following day, the hall of the legislature was crowded to capacity with town officials, families of rank, relatives, and neighbors as Patrick stepped up to the speaker's rostrum.

He stood silently for a moment in all the sparkle of his youth. Then he declared: "Thank you, Fathers, for the honors you have offered me. But I cannot remain with you. I have business to attend to in Ireland. . . ."

He had heard the voice. He knew what his life's work was to be. But he was no scholar in church doctrine. To be sent on a mission with the backing of official Christendom, he needed training for his office. Laying aside his toga for the pilgrim's staff and cowl, he left Bannaventa and sought schooling in the quietest places on earth—the monasteries.

Years before, Honorius, a man of great fortune who belonged to one of the noblest families in the Empire, had abandoned a brilliant worldly career for the peace beyond riches. Looking for an area in which to establish a monastic retreat away from the wars that were devastating the continent, he settled on the Island of St. Lérins in the Mediterranean, off the coast of southern Gaul.

It was an island choked with underbrush, and crawling with snakes who emerged from their holes when the tides swept inland. But Honorius and his monks cleared the broom, planted fields, cultivated gardens, and turned the wilderness into a semitropical paradise. To Lérins flocked diplomats and barristers, high court officials and generals, rakes, war refugees, and gentlemen of fortune—men broken by the tragedy of living. From all parts of the world they came, selling all they owned, giving up homes, careers, families, to devote their lives to a quiet investigation into the meaning of existence. And to this remarkable little island, after a sojourn in a cell at Tours, came young Patrick. He lived here in a stone hut, meditating, tilling the vineyards, and taking his single meal at midday in the shade of olive trees.

The elder monks devoted their time exclusively to prayer, but many of the younger brethren were employed as librarians. For scholars and teachers, fleeing the barbarians, had brought their precious manuscripts to Lérins to be kept in sanctuary and passed on to future ages.

Unlike many of the others at Lérins, Patrick did not consider withdrawal from the world the supreme goal of life; it was merely the preparation for a higher mission. Often he stood on a knoll on Lérins and looked north across the water to the distant, snow-covered Alps—the gates to another world where people were toiling and suffering in the competitive sweepstakes of living. And he never forgot that he was meant to share in their suffering. To the brethren who noticed his impatience to be off into the world again, he would relate a parable of the Greek philosopher, Plato:

"The world is a cave. Beyond its mouth is a landscape with flowers and trees and meadows sparkling in the sun. But we men are chained with our backs to the light. We mistake the shadow landscape flickering on the wall for the true outdoors. A few of us by great energy of will manage to break our chains and grope to the entrance to the cave. At first when we look into the sunshine, our eyes, accustomed only to the darkness, are blinded by the light. But gradually we perceive the true color of a tree, a blade of grass, a flower. We climb to the top of a hill and see before us in its true dimensions the total meaning of life.

"Some are content to stay here aloof in our enlightenment. But others of us choose a harder course. We descend into the valley again and return to the cave to lead our fellow men to the hill.

"For our efforts we are usually abused and rejected by our brothers in bonds. To them we seem foolish, for no longer used to the shadows, we stumble about uncertainly in their narrow little cave. They call us idiots, misfits, and worse. Often we suffer martyrdom at their hands. But if, before we pass from the shadows, we have helped a handful of men to turn toward the sun we have lived to the very limits of our abilities. And who can desire more?"

Patrick stayed nine years at Lérins, then continued his studies for another fourteen years. Part of this time he preached in villages and country crossroads in western Europe. And then the day arrived for which he had so painstakingly prepared—the return to Ireland.

In 431, when Patrick was already a man of forty-four, Palladius, a bishop, was sent to get in touch with the underground Christian communities in Ireland. A year after his arrival there, news was received on the continent that he had been murdered. Patrick heard the report in Auxerre, in Gaul. He felt that he must hasten now, without delay, to Ireland to aid the Christian community in its hour of crisis.

Friends warned him that he was taking his life into his hands in volunteering to carry on the dangerous mission that had resulted in the death of Palladius. But Patrick was unconcerned about his own safety. He departed for a port

in Briton where, in the fall of 432, he assembled a hand-
picked company to embark with him for Ireland.

Boarding the little ox-hide vessel were men of various
occupations, speaking different tongues but united in a bond
of common devotion. There was a ship's mariner, an assistant
priest, a judge, a bell ringer, a cook, two table attendants,
a table chaplain, a brewer, a woodsman, a cowherd, three
embroidery workers, and three artisans. And, pacing the deck
restlessly, was Patrick—a stocky man with hair prematurely
silvered and deep-set hazel eyes under shaggy brows, dressed
in a gray woolen tunic, a chasuble, and sandals.

The vessel sailed for Ireland over the route taken by the
martyred Palladius, putting in at Inver Dea, near the hills
of Wicklaw, in southern Ireland. Immediately the party encountered trouble. The chieftain of the area gathered with
his people on the beach and stoned the travelers as they
disembarked. The first ashore, a brewer by the name of
Manton, was struck in the mouth by a rock that split his
lip in two and smashed his teeth. He survived, but from
that time on he was called the "toothless one."

To avoid further casualties, the travelers again put to
sea. They continued northward along the coast, living on
the fish caught on the way, and finally reached the mouth
of the Strangford River in Sabhal. Here they went ashore
to stretch their limbs. Some of the company had just begun
to entertain the others with songs to the accompaniment of
a harp when the barking of dogs was heard, followed by
men's voices. Patrick leaped to his feet. His party was a
mere handful and unarmed. There was no time to ready
the vessel for departure.

Suddenly a giant of a man emerged from the brush with

a wolfhound. He was Dichu, a local chieftain. Only a few
minutes before, his swineherd, peering from the thicket,
had seen Patrick's group debarking from their vessel. He
was astonished at their shaven heads, their unfamiliar
language. Believing them to be pirates, he had rushed to
warn his chieftain, and Dichu had hurried to the shore
with an armed group. His men were even now at his rear,
hidden by the brush.

He stood for an instant observing the strangers. His beast
growled, ready to leap. Patrick stepped forward and called
to the dog in the soft, musical Gaelic he had used with his
own hounds on Slemish. The dog paused in his mutterings
and stretched his legs. Although still suspicious, he permitted Patrick to pat his head.

The chieftain disappeared into the brush for a moment
and returned with two of his men. The three of them conversed with vigorous gestures. It was obvious they were
discussing what to do with these newcomers.

Suddenly—according to some chroniclers—the foliage
parted and a young woman appeared, the wife of Dichu.
She had hurried down to the landing, curious to see what
the strangers were like. Patrick looked at her in surprise. He
had seen this face before—it had been very much younger
then. But where?

Then he remembered. He could hardly believe his extraordinary luck. "Bronach!"

She turned to him. Tears of joy came into her eyes. She
remembered, too.

In an instant she was in his fatherly embrace. She was the
daughter of Miliucc who, together with Guasacht years before, had brought food to the young shepherd on Mt. Slem-

ish. And now she was married to Dichu and had a son of her own, having left her father's dun and moved south to this region.

So Patrick's encounter with Dichu ended happily because of this chance meeting with his wife. The travelers remained with Dichu and Bronach through the winter months. The couple became Patrick's first converts to Christianity, and Dichu donated a barn which Patrick used as his first church in Ireland.

Dichu frequently warned the missionary of the dangers that would confront him if he persisted in challenging the power of the druids, the high priests of Ireland. "They wield tremendous political influence, Patrick, because of the people's fear of them. They are reputed to possess magic powers over one's life. The people are convinced that they can turn a person into a lunatic simply by uttering a curse over a blade of grass and flinging it into his face. It is alleged they can strike an opponent dead by roasting a dog on a spit and muttering the victim's name over the fire.

"The druids have persuaded the kings that the Christians are attempting to incite the masses to treason. Your own life is in jeopardy, Patrick. The druids will never rest until they have destroyed you."

But the missionary continued with his plans. One spring morning, he ordered his men to prepare to leave immediately. When Dichu asked him his destination, Patrick replied, "I am going north to hunt up Miliucc, my former master. He lost his investment when I ran off. I wish to pay him a price for my ransom."

And he added, "I'll offer him something more besides—the chance to become my brother in the family of Christ."

So Patrick traveled north to Slemish through forests and glens ablaze with golden trefoil. But spies had already learned of his coming. They rushed to Miliucc, bringing him the news.

The chieftain was panic-stricken. His former slave was returning with a band of men! Miliucc was now old and feeble and in retirement with only a few scattered retainers. Patrick could be coming for only one reason, he believed— to confiscate his property and sell him into slavery.

When the missionary reached the slopes of Slemish and looked across the valley, he was stunned to find the dun a blazing heap of ruins. Poor old Miliucc, knowing nothing of the Christian doctrine of forgiveness, had committed suicide. Barricading himself in his house, he had set fire to himself and all his possessions. He died by the only code he understood.

News of Patrick's coming had passed rapidly through the Christian communities on the island. The people sang *Alleluia* as if another Messiah had arrived.

In his campaign to liberate them, Patrick decided to strike at the very heart of political power. At this period, Ireland was divided into tribes governed by kings and chieftains. And the high king of all was Laoghaire who ruled at Tara in Meath, in northern Ireland.

With his followers, Patrick traveled northward to Tara. He arrived at the mouth of the River Boyne, ten miles from the royal court, and at twilight climbed the wooded Hill of Slane. It was the evening before Easter, 433. He pitched his tent and looked across the pastureland toward the purple hills. Upon one of them where the King's residence was situated he saw lights in the gloom. Beginning on this eve-

ning annually, the highest holiday in pagan Ireland, the
Feast of Tara, was celebrated. At the royal court, all the
priests and nobles of the kingdom assembled to record laws,
to settle outstanding legal claims, and to celebrate the beginning of the Irish New Year. To launch this marathon
festival which lasted six days, the King lit a fire that could
be seen for miles around. By royal proclamation all other
hearths must remain cold until the King's fire had been
started. Infraction of the law meant death.

But on this night of 433, an unprecedented event took
place. The fire of Tara had not yet been lit when Patrick
summoned his companions to prepare his own Easter fire.
A pyre was built. The spark was struck from tinder. The
holy candle was blessed and set to the wood, and flames
roared up from the hill.

King Laoghaire observed the flames from a window of his
manor house and summoned his chief druid in a fury.

"Who has had the audacity to light his fire before mine
tonight? Does he not know the penalty for this?"

"Sire, I do not know who the lawbreaker is," the other
replied.

"I shall go after him! He shall be taught a lesson!"

The druid replied craftily, "Sire, do not go to him. Order
him to come to you. In this way, he will know who is the
King and who is the subject."

"You are right, Lucatmael. Bring him to me!"

Lucatmael ordered horses yoked to nine chariots, and he
loaded them with helmeted soldiers. Then, accompanied by
fellow druids and nobles, he led the column to the Hill of
Slane. They dismounted on the outskirts of Patrick's encamp-

ment. Lucatmael strode up to Patrick's tent and challenged him to appear.

The flaps parted, and Patrick stepped forward. In a semicircle, silhouetted against the flames, stood rows of armed men, their chins resting on the rims of their shields, their spears upright at their elbows. Behind them, the flames cast grotesque shadows on the carved chariots. The pawing of the restless horses added to the ominousness of the scene.

"Who are you, Stranger?" called out Lucatmael. "Why have you lit a fire in defiance of the High King of Ireland?"

Patrick was silent a moment. "I am celebrating the festival of a still greater King."

The druid looked at him blankly. "Who can be a greater ruler than Laoghaire of Tara?"

"Jesus of Nazareth."

The druid paused to consider this reply. Whoever that monarch may be, this fellow was cunning and impudent. No doubt of it. It was necessary to handle him with the utmost subtlety.

"The King invites you and your company to Tara as his guests," said Lucatmael softly. "No doubt your reasons for lighting a flame on this holy night are excellent, and we will listen with interest to them. Tomorrow at a great banquet you will be welcome to address us."

The druid ordered his party to lead the newcomers back to Tara. He gave other orders—secret ones—for troops to patrol the way to cut off any attempt at escape.

The following morning Patrick rose from bed within the royal settlement. On the way to the King's residence, he passed through streets of timber houses with roofs daubed

in carnival colors, the most gaudy building of all being reserved for Laoghaire's ladies of pleasure.

Patrick entered into the Teach Miodchuarta, the banquet
hall, accommodating a thousand warriors. Even at meal-
time no man trusted his neighbor. Lords and captains sat
facing one another, their weapons within instant reach.
Many a tragic quarrel had broken out under the stimulus
of heady ale. Hanging from the ceiling at regular intervals
down the middle of the hall were spits on which the joints
of boars were roasted over open hearths. Columns of smoke
rose and escaped through holes in the ceiling.

Patrick walked directly up to the King, who sat in the
upper end of the hall with his druids and bards. Laoghaire
rose to greet him.

"Welcome to Tara, Beardless One."

At the suggestion of his chief advisors, the King had prepared for this audacious stranger a quick exit from life. At
his elbow for the ceremonial toast stood two porringers of
ale. Into Patrick's he had instructed his cupbearer to pour
poison.

As Patrick acknowledged the royal welcome, a chorus of
muttering was heard through the hall. Voices cried out,
"Who is this man? What is his purpose in coming here?"

Patrick turned to the assembly and said in a clear, firm
voice, "I have come with a message of peace."

From a nearby table a druid shouted, "The man lies. He
is here to spread treason against the King!"

Throughout the hall men leaped to their feet and beat
menacingly on their shields.

The King silenced the assembly and motioned for the missionary to proceed.

"I have come," said Patrick, "not to speak treason, but to teach loyalty—loyalty to the spirit of God. There isn't a man among you who doesn't live in fear. Even now as you eat, each of you sits trembling under his shield! And what do you live in dread of? War! The continual, ruinous warfare of your own making. I have come to build schools, to educate your young, to teach you the law of love!"

Laoghaire rose. "These are strange words you speak. I do not pretend to understand your motives for lighting a fire against my orders. However, let us be friends." He picked up the flagons. "We shall toast to our friendship."

He handed one to Patrick and fingered his own nervously. Patrick nodded and raised the ale to his lips. Suddenly a strapping individual with brick-red hair leaped to his side, snatched the mug from him and hurled it to the ground with a clatter. He was Dubtach, the chief poet of Ireland. For several moments he stared at the tankard as if astounded at what he had done. Then he raised his eyes to the King.

"Sire, forgive my impudence. I know I have jeopardized my life. But I have felt from the first that if we poison this man, we shall bring a calamity upon Ireland."

There was a silence in the great hall, broken only by the hissing of the spits. Then young Fiacc, the favorite pupil of Dubtach, rose to his feet.

"I agree with you. This stranger is our friend."

Laoghaire did not immediately answer. Never before had anyone flaunted a decree of King Laoghaire, son of Niall of the Nine Hostages. Clearly there could be only one reason for this rebellion by Dubtach and Fiacc. They had suddenly come under the spell of a mighty deity who had placed this stranger Patrick under his protection.

Laoghaire was nothing if not a realist. He said to Patrick in quiet, resigned dignity, "What I have just witnessed makes it evident to me that you have entered my hall under the protection of a supernatural power. I am not going to dispute it by tampering with your life. We've had enough quarreling. Let's get on with the feast."

Over a platter of fried trout, the King turned to Patrick and declared in high spirits, "After all, how can a fellow like you be a menace to my throne if you go through the kingdom teaching the power of love!"

And so the momentous meeting with the King ended in success. Before they parted, Laoghaire gave Patrick his permission to teach Christianity in the northern half of Ireland which was under his immediate control.

Young Fiacc became Patrick's first convert in Tara. Many others of Laoghaire's subjects followed suit. But not the King. Laoghaire did not object to most of the tenets of Christianity, but to have become a Christian would have meant his having to "forgive" his major enemies, the Leinstermen with whom he and his ancestors before him had been feuding bitterly. He remained a pagan to the end, and, like his forebears, was buried standing upright, spear in hand, facing the hated Leinstermen to the south.

Five roads led from Tara to all parts of Ireland, and over these Patrick now traveled making converts. He spent about a fortnight in each region, measured out with his crozier an area for a wooden chapel, preached and baptized. Leaving a native convert in charge of the district, he passed on to a new region. A shrewd strategist, he outmaneuvered the druids by going directly to the kings and leading chieftains of each clan. He offered them gifts, turned their sons into disciples, and with their backing, or at least tolerance, succeeded in winning large numbers of their followers to Christianity. In this thoroughgoing manner the tireless crusader promoted the gospel from one end of Ireland to the other.

Many of the details of Patrick's mission are obscure, and some are in dispute. But what are specific facts before the magnificence of his achievement! See this sturdy fisherman for souls traveling from Meath to Killala, from Donegal to Leinster, from Munster to Armagh to Killarney by ox-drawn chariot, wading or swimming or ferrying across swift rivers in which the pearl mussel abounds, stopping off for milk and wild honey at a wayside hostel, judging disputes with the homely wisdom of Solomon, confounding his opponents with the eloquence of the old Hebrew prophets.

Traveling over the countryside is a rough, uncomfortable life, and numerous incidents try his patience. "By the Lord's doom!" he shouts angrily when his chariot overturns, or his oxen are stolen by highwaymen, or one of his teeth is knocked out on a boulder when he stumbles while fording a stream.

Yet how gentle he can be! He blesses a brook near a church he has established and puts two small trout into it. "Angels will keep them here forever."

Once, while he is preaching to a crowd of villagers, a small girl falls asleep. He puts his finger to his lips and forbids anyone to awaken her. And finally when she opens her eyes, he kneels beside her and murmurs, "Tell me all about your dream, little one."

As the years pass and members of the original party that came with him to Ireland grow tired of their travels, Patrick settles them in parishes to carry on his teachings. Each church he establishes is a self-sufficient community. The clerics do their own building. They fish, plant corn, brew ale, spin their clothes, shoe the horses, erect altars. At Armagh, Patrick's largest parish settlement, a school is erected beside the church, and a library, too, for the preservation of valuable manuscripts.

Patrick is influential in transforming the Irish law—the Senchus Mor—into a vehicle for Christian justice. He outlaws slavery. On one occasion, Coroticus, a British tyrant who had established his rule over western Britain after Roman protection had been withdrawn, raided Ireland and carried off a group of Christian converts while they were still in their baptismal robes, killing those who resisted. To Coroticus, Patrick sent a messenger demanding the release of these captives. And to the public he issued a denunciation of the raid in words that have survived to this day as a ringing testament to freedom. But, despite this pressure, Coroticus turned his back on Patrick's demand.

Periodically, Patrick, feeling the need to replenish his inner resources, retreated alone to the mountains. On one occasion, he climbed *Cruachan Aigle*—the Hill of Eagles— overlooking the Irish Sea, and remained on the summit for forty days, praying and fasting. According to folk legend, it was here that he banished the snakes from Ireland.

As the years sapped Patrick's energy, and his longing to settle down grew overpowering, he would fall to his knees whenever he came to a particularly lovely area. "I want to remain here. I am tired. I do not wish to go further."

But a voice within him replied, "You must go on. Although you are weary, you must go further!"

And then one winter morning, the family of Dichu, the

chieftain who had contributed his barn to be used as Patrick's first church in Ireland, was surprised and delighted to see the missionary once again. He was very old now, and he leaned on his crozier for support, but his eyes had not lost their sparkle.

"This is where my mission was first welcomed with love," he announced. "I have returned to Sabhal to die."

There were others to carry on his work—his disciples, the native converts, and the bishops sent by the Church. Christianity was in Ireland to stay.

Patrick died on the seventeenth of March—the exact year is unknown. A few days before the end, according to chroniclers, his attendants asked him, "Master, where do you wish to be buried? Many towns are competing for the privilege of erecting your tomb."

Patrick replied, "I shall not select a burial site. That would only create rivalry among my followers. When I am gone, place my body in a wagon and hitch two oxen to it. Turn the animals into the fields. Wherever they lie down to rest, there you shall dig my grave."

And so, when Patrick had passed on, the coffin was placed in a wagon. The unguided oxen turned into the meadow with it, carrying also the grave diggers and a priest assigned to perform the burial service.

But two rival clans—the Men of Ui-Neill and the Men of Airthir—who had been vying heatedly for the honor of burying Patrick within their respective territories sent armed patrols to hunt down the wagon. The Men of Airthir overtook it as it came to the bank of the Strangford River. They seized the coffin and started back with it to the headquarters of their chief. But on the way, they became suspicious of the lightness of their burden. They opened the coffin and received a shock. It was filled with straw. Patrick's loyal attendants had outwitted the body-snatchers by burying the master secretly the night before and sending out the ox cart as a decoy. To this day the grave has not been found.

But the location of Patrick's dust is of little importance. His soul is everywhere in Ireland. Her people have never forgotten in their periods of deepest despair this pioneer crusader for freedom.

8

Adventurer in Cathay

MATTEO RICCI

〰〰〰〰〰〰〰〰〰〰〰〰〰〰〰〰〰〰〰〰〰〰〰〰〰

It is late afternoon in the Chinese city of Chao-K'-ing. The streets are thronged with shoppers. Under green and yellow awnings painted with dragons and deer, alchemists offer to turn base metals into silver, and women of pleasure peer beckoningly from behind sweet-scented fans. Mandarins in winged caps and shiny black leggings ride arrogantly on the shoulders of attendants who open a way through the crowds with bastinados.

Under the great carved bridges, through canals that run up to the very doors of their customers, peddlers navigate their junks, selling fruits, vegetables, catfish, and carp. The great Sinkiang River swarms with families who have never set foot on land. They drift for a lifetime in flat-bottomed houseboats on which they raise ducks and pigeons, breed livestock, cultivate orange saplings and flowers in earthen pots, and earn a meager living ferrying passengers.

Aloof from this bustling river populace are the houses of the magistrates, surrounded by magnificent gardens in which bronze-carved deer and magpies spout jets of water into the air.

In the living room of one such residence, a tea party, typical of those held in Chao-K'-ing at this hour, has just come to an end. The host and guests are saying their goodbyes with elaborate ceremony. They bow to one another, inclining their heads until they touch the ground. And when they approach the exit, they turn and bow to the door in an additional gesture of farewell. One of the visitors lingers behind the rest. As he steps leisurely into his sedan chair, his host bends over to him and murmurs, "We always have a pleasant chat together when we meet. Do we not?"

The guest smiles and inclines his head in agreement. He is tall, lantern jawed, with long flowing hair and a profuse black beard. His gown is embroidered with a floral pattern and girdled by a sash whose insigne attests to his being a mandarin of the highest rank. But there is one startling feature about him—his eyes. They are not slanted in the Oriental fashion. And they are blue!

"It was a very pleasant gathering, Tchu-ain," he replies to his host. "I particularly enjoyed the actors you hired to entertain us. I haven't seen a more amusing comedy in years."

He bows slowly once again, his hands concealed within his wide-flowing sleeves, and motions for his attendants to carry him home. He is borne through the streets as the dusk gathers over the city, crosses a bridge over the Sinkiang, and arrives at a one-story building of European design that seems strangely out of place in this city of Buddhist temples.

He alights, passes through the entrance into a spacious circular hallway, and enters one of the adjoining rooms. This chamber is furnished in an amazing fashion. Packed densely from wall to wall are celestial globes of various shapes and sizes, clocks wrought in metal and alabaster and fashioned in the images of windmills and church spires, prisms sparkling with the colors of the rainbow, a variety of music boxes, sun dials, quadrants, and astrolabes. On the walls hang oil paintings executed by the finest painters of Europe.

The mandarin walks over to a large metal sphere of the heavens. He spins it until the stars and planets merge into a blaze of silver. Then he puts his finger on a wall map at his elbow, moves over the contours of land, and comes to rest on the huge, bulging mass of China.

An assistant behind him speaks. "Father Ricci, I am relieved every time you return safely. How long can we keep up this double life? I don't have to remind you of the fate of any foreigner discovered inside China. It's true we've managed to slip inside this city, that you have won over the Governor with your astronomical instruments, and we have made friends with the influential mandarins. But suppose the Governor is removed from office tomorrow? And what if the Emperor in Peking learns of our presence?"

Father Ricci is heedless of the other's remarks. He is bent over, absorbed in the examination of one of the clocks, a table model carved to represent a Neapolitan galley. When the hour strikes, the crew on deck dances a comical jig.

Then he straightens up. "Bruneschelli, I am afraid that this clock is several minutes slow. You know it's one of my favorites. Hereafter, see that it is wound properly. We must have every instrument—*every* instrument—striking the hours in unison!"

"Father, you are taking matters much too lightly. We are surrounded by enormous pitfalls. One false step . . ."

Father Ricci regards his assistant with a twinkle. For months he had heard this complaint from him. "But I am not a foreigner, Bruneschelli. I speak Chinese as well as the Emperor. I know the books of Confucius better than most native doctors of philosophy. And besides," he shrugs his shoulders, "we all live as long as we can and then we die. Do you know any other prescription for happiness?"

He walks over to the window and looks out over the river. Numerous lanterns light up like fireflies on the moving junks. The sky is a deep twilight blue, as delicate as glazed porcelain. Now Matteo Ricci's thoughts go back to another body of water—the blue Adriatic that washes the shores of Italy near the village where he was born in the year 1552.

It had been an exciting boyhood growing up in an Italy where Titian had caught the glory of the sunset and Dante had written of Paradise and Hell. Matteo's father was a high official in Macareta, one of the Papal states. In his villa he wined and dined politicos from Rome, a senator or two from Venice, and even influential men from Piedmont. His heart was set on his son's becoming a lawyer and following a career in government.

He sent Matteo to Rome at sixteen to study law. For three years all went well. And then, suddenly, the boy returned to Macareta and told his father he was abandoning his profession.

"What then will you be? A strolling actor?" asked the father sarcastically.

The young man walked quietly over to the clavichord, sat

down, and ran his fingers over the keyboard. He picked out a fragment of a theme from Palestrina. "I want to enter the Church."

His father's face reddened. "But that's preposterous. I have a career all mapped out for you! I have all the necessary connections to make you a man of influence, of wealth. How dare you leave your studies without consulting me?"

The young man stood up. In this room was all the luxury, the aesthetic satisfaction money could buy. Here were exquisite heads by Donatello and Della Robbia modeled in Carraran marble, paintings by Tintoretto to delight the eye, wines from Capri to stimulate the senses. But there were some things money could not buy; there were some things more necessary to men than success.

"I want to serve the Church as a missionary overseas. I want to enter the Jesuit order and become a master in theology and science, to learn all I can about the physical world and bring my knowledge to people whose minds are sealed."

And so despite his father's protests, Matteo Ricci entered the Society of Jesus at Rome. Like St. Patrick eleven hundred years earlier, he gave up his chances of worldly advancement to devote himself to his fellow men. For twelve years he studied the movements of the planets as explained by Father Clavius, the brilliant astronomer. He investigated the latest advances in geography made possible by the explorations of Da Gama, Columbus, and Magellan. He examined the science of architecture handed down by the ancient Greeks and expressed in the beautiful buildings of Bramante and Sansovino. He steeped himself in the politics and ethics of Aristotle and the poetry of Ariosto. Methodically, painstakingly, he sharpened his intellect on the whetstone of the Renaissance until he became an expert interpreter of the intellectual awakening that had, since the fifteenth century, directed the thinking of the Western world.

And at twenty-six, the young Jesuit was ready to bring his knowledge into remote places. Volunteering for service in the Orient, he embarked for India whose shores Vasco Da Gama had first reached seventy years before, opening up the way for trade and an interchange of ideas between Europe and the Far East.

The voyage was rough for even the hardiest sailors, let alone for a scholar who had never before been to sea. The Portuguese carrack in which he sailed was a squat, clumsy vessel that was swamped by even moderate tides. Passengers were herded like cattle under the hatches, where they lay for weeks. The salt pork served them crawled with worms, and the water had such a stench that one could drink it only when holding his nose.

Upon arriving at Goa, a Portuguese trading center on the west coast of India, Father Ricci went to work teaching in the Jesuit College of St. Paul. He also served for a time at Cochin. And then, four years after arriving from Europe, he was sent on a special assignment to the Portuguese colony on the island of Macao.

Macao was one of the strangest places on earth. It was a toehold on the mainland of China whose millions of people had for centuries been shut off from the rest of the world. Though the Chinese government despised foreigners, it had permitted Portuguese traders to settle on the rocky island of Macao, situated at the mouth of the Canton River, in return

for Portuguese protection of Chinese ships against pirates
raiding the coast. However, the colony was sealed off from
China proper by a guarded wall that had only one gate.

The Portuguese in turn had permitted the Jesuits to establish a training school for missionaries on the island. Ricci
was introduced to Father Alessandro Valignani, the superior-
general of the order, a man of tremendous drive and practical intelligence, who since his own arrival in Macao years
before had been absorbed in the problem of trying to establish a mission in China.

His glittering black eyes fastened on Matteo Ricci as the
young missionary entered his study. He gripped him by the
hand and led him to a window.

"There she is, the vast, mysterious land of Cathay," he
said. "For seventeen years we have been looking at her
through this window, and always the gate is shut. To the
north there is the great Chinese wall that holds back the
world for twelve hundred miles; to the west, the desert and
lofty mountain peaks; to the south and east, the sea. For almost three hundred years, ever since Marco Polo left Peking,
we have been trying to get inside. Many missionaries have
made the attempt. Most have never been heard from. A few
have returned to announce their failure."

He turned from the window and faced Matteo Ricci.
"To attempt to infiltrate into the Empire would mean prob-
able death. The Portuguese would not risk losing their trade
with China by lifting a finger to help free any missionary
seized by the Ming Emperor. We are recruiting the very best
minds to find a solution to this problem, and that is why we
have sent for you, Father Ricci."

The young Jesuit immediately plunged into the training

that was required of all missionaries at Macao. For two years he applied himself to the Chinese language spoken at the court. He familiarized himself with the writings of Confucius. Day and night he analyzed the problem of gaining entrance into the Celestial Empire.

There was one exception to China's inflexible rule against foreigners. Twice each year a limited number of Portuguese traders from Macao were permitted to come ashore for a month at Canton to set up bazaars and barter goods. Daily, at sundown, the traders had to be back in their ships. And promptly, when the month was over, they were required to sail home.

Thus custom set Ricci's mind to working. Gradually, he developed a plan.

"On the next trading date, I'd like to go ashore as a Portuguese merchant," he told Father Valignani.

The superior-general smiled. "A clever idea, Father Ricci. But it has already been tried and found wanting. Father Ruggeri went ashore that way. He was kept under surveillance by the Chinese, ordered to his ship each sundown, and sent home with the others. He could find no way to remain on the coast permanently."

"What do the Portuguese sell the Chinese?"

"The usual commodities—amber, furs, jewelry."

"Do the traders meet any officials during their stay?"

"Representatives of the provincial Governor frequently visit the bazaar to make purchases for him."

Father Ricci mulled over this and said, "I have a plan. It's worth a try." He added with apparent irrelevancy, "Often it is best to introduce oneself with a melody. A tune has an irresistible appeal."

Father Ricci sought out his colleague Father Ruggieri, who had previously been ashore in an effort to bargain with the Governor's agents. And with Father Ruggieri's cooperation, he worked out the details of his project. Six months later, Ricci stepped ashore at Canton with the Portuguese, and set up a colorful booth. But he did not display the conventional wares of his fellow traders. Instead, on a mahogany stand painted in floral marquetry, he presented a novelty that caused a sensation with the crowds, something that had never been seen by the Chinese. It was a clock carved in alabaster to represent a merry-go-round. Figurines on horseback were spaced around the circular dial. Every sixty minutes, after the final note of the hour was struck, the horses revolved around the dial, accompanied by a lively tune.

The clock had been designed by a famous horologist in Venice and presented as a gift to the Jesuit order in Macao. But the inspiration for making this very practical use of it was Father Ricci's.

Whenever the amazing clock struck the hour, the other booths were deserted by the crowds who gathered about Father Ricci in astonishment. His clock became the talk of the town. One morning two magnificently dressed officials strode into the missionary's booth.

"The Governor has heard about your wonderful machine," said one. "He has asked us to make inquiries about it."

Father Ricci bowed low. "I will be happy to explain everything."

The first official folded his fan with a snap and pompously thrust out his chest. "Who sings the merry music when the hour strikes, the god of earth or of heaven?"

"The god of mathematics," replied Ricci wryly. "This works on the principle of a pendulum."

The officials looked at him blankly. Then they asked several more questions and were given equally bewildering answers. They turned on their heels and strode off.

The month's stay was rapidly nearing its end and the merchants were making preparations to depart for Macao when the officials returned to the booth and announced that the Governor desired to buy the wonderful clock. They were prepared to weigh out whatever amount of silver was necessary for its purchase.

"His Excellency may have it as a gift," replied Father Ricci. "I am pleased it has made such an impression on him."

But when the officials left with the clock, the missionary recalled soberly that this was his last day in China. The ships were sailing at dawn. Late that afternoon, as he was disassembling his booth, the officials appeared again in tremendous excitement.

One of them blurted out the dreadful news. "The beautiful clock has stopped. The god of song is silent. The Governor waits in vain for the striking of the hour and for the tune that has thrilled his heart."

The other snapped his fan vigorously. "Our political careers are finished unless this clock finds its voice immediately. What spell have you cast over it?"

A sheepish look came over Father Ricci's face. "I must have forgotten to wind it," he answered. "The clock has run down, that's all."

The officials looked at him blankly. "The Governor has set aside a suite in the palace for your immediate occupancy.

You are exempt from the order to leave China until you have made the clock sing again."

And so Father Ricci moved into the Governor's palace in Chao-K'-ing, the capital of the province, on the tune of a merry-go-round. Once there, the ingenious man remained. It was possible for the Governor to overlook, for a time at least, the Emperor's ruling against foreigners because communication with the interior of this vast, diffuse kingdom was very poor. The Emperor, shut away in his palace in Peking, had of necessity delegated immense authority to his provincial governors. As a result he remained ignorant of much that went on in his country.

Father Ricci kept the Governor spellbound with his learning. He taught him how to wind the clock. Through the co-operation of customs authorities under the influence of the Governor, he was able to import numerous other novelties with which to bedazzle his patron. He even succeeded in bringing several lay assistants into Chao-K'-ing.

Even when the Governor suffered a reverse of political fortunes and was removed from office, Father Ricci succeeded in winning over his successor.

One day he said bluntly to the new Governor, "I am a priest. I would like to build a temple here in Chao-K'-ing in which to worship God."

The enthralled politician could deny this man nothing. "There is a Buddhist temple called the 'Flowery Tower' on the left bank of the river. You may move into it. But whatever god you worship, you must always obey the laws of China."

With the help of native labor and under the scrutiny of curious onlookers, Father Ricci renovated the "Flowery

Tower" into a one-story building that blended harmoniously
with the orange and pomegranate trees that surrounded it
and the brightly colored lanterns of the houseboats that
passed and repassed on the lazily flowing river.

There were, however, political factions in Chao-K'-ing
who looked on Father Ricci with jealousy. They didn't like
the prospect of white men moving permanently into the city.
They whispered warnings into the Governor's ear. "These
men are spies in league with the Portuguese traders. The
house they are constructing is not a temple. It is an arsenal
for secret weapons. At the suitable time they will blow up
this city!"

The Governor shook his head. "I do not believe they are
smuggling in secret weapons," he said. Yet he was disturbed.
Among folk high and low, agents of the mandarins whispered these warnings, and orators stood on street corners
making charges publicly.

Rumors spread through Chao-K'-ing. A watchman declared under oath that one night he had seen the foreigners
move secretly into the temple a huge object wrapped in
skins. Several witnesses corroborated the testimony. Finally
the Governor summoned Father Ricci and questioned him.
Why was he taking so long to finish the temple? Why had
he not opened the doors and permitted the public to enter?

The missionary appeared ill at ease under the questioning.
He seemed to be holding back something. Eventually he
admitted that he did have some unusual equipment hidden
behind locked doors. "But I will open the temple when I am
ready. Until then you must trust me."

But the populace was panic-stricken. A few hours after
Father Ricci was questioned at the palace, citizens of all

classes, from every section of the city, advanced on the "Flowery Temple," armed with stones and clubs. They swarmed up to the doors of the temple. Father Ricci appeared and raised his hand. Eventually he quieted the mob.

"Friends," he said, "I will confess: I do have a secret weapon. But you are forcing me to reveal it before the finishing touches have been put to it. Since you so desire, it shall be secret no longer!"

He asked a half-dozen leaders of the crowd to step forward. He conducted them into a large central hall. "There!" said Father Ricci. "See for yourselves!"

Covering the entire wall from floor to ceiling was a huge, brilliantly colored map of the world. It was the first comprehensive map of the world ever to appear in China. Each of the five continents was set off from the others in a dazzling hue. Every known country was labeled, each with a description of its people, its customs, language, industries, and its geographical resources. Meridians had been drawn accurately from pole to pole. The shape and relationship of all known land and water areas were graphically depicted. Father Ricci had been in the final stages of translating this into Chinese when the riot had broken out.

The map was extraordinarily accurate within the limits of knowledge available to sixteenth-century Europe. It was, as Father Ricci had declared, a revolutionary "secret weapon"—in the war against ignorance.

The Chinese were astonished by it. Savants from all over the province flocked to the temple to observe the missionary's latest "miracle." Their own maps contained no accurate knowledge of the outside world. Theirs had portrayed the Celestial Empire as a tremendous, centrally located land mass, surrounded by a few scattered islands representing the several nations they had heard of. They had no idea of the actual shape, the distance, or direction of any foreign country. But Father Ricci's map changed all this. It gave the Chinese their first concept of the unified world they lived in. It demonstrated to them, among other things, that the earth was round. The Chinese scholars conceded that Father Ricci had opened their eyes to amazing truths of geography, and the Governor was so pleased with the map he requested that copies be made and distributed to other provinces.

Following this revelation, Father Ricci constructed a calendar embodying the latest scientific knowledge of the months and seasons. He gave lectures on astronomy and translated the theorems of Euclid into Chinese.

The missionary found Chinese civilization to be a curious mixture of enlightenment and barbarism. China had developed a remarkable system of civil service. The highest administrative offices were held by doctors of philosophy, mandarins, and literati of great learning who won their positions in competitive examinations. Their scholarship entitled them to the highest social status—similar to that of a duke or count in Europe. The people were comparatively unwarlike. Their chief use for gunpowder was in the fireworks with which they celebrated national holidays. Despite huge manpower resources, the Emperors made little attempt to annex the smaller nations at their borders. They were, on the whole, content with what they possessed, an attitude rare indeed for the times.

However, combined with this enlightenment was the practice of polygamy, the bartering of children into slavery, the drowning of female babies to cut down the size of families, the binding of women's feet to keep them "fashionably" small.

Father Ricci admired certain aspects of Chinese life and courageously opposed what he disapproved. He traveled to several localities outside Chao-K'-ing to lecture and teach. On one occasion he moved into a "haunted" house to explode the popular superstition about ghosts.

But he had his political troubles, too. Once, the Governor, in a fit of anger, banished him to Shao-Chow, a city with a notoriously unhealthy climate. Here one of his assistants died of yellow fever, and only Father Ricci's vigorous constitution saved him from a similar end. Eventually he managed to make his way, with his lay assistants, to Nanking where for a time he lived and taught unmolested, having become in dress and psychology as Chinese as the most provincial literati.

However, he eventually became persona non grata to the officials here. Jittery because of the threat of a Japanese invasion, he was suddenly accused of being a spy in the pay of Japan!

The Governor summoned Father Ricci. "You must leave China immediately! If the Emperor discovers that I have been harboring foreigners, I will suffer more than mere loss of office. Go now, and you may escape with your lives."

The blow was a bitter one to Father Ricci. It meant that he had to steal off like a thief in the night, abandoning his scientific equipment, his globes and astrolabes, his sundial and prisms, for in flight one had to travel as lightly as possible. Yet there was no alternative.

And so with a broken heart the missionary closed his school, and together with his assistants left the city.

They passed through towns and villages, mingling in crowds, disguised as peddlers to avoid seizure by the police. They wangled rides on river craft, and slowly made their way south toward the coast. Once there, they hoped to be picked up by a Portuguese carrack patrolling the sea. Father Ricci was depressed. He continually muttered, "We must not leave China. If we fail to maintain our mission, no other Westerners may enter this kingdom for centuries!"

"But there is no possible way of staying," his assistants pointed out. "You no longer have your clocks and maps and calendars. With what else can you buy your way?"

One evening while hiding in a barn on the outskirts of Nanchang, waiting for the arrival of darkness, Father Ricci seemed even more dejected than usual. In an effort to cheer him up, one of his assistants declared, "Well, we've come this far without being caught. A few miles more and we'll be out of reach of the police."

The priest's face brightened. An idea had struck him. "Yes, the police! Why, the obvious solution to our predicament has been staring us in the face right along! Instead of stealing away, we should give ourselves up to the police immediately. It is our one chance of remaining in China."

His companions looked shocked. But the missionary continued. "The Emperor does not want a foreigner who has set eyes on his country to return to the outer world with this information. If we hand ourselves over to the authorities, the whole machinery of the law will be set in motion to detain us permanently."

"But we'll be put to death!"

"Possibly. That's the gamble we take. But we may be able to convince the court, as we have already persuaded several

of the provincial governors, of our usefulness to China as
scientists.

"And if we can, and we are spared, the officials will un-
doubtedly see to it that we never again pass over these
borders. We'll be sentenced to remain here for life by official decree, and that, after all, is what we have been striving
for from the beginning—an official guarantee of our remaining. Isn't it worth the risk? Live or die, we'll be certain to
end our days here!"

Father Ricci offered his assistants the opportunity to continue on to Macao if they so desired. But to a man they
decided to remain with him. And so they walked into the
nearest town and surrendered themselves to the police. They
were immediately thrown into jail where they remained for
a week. And then they were brought before the head magistrate of Nanchang.

The reception chamber was crowded with officials. In
the audience were several mandarins who had stopped off
in Nanchang on their way to Nanking and other centers.

"What are you doing in the Empire of Heaven?" the magistrate asked Father Ricci severely.

"I am a priest. I have been teaching for several years in
Chao-K'-ing and Nanking."

Immediately an elderly, austere looking mandarin stood
up in the assembly. "I recognize this teacher. For three years
my son sat at his feet in Chao-K'-ing. He constructed a map
that proves beyond a doubt that his mother country is so far
away, no army can possibly be launched from there to do
us harm. Indeed, his knowledge of the planets makes him
especially useful at this moment."

The mandarin went into a huddle with the presiding magistrate. They conversed in low tones for several minutes. The magistrate then addressed the missionary. "You have appeared at a critical time, Father Ricci. My colleague here informs me that the royal astronomers in Peking are in danger of falling into eternal disgrace. On the moon of the feast of the dragon they made a prediction to the Most August Emperor of an eclipse of the sun to take place on the first day of the new year. A proclamation was issued by the court. On the designated morning the peers of the kingdom assembled at the Peking Observatory in their robes of office, making the ceremonial noises with cymbals to encourage the sun in his life and death struggle with the moon. But incredible as it may seem, nothing happened. The sun continued to shine!"

The mandarin now took up the story. "The Emperor dismissed the president of the Tribunal of Rites. I have been appointed to that office. And I am on my way to Peking now. I have been ordered to correct the errors of the royal astronomers. But how do I know why the sun continued to shine on that tragic morning? You alone, Father Ricci, of all men in China, can unlock this secret! It was destiny that brought you into court today."

"But my scientific instruments were left behind at Nanking. By now they certainly have been plundered by the mob."

"You can build new ones. As president of the Tribunal of Rites and honorary chairman of the Royal Order of Learning, I will place all the facilities of the Royal Observatory at your service."

"Do you dare to introduce a foreigner into Peking?"

"What choice do I have? If I do not correct the blunders

of the royal astronomers, I am undone. You are famed for your knowledge of the planets. With your learning, you will make yourself indispensable to the Emperor. In any event, I must take the chance!"

And so it was decided that Father Ricci would go to Peking. In preparation for the trip, he sent to the Portuguese at Macao a list of the presents he wished to take along for the Emperor, Wan-Li. He devoted his time to teaching while waiting for the gifts to arrive, and then, under the direction of his powerful new patron who had gone on ahead of him to prepare the way, he boarded a houseboat with two lay brothers, and left on his visit to the Emperor.

In 1598, he entered the "Forbidden Purple City of Peking," the first white man to pass within its gates since Marco Polo, three hundred years before.

Father Ricci was escorted to the throne room through one of the four entrances to the great palace. His eyes were almost blinded by the glaring shade of yellow with which the hall was gilded from floor to ceiling. Yellow was the royal color, and no one else was permitted to wear this color or furnish his home in it.

The throne stood in the middle of perforated gold columns from which incense rose, mingling with the odor of myrrh from censers set on ivory stands. Opposite the throne was a huge mirror in which the heavy-jowled Emperor surveyed himself in all his magnificence. A thousand lanterns screened in yellow cast light on him. His courtiers were dressed somberly, even shabbily, so as not to detract from the presence of the Son of Heaven.

The Emperor received Father Ricci's gifts without comment. The finest that Western art, science, and ingenuity could produce was placed before him, to no apparent effect. But when the missionary had reached the end of his resources, the Emperor leaned forward and took him by the beard. He ran his fingers through it, slowly, sensuously. His eyes, black as midnight, grew strangely luminous.

"Man of science, can you show me how to live forever?"

Father Ricci was taken aback by this unexpected question. He was silent.

The Emperor rose to his feet. "My royal command is that I live forever. I have searched throughout my kingdom for the physician, the astronomer, the philosopher who will prepare the proper drug. I have not found him. If you cannot supply me with the formula, you are useless to me."

Father Ricci turned to one of his lay brothers and took from him a final gift, one he had withheld until now. It was a large painting of the Madonna and Child executed by a Renaissance master. He set it up for the Emperor to see. "Your Majesty, you ask for eternal life. I do not have it to give. But look at this child, born over sixteen hundred years ago. He is living today. He has the secret to eternal life."

"Bring the child to me immediately."

"Your Majesty," replied Father Ricci, "you must go to Him."

"That is impossible."

"Not at all. You may reach Him without ever setting foot outside this palace. Let me settle in this city, and I will show you how."

And then Father Ricci walked over to a clavichord, one of the gifts he had brought with him. He sat down and played very softly as he spoke. "There are various kinds of immortality. Consider this musical theme. It was written by a man named Palestrina. *It* will live as long as someone wishes to play it. And the heart of a man who has laid down his life for a friend surely beats forever. And those who have learned why the planets move in their orbits—do you suppose they ever close their eyes to truth?"

The Emperor looked at this stranger who spoke so persuasively. Then he smiled. "Man of science, I like your tune. Stay with us in Peking!"

The Emperor was a temperamental man, and at the beginning the association was a tempestuous one. Father Ricci was exiled from Peking when politicians unfriendly to him infused the Son of Heaven with their prejudices. But the resourceful Jesuit succeeded in regaining the Emperor's favor, and he returned to Peking, residing in the Imperial City for nine years until his death.

He constructed new astronomical instruments for the Peking Observatory and corrected the errors of the royal stargazers. He opened an academy of physical sciences. He introduced European architecture, building a chapel that incorporated the arches, cornices, and pillars of Renaissance design. His reputation as a teacher grew to such proportions that the scholars of China gave him the title of "Ching-Jeu," the "Holy One of the West." The title of "Holy One" had hitherto been bestowed only on Confucius and a handful of other Chinese heroes.

Daily, symposia were held at the Academy of Physical Sciences at which the master and his disciples ate their food with ebony chopsticks and discussed the solar system of Copernicus, the anatomy of Vesalius, the poetry of Petrarch. In addition, Ricci printed and distributed by the thousands a catechism on Christianity explaining to the Chinese that the teachings of Christ were at many points simply a dynamic expression of all that was best in Chinese morality. Confucius had declared, "What you would not have others do unto yourself, do not unto others." Jesus had turned this philosophy of passive tolerance into a positive rule of love.

Ricci pointed out that Jesus, like Confucius, believed that human society must be rooted in the moral strength of the individual and that a person's spiritual salvation was assured only when he loved virtue as instinctively as he loved beauty. Hounded and abused by the princes and ministers he had sought to reform, Confucius had replied, even as would have Jesus, to the advice that he retreat from the world and live as a hermit, "But if I may not associate with suffering mankind, with whom am I to associate?"

And certainly Matteo Ricci, who had devoted his life to a study of the Chinese, felt a kinship with Confucius when he said, "I am disappointed, naturally, when men do not understand me. But my greater concern is when I do not understand *them*."

Christianity, emanating from the heart of this Jesuit who had made such a painstaking effort to become one with them, made a deep impression on the Chinese. In converting many of his pupils to Christianity, Father Ricci prepared the way for other missionaries to reap an even greater harvest.

Carrying out his tremendous role as the Western world's ambassador of good will to the East seriously undermined Father Ricci's health. In 1610, the leading scholars in China made a pilgrimage to the Imperial Palace to pay homage to the Emperor. As a matter of course, they called on Peking's leading private citizen as well. The round of entertaining exhausted Father Ricci's already overstrained constitution. He took sick and died. He was fifty-eight.

The entire nation paid tribute to "Ching-Jeu." A Buddhist temple was converted into a Christian church to accept his body, and his converts prayed for his soul. The missionary who had introduced modern science into China died convinced that other Westerners would find their way into the Celestial Empire and carry on his work. He had written to Rome, just before his death, describing the kind of missionaries to be sent: "Let them be good astronomers."

Immediately after his forceful personality left the scene, the outlook became bleak. His assistants were banished to Macao. Nevertheless, the rebuff was a temporary one. Jesuit missionaries succeeded in entering China again to carry on the spiritual and temporal work of their predecessor. Leibnitz, the great German physicist and co-inventor of the calculus, corresponded with Jesuit scientists in China and obtained valuable information from them.

Today a new Chinese wall has been erected against the spirit of free inquiry. But the intellectual freedom for which Matteo Ricci stood is certain to be born again in the country of Confucius.

Jesus said: "Go ye therefore, and teach all nations . . . and, lo, I am with you always, even unto the end of the world." And none of his disciples carried out this command in a more spirited manner than the blue-eyed mandarin from Italy who was buried with Chinese national honors in the Forbidden City of Peking.

9

Healer in the Tropics

ALBERT SCHWEITZER

〰〰〰〰〰〰〰〰〰〰〰〰〰〰〰〰〰〰〰〰〰〰〰〰〰

FORTY MILES from the Equator, in the creeping, humid African jungle where the rains pour down in a tidal burst and layers of suffocating moisture drain the energy from a white man, there is an entire community built on stilts like the villages of the lake dwellers before the dawn of history. To this "modern prehistoric" settlement perched over the sunbaked earth come natives from scores of grass hut villages within a radius of five hundred miles. They come in dugouts down the crocodile-infested Ogowé River, and they carry patients suffering from strangulated hernias, leprosy, sleeping sickness.

At the landing area they are met by a bulky, slightly stooped European, with friendly gray eyes and a large drooping mustache. He wears a sun helmet. His shirt is open at the collar. Flanked by interpreters to translate the various dialects spoken by his patients, he listens to their complaints.

"I have a singing heart and a running ear, doctor."

"I have crabs living in my stomach."

"My body is turning all soft—the blood is going to my head."

He assigns each arrival to one of the dozens of well-equipped rooms, for an emergency operation, for medication, or—in the case of the insane—for psychiatric therapy.

Dr. Albert Schweitzer, the energetic head of this extraordinary hospital in the Gabon territory of French Equatorial Africa, has been at his trade of healing for forty years. The natives affectionately call him "the Big Abdomen," and by this they're not referring to his stomach. The quiet, self-effacing doctor is their "Mr. Big"—the most important person ever to come into their lives. Before Schweitzer arrived, the natives had only their medicine men to rely on. Today, five thousand patients annually are treated by the doctor and his competent staff. Mothers arrive from remote settlements, where jungle drums are still beaten in primitive rites, to have their babies delivered by modern methods in Dr. Schweitzer's hospital. Chieftains who have lived a lifetime in a world of fetish worship flock eagerly to the hospital to receive shots of penicillin and up-to-date surgical treatment. The jungle itself remains ancient, changeless, impenetrable, but the people along the Ogowé have undergone a remarkable change in their physical habits, thanks to Dr. Schweitzer and his mission.

The development of the hospital at Lambaréné from a single shack to a community of forty buildings is an amazing enough story. But even more extraordinary is the personal story of the man who directs this enterprise. It is the record of one man's rebellion against the self-seeking, materialistic spirit of the times.

Albert Schweitzer was born in 1875, the son of a pastor in upper Alsace, which at the time was a German province. His grandfather was a schoolmaster and an organist, and from him he inherited a passion for music. At nine, he performed on the organ in the loft of the village church; in his teens he came under the instruction of the organist, Charles Marie Widor, in Paris. His playing won praise from distinguished people in the musical world, including the composers Faure and D'Indy, and the widow of Richard Wagner.

But there was another strain in Schweitzer that sought expression as well—a strong religious feeling, coupled with a remarkable aptitude for scholarship. At twenty-four, already launched on a successful career as concert organist, he received the degree of doctor of philosophy, having published a strikingly original analysis of Kant's system of thought. He entered the theological school at the University of Strasbourg, contributed a brilliant new interpretation of Christ's Last Supper, and earned a degree of Licentiate in Theology. He was appointed director of the theological school of the University. The same year, he was ordained a preacher.

Renowned throughout Europe as a musician, philosopher, and theologian before he was thirty, Schweitzer, like Goethe's Faust, seemed destined to enjoy the last scintilla of worldly good fortune. Unlike Faust, however, Schweitzer was not enslaved by the fleshpots. One morning, as early as his twenty-first year, while he lay in bed, a disturbing thought came to him. "It struck me as incomprehensible that I should be allowed to lead such a happy life, when I saw so many people around me wrestling with care and suffering.

There occurred the thought . . . that I must not accept this happiness as a matter of course, but must give something up in return for it!"

Even as a child, Schweitzer had had an extraordinary sensitivity toward others. Although he was the son of the village pastor, he refused to dress differently from the sons of uneducated, poorer people. He refused to wear leather shoes while the other boys wore wooden sabots, or to wear mittens during the cold weather when the hands of others went exposed. He felt guilty of eating food that was not available to the less fortunate.

And now while lying in bed in his native Günsbach in Alsace, he analyzed these feelings of guilt calmly and decided he could not go on indefinitely living for himself. "I settled with myself before I got up that I would consider myself justified in living till I was thirty for science and art, in order to devote myself from that time forward to the direct service of humanity."

In the next nine busy years he never lost sight of his master plan for serving the needy. Then one morning he came across a magazine published by the Paris Mission Society. He read an article written by its president, rueing the lack of doctors in the Gabon territory of the French Congo. When Schweitzer put down the magazine, he knew what his life's work was to be.

A few months later, on his thirtieth birthday, he was in Paris. He dropped a letter into a mailbox on the Avenue de la Grande Armée announcing to his family that he was going to become a doctor and practice among the natives of the French Gabon. His family and friends were dismayed. For a man to enter medical school in his thirties was difficult enough. For the principal of the theological college at Strasbourg, a man who had already won worldwide fame in music and philosophy, to enroll as a freshman medical student was almost beyond belief. But what caused them the most concern was Schweitzer's determination, after getting his medical degree, to disappear into the equatorial jungle, to bury himself among primitive black tribes for life—he who had written a definitive study of Bach!

Some of Schweitzer's friends believed that he was reacting from an unhappy love experience. Others uncharitably laid the decision to a rebuff in his professional career. Charles Widor, his organ teacher, threw up his arms in despair. "The general does not go to the front lines with a rifle! You cannot bury the talent entrusted to you!"

One fashionable young lady, very much in evidence at rallies for the "betterment" of mankind, told him that he could do more good by *lecturing* on medical help for the natives than by going out as a doctor himself. "Propaganda is the mother of happenings," she declared.

Schweitzer was deeply disturbed by the attitude of his friends—"people who professed to be Christians." However, he was philosophical about them. "Anyone who proposes to do good must not expect people to roll stones out of his way, but must accept his lot calmly if they even roll a few more upon it."

The truth was, he shared, in a sense, the misgivings of his associates. He looked ahead to his years as a medical student with anxiety. In spite of his intelligence and determination, he realized that the memory of a man of thirty was not nearly as efficient as that of a twenty-one-year-old student.

The next four years were ones of great strain. Schweitzer

didn't have the heart to give up his theological teaching or his preaching, and so he continued with these activities while studying medicine. Furthermore, he traveled regularly to Paris to play the organ at the concerts of the Bach Society. And he gave concerts in Barcelona as well. On these train trips he prepared his sermons, his lectures to his theology students—and his own lessons as a medical student.

The ordeal finally came to an end. "When . . . after my final examination conducted by Madelung, the surgeon, I strode out of the hospital into the . . . winter evening, I could not grasp the fact that the terrible strain of the medical course was now behind me."

Madelung, who walked beside him that evening, declared, "It's only because you have such excellent health that you have gotten through a job like this."

While at medical school, Schweitzer had fallen in love with a woman who was ideally suited to be his wife. She was Helene Breslau, the daughter of a history professor, an experienced teacher and social worker. Schweitzer married her the year he interned in a hospital following his graduation. To become even more valuable to him, his wife took special training as a nurse.

Even after Schweitzer received his medical degree, there were other obstacles to be cleared before he could depart for Africa. Since he desired to go as a free agent, he had to raise his own funds for his mission. With characteristic energy, he gave a series of benefit concerts. The German professors at Strasbourg and members of his own congregation contributed generously to this fund. When he had finally achieved financial independence, he went before the Paris Mission Society and requested permission to establish his medical mission in the Gabon territory. The last difficulty was overcome when Schweitzer received permission from the French Colonial Office to practice medicine at Lambaréné. The cooperation between Frenchmen and Germans making the doctor's project possible—less than twenty-four months before the outbreak of World War I—is a striking commentary on Albert Schweitzer's ability to summon forth the best in men even in times of national chauvinism and tribal hatreds. This was to be a unique quality of the man.

Now that departure was imminent, Schweitzer felt immeasurably saddened. "Until I left for Africa I avoided as far as possible going past either St. Nicholas' [his church], or the University, because the very sight of the places where I had carried on my work which I could never resume was too painful for me." And twenty years later, when he was in Europe on vacation, he wrote, "I cannot bear to look at the windows of the . . . room to east of the entrance of the great University building, because it was there that I most often lectured."

In February, 1913, the last of seventy packing cases was loaded with supplies. Together with his wife, Schweitzer left Günsbach for Bordeaux, and in March sailed for Africa. On arriving at Lambaréné, he took up lodgings in the protestant mission founded by an American missionary who had recently retired. Three times the natives had burned down the American's house and robbed him of his books. Finally, for protection, he rebuilt his home on a hill. And it was here that Schweitzer commenced his practice.

Lambaréné is a small village situated on the Ogowé River which runs through the heart of Equatorial Africa and with its tributaries provides a waterway linking hundreds of jungle villages together.

The conditions he met were deplorable. The first native patients who came to Schweitzer had to be treated in the open, or, when it rained, on the veranda of his home. Within a few weeks, he moved into an old hen house. It had no windows. But there were so many cracks in the roof, Schweitzer had to wear his helmet indoors for protection from the sun. The following autumn, with native help, he built a corrugated iron building down by the river. It consisted of an examining room, an operating room, a dispensary, and a room for sterilizing instruments. Around this building he erected a number of bamboo huts to be used as wards.

The natives at first regarded Schweitzer as another "medicine man." As in the case with their own "healers," they believed he had the power not only to cure but to implant diseases, if he chose. Because of this conviction, Schweitzer's first native assistant advised him not to accept for treatment any patients whose recovery seemed doubtful. Should a native die under his care, there might be retaliation by his relatives. Another thing that added to the natives' distrust was Schweitzer's policy of maintaining open graves on the hospital grounds. He prepared graves beforehand because corpses decomposed so quickly in the climate. But some of the natives feared that he planned to murder them.

These *indigènes* at first visited him reluctantly. But when they returned to their villages cured of their aches and pains, others followed. Before the first year was over, Schweitzer had treated about two thousand people. Fortunately all his surgical operations were successful. From then on his reputation was assured.

Malaria, leprosy, elephantiasis, dysentery, and syphilis were prevalent among the natives. For fifteen years Schweitzer had the main responsibility for treating and curing sleeping sickness in the region. After 1928, government agencies directed the campaign. Strangulated hernias were common, and until Schweitzer's coming, almost every family in the area had lost a member from this ailment. The natives were also highly susceptible to pneumonia, bronchitis, rheumatism, and the common cold. Periods of great humidity and rain, followed by sudden dry spells, provoked violent chills. There was more rheumatism here than in the Western world. Heart disease was also fairly common. The children were especially susceptible to intestinal parasites. Curiously enough, in forty years Schweitzer has never seen a native case of cancer or appendicitis.

Patients came to him with injuries caused by attacks from buffaloes, elephants, and gorillas. River dugouts were frequently attacked by hippopotami. Snakes also were a constant threat, and Schweitzer never entered the forest unless natives carrying machetes preceded him.

Patients sometimes came to him with wounds inflicted by "leopard-men," members of a secret society organized throughout Equatorial Africa, who believed they were the reincarnation of the leopard. They leaped from ambushes dressed in the animal's skin and wearing metal claws.

In keeping with his policy of hardboiled idealism, Schweitzer insisted that the *indigènes* pay for their treatment. From them he accepted bananas, poultry, livestock, eggs, or any other produce they wished to donate to the hospital. He knew that people rarely value what they get for nothing.

Before Schweitzer's departure from Europe, the Paris
Bach Society had presented him with a piano especially
constructed for service in the humid tropics. For months,
however, the doctor didn't have the heart to play it. He
felt that the break with his musical past would be easier if
he allowed his fingers and feet to "get rusty." Nevertheless,
one night when he had made his final round of the wards,
he retired to his study in a nostalgic mood and limbered up
his fingers on a Bach fugue. As the mellifluous sound filled
the room, he realized that he could best use his free time
by continuing to practice on the piano and deepening his
musical conception. Hereafter, although the average day
allowed no more than a half hour for practice, he kept at
it steadily, playing the music of Handel, Mendelssohn, and
Reger in the primeval forest.

Schweitzer had spent a little more than a year in Africa
when events suddenly altered his life. War broke out in
Europe. As a German national in a French colony, the doctor found himself in a delicate position. On the evening of
the day the news of war reached Lambaréné, French colonial
officials made him a prisoner. "You may remain in your home
for the present," they told him, "but you must discontinue
all communication with Europeans and natives, and you
must unconditionally obey the African soldiers who will be
assigned to guard you."

The *indigènes* were baffled. They didn't understand why
the doctor should suddenly be treated as an "enemy." When
word was received of the death in overseas battle of ten
Europeans who had lived in Lambaréné, they shook their
heads dubiously. "Why don't the white folk meet in a palaver
to straighten out their affairs peacefully? How will they ever

pay for all these dead men?" In native wars, a price was exacted of the opposing army for each man killed in battle. This kept the slaughter to a minimum.

Since he was forbidden to work at the hospital, Schweitzer sat down and, as in the old days, started work on a book. But this time he was not concerned with Bach's music or the philosophy of Immanuel Kant. He was concerned with nothing less than civilization itself. Like every feeling person, he was profoundly shocked by the war. He who had interpreted the teachings of Christianity so literally was horrified to observe his fellow Europeans mobilizing for mass annihilation. It could have happened, he believed, only because his contemporaries—in developing their intricate industrial machines, their marvelous scientific formulae, their iron and steel foundries, their great commercial cities—had lost their reverence for life.

Five months after his internment, aided by the protests of his musical friends in Paris and the complaints of the natives who required medical attention, he was permitted to practice medicine again. But in every free hour he continued with his analysis of the decline and fall of modern civilization. He surveyed earlier civilizations, the major religious and political groupings, their dominant cultural values and philosophical concepts, for the light they could throw on the present predicament in which humanity found itself.

He decided that the most successful societies had been those in which ethical values were esteemed above all else. The tragedy of modern society, Schweitzer felt, was caused by its basic atheism, its worship of expediency above principle, its flippant disregard of moral absolutes.

"Many a night I sat at the book . . . writing with the deepest emotion as I thought of those who were lying in the trenches."

In the fall of 1917 the French government issued new regulations concerning aliens. The doctor was notified that he and his wife were to be deported to a prison camp. He had already completed part of the writing of *The Philosophy of Civilization*. But so hysterical was the mood of the times that he didn't dare take the manuscript with him for fear it would be confiscated at the customs inspection. He left it in the care of an American missionary, preparing a brief summary and topical outline to take with him. So that the subject might appear to the censors to be remote from the political present, he inserted chapter headings related to an historical study of the Renaissance. In this way he saved the manuscript from confiscation on several occasions.

Schweitzer kept busy diagnosing, operating, and giving medication to his patients up to the day of his departure. When he boarded the river steamer, the natives gathered at the shore to say goodbye. The father superior of the Catholic mission across the Ogowé River boarded the steamer and, waving aside the soldiers who tried to prevent his approach, shook hands with the doctor and his wife. "You shall not leave this country," he declared, "without receiving my thanks for all the good you have done."

On the ship to France, Schweitzer was kept in confinement. But he continued his music exercises, using a table in his cabin for the keyboard and the floor for pedals, as he had done as a boy. He learned some Bach fugues by heart and Charles Widor's Sixth Organ Symphony.

When they reached Bordeaux, the Schweitzers were interned in temporary barracks. The doctor came down with dysentery, but fortunately he had medicine with him, and he successfully fought the attack. From Bordeaux, the couple were transferred to a large prison camp at Garaison in the Pyrenees. As the doctor's luggage was being inspected, a guard happened across his French translation of Aristotle's *Politics*. "Here's a fellow trying to smuggle a political book into a prisoner-of-war camp!" he reported.

"This book was written years before the birth of Christ," Schweitzer pointed out.

"Is that true?" The guard turned to a fellow soldier with a reputation for scholarship. The other verified the doctor's statement.

"What! People talked politics as long ago as that?" pondered the *poilu* in amazement. "Well, anyway, we talk politics differently today from what they did then. So keep your book."

The prison camp teemed with internees of all backgrounds. There were German and Austrian painters, lawyers, and professors who had been caught outside their national borders when the war broke out; missionaries and traders from West Africa; merchants arrested on the seven seas; members of religious orders from the Sahara; Turks whose wives went about veiled.

Schweitzer was permitted to keep his instruments and medicines, and he became the camp physician. Since nearly everyone suffered from malnutrition and from exposure to drafts in unheated rooms, Schweitzer was kept busy. Displaying his characteristic interest in people, he struck up an acquaintance with individuals from all walks of life, acquiring a variety of specialized information that broadened his understanding of human affairs. He became friendly with a group of gypsy musicians who had been playing in the fashionable cafés of Paris when war broke out. They had been allowed to keep their musical instruments, and they serenaded the Schweitzers.

The prisoners who suffered the most from their enforced idleness were the artisans. When Mrs. Schweitzer obtained material for a dress, several tailors begged to be allowed to sew it free of charge, so that they could feel once more the needle and thread between their fingers.

Finally, the Schweitzers were transferred to a camp for Alsatians at St. Rémy in southern France. When the doctor entered his new lodgings, they seemed unaccountably familiar to him. He had seen that bare, ugly iron stove, that flue pipe somewhere before. And then he recalled where. He had seen them in a painting by Vincent Van Gogh. This was the very room in which the great Dutch artist had been confined when he went mad. So here, in a former insane asylum, Albert Schweitzer now resumed writing his book on civilization.

Five months later the period of imprisonment suddenly came to an end. The Schweitzers were put aboard a train for Switzerland, and there they were released in an exchange of prisoners.

After a short visit to Strasbourg, the doctor returned to his native Günsbach which he had left in 1913. The change the town had undergone since he had last seen it amazed and saddened him. From the mountains he had climbed as a boy came the roar of artillery. On the roads, one walked between high banks of wire netting packed with straw that masked the position of the townspeople from enemy guns. Every few yards were emplacements for machine guns. The woods in which Schweitzer had played in his youth had been razed to a few skeleton tree stumps. The Kaiser's troops were quartered in many of the houses. People carried gas masks with them everywhere, and huddled in their cellars during the frequent bombardments. To this level the world had fallen nineteen centuries after Jesus!

Schweitzer's health, seriously weakened by his attack of dysentery and his subsequent long confinement, now broke down. Realizing he needed surgical attention, he set out, with a high fever, for a hospital in Strasbourg. Practically everything on wheels had been requisitioned by the army, and the doctor traveled several miles by foot before he was able to find transportation. On his arrival at Strasbourg he was operated on.

Shortly after his recovery, the mayor of the city offered Schweitzer a position at the municipal hospital, and since he needed money badly, he accepted. He was also reappointed pastor of St. Nicholas'. It seemed as if his life had completed a cycle.

When the war ended and the peace treaty was signed, Schweitzer found himself a French national. But it was impossible to bottle up this citizen of the world behind any national border. Weekly, for two years after the armistice, he crossed the Rhine River with baskets of food for his friends in Germany who were on the verge of starvation. Among them were Cosima Wagner, the widow of Richard Wagner, and Hans Thoma, the elderly painter.

Now that a temporary measure of sanity had been restored to the world, Schweitzer made plans to return to Lambaréné. Volumes I and II of *The Philosophy of Civilization* had been published, together with a book on his African experiences,

On the Edge of the Primeval Forest. He felt that it was time to be getting back to his natives. Once more he had to raise funds "from scratch." He gave lectures and organ recitals, drew upon the royalties from his books, gratefully accepted the donations of friends all over Europe.

In February, 1924, he left again for the tropics. This departure was a particularly sad one, for he was compelled to leave his wife behind. Ill health made it impossible for Mrs. Schweitzer to live in Africa during the wet season. However, in the years ahead, as often as she was able to, she joined her husband during the dry season.

A terrible disappointment was in store for Schweitzer when he arrived in Lambaréné. All that remained of the hospital he had so laboriously developed in four and a half years was one small building of corrugated iron and the shell of one of the bamboo huts. The other buildings had collapsed. The path leading from the main hospital building to the doctor's bungalow on the hill was overgrown with creepers.

Yet the moment Schweitzer arrived, the sick flocked to him clamoring for treatment. And he plunged into work. Mornings he attended his patients. Afternoons he assumed the role of a master builder. With native labor he cleared the jungle and rebuilt walls, roofs, and floors for the physically ill, and examining rooms and quarters for the insane. For more than a year he was at this exacting labor. But no sooner was the job completed in the autumn of 1925 than an epidemic of dysentery broke out along the Ogowé River and the natives rushed to Lambaréné in greater numbers than ever. Instead of a hospital of fifty beds, Schweitzer needed space for a hundred and fifty. And when this epidemic passed there would be other emergencies. The hospital could not be expanded further on its present site, for the land was confined by a steep slope on one side and a swamp on the other. It was necessary to find a new location.

Although he was in a state of exhaustion, Schweitzer looked about for a more suitable site. Three miles up the Ogowé River he found one. He received a grant of a hundred and seventy-two acres from the district commissioner, and set to work clearing the underbrush. The building was painfully slow. Often it took workers several days just to cut down one giant jungle tree. And several more days were required to cut it into sections for use. In this new settlement the buildings were placed on piles to protect them from the river floods and from the torrential rains that poured down from the hill slopes.

At the beginning of the short dry season in 1927, the transfer of the patients to the new hospital was begun. For days Schweitzer was on the river piloting dugouts packed with passengers, furniture, and medicines. It was a tremendous job, but at night when the doctor made his rounds of the new wards and heard the comments of the sick, he felt rewarded.

The new hospital had space for two hundred patients. In place of the damp earth of the earlier hospital, the new one had wooden floors. Instead of dark, stuffy rooms there were well-lighted, properly ventilated wards. There were eight cells for mental patients where before there had been two. The surrounding jungle was cleared with ax and machete. Tropical fruit trees of every variety were planted. Indeed, Schweitzer cultivated citrus fruits in such quantity that he was able to trade the surplus crop for rice—a basic food of the natives—which he stored up against hard times.

Schweitzer sent out a call for volunteer doctors and nurses. The response gladdened his heart. Today he has three physicians and three nurses assisting him the year round.

In a short time, the doctor's village took on impressive dimensions. New buildings were built with donations sent in by people all over the world. One addition, called the "Necklace Building," is so named because an Englishwoman paid for it by selling her jewelry. Another is called the "Emmy Hopf Building" after a Swiss organist who raised money for it by giving a series of benefit concerts. A building for the insane was donated by the Guild House in London.

The doors and windows of the hospital are heavily barred against the panthers, gorillas, lions, and elephants that roam through the surrounding jungle at night. On more than one occasion the doctor has looked up from his writing table into the luminous eyes of one of these savage visitors pressed against the bars.

His own headquarters, built where the palace of an old native sun king stood, is a striking demonstration of how the primitive world can be adapted to the needs of a highly civilized mind. Over his bed is a mosquito net, and against the wall stand dugout paddles, a hammer, and a saw. Within reach, hung from a nail—"the way a hunter strings up pheasants," Schweitzer says—are the latest chapters of his epic study of civilization. Sections of pages have been chewed off by Léonie, a baby fawn who sleeps in a pen at his elbow. Schweitzer writes by the light of a kerosene lamp, sitting on a wooden bench (though when he reached his seventieth birthday, he permitted himself the luxury of a cushion). Adjoining this study is his music room. Here is his famous piano with organ pedals. When he is not playing, the doctor keeps a rug over the pedals to protect his fawn from breaking her legs. Once he kept a porcupine in the room and was delighted to find her gravely dancing in time to a Chopin étude.

In this room too are rows of books, many of them mildewed from the dampness, some crawling with termites. But the ideas remain inviolate. The works of ancient Chinese and Indian philosophers predominate. They are, in many respects, the spiritual ancestors of the doctor.

In this jungle where Schweitzer has declared that he has found his deepest, most penetrating insight into the music of Bach, he also feels a subtle, lively kinship with the chimpanzee. A family of them romp on his grounds. The bee, the tiger, the ant—all are precious to him. His reverence for life extends to everything alive. "I never burn a field. Just imagine all the insects that would perish in a fire. When the natives burn large areas of brush and forest to make room for their plantations, when night after night I see the light of these great conflagrations from my window . . . my heart is filled with pity." He is convinced that only when men take upon themselves the burden, not alone of other men's trouble, but the pain of every living thing, will genuine moral health be achieved.

Schweitzer runs his hospital against almost insuperable odds. The extreme humidity makes precision instruments useless. He cannot, for instance, operate X-ray machines or electro-cardiograph equipment; he cannot take metabolism tests or many other laboratory findings that are routine in modern medicine. His medicines must be carefully stored away in metal boxes which are proof against the weather and the incessant termites. The climate is so debilitating to the white man that European members of Schweitzer's staff, after serving two years in Lambaréné, are sent home for a long vacation. Schweitzer estimates that his staff accomplishes daily only half the work it would normally get done in a temperate climate.

In addition to the natives, the hospital serves the white residents in the area, many of whom have become anemic from a long stay on the equator and a lack of calcium in their diet.

Even today, the *indigènes* regard the doctor's work with awe. To undergo an operation at Lambaréné adds tremendously to a native's prestige in the eyes of his followers. The knife is worshiped by them as if it were a deity. It is believed to be much more powerful in driving off evil spirits than drugs, and many an *indigène* expresses disappointment when he receives only a medicine for his ailment.

More than once, the doctor in making his rounds has found a patient sleeping on the floor and the relative who brought him to the hospital sleeping in his bed. The father, brother, uncle, anxious to experience for perhaps the only time in his life what it is like to sleep like a white man, has persuaded the patient to give up his bed for the night.

The hospital has frequently taken on the appearance of a home for orphan children. There is a superstition among the natives that a woman must not give her breast to an infant whose mother has died, for fear she will suffer the same fate. Since cows cannot survive in the equatorial jungle because of the tsetse fly, motherless infants before Schweitzer's coming often starved to death. Now such infants are brought to the hospital to be fed on canned milk. The nurses have dozens of children on their hands at all times.

Schweitzer's sermons on Sundays are as informal as the shirt he wears open at the collar, and as muscular as his arms that emerge bare at the elbow. He speaks in the open air in front of the hospital wards while the natives sit listening on the doorsteps or gather in little groups before the entrances. As he preaches, mothers nurse their babies, dogs roam through the streets along with hens, ducks, and sheep. Even the monkeys chattering in trees and men from the insane ward dancing jigs are included in the congregation. Nothing that breathes is banished from the Sermon on the Mount and the message of Saint Paul.

The experiment at Lambaréné has become widely publicized despite Schweitzer's personal dislike of publicity. He has received invitations to lecture all over the world, and since this is his chief method of raising funds he has met as many of these requests as possible. Leaving his hospital in the care of his competent staff, he once visited America—to deliver the major address on the Centennial of Goethe's death, in Aspen, Colorado, in 1949.

The doctor doesn't know the meaning of idleness. So overwhelmed is he with mail from admirers that he carries two linen bags crammed full of letters wherever he goes. Every spare moment he devotes to his correspondence.

One Christmas Schweitzer was invited to Zutphen, Holland, to deliver the holiday sermon. He arrived at the little town a week before Christmas, then disappeared for five days. The residents were mystified. Finally one of them, the journalist Pierre Van Paassen, happened to be passing a cathedral when he heard the notes of an organ. He entered and found the doctor covered with sweat, cleaning the pipes in the loft. This is how he had been "resting up" for his sermon.

In Edinburgh he met his celebrated colleague, Dr. Wilfred Grenfell, for the first and only time. Grenfell was then in Europe for a rest. The two physicians immediately began talking shop. Grenfell declared that his chief trouble was caused by the straying off, during their periodic migrations, of the reindeer he had imported from Siberia for milking. Schweitzer spoke of his loss of goats through theft and snake bites. Suddenly they both laughed. They had been talking, not as doctors concerned about their patients, but as farmers dealing in livestock.

Just before they parted, Schweitzer wrote in the guest book provided by their host, "The hippopotamus is delighted to have met the polar bear."

Once, when the chairman at a lecture asked Schweitzer how he would like to be introduced to the audience, he replied, "Just say that this fellow who looks like a Scottish collie is Albert Schweitzer."

The outbreak of World War II found him at his post in Lambaréné. He had been in Europe on business in February of that year, but, convinced that war was imminent, had hurried back to Africa. He began immediately to stockpile hospital supplies and set by food reserves. Most of his vital medicines and drugs arrived from Europe just before hostilities began, although the vessel carrying the last shipment of supplies was torpedoed off Cape Finisterre. In 1940, the fighting reached practically the front yard of the hospital when De Gaulle's Free French battled the Vichy Forces for the village of Lambaréné. The staff prepared for any eventu-

ality, covering the sides of the buildings with sheets of gal-
vanized iron. They took refuge in the concrete cistern from
which the water had been emptied. Luckily the hospital was
three miles up-river from the town, and it was not bombed,
although a number of stray shells and bullets did fall on the
grounds.

A few months later, with Europe sealed off as a source
of supply for medicines, Schweitzer received a message from
friends in the United States offering to send him supplies if
he would prepare a list of his needs. This shipment arrived
at the very moment his reserves had reached a perilously low
point.

On May 8, 1945, just as he was sitting down to his daily
correspondence, Schweitzer received word that an armistice
had been signed in Europe. He finished his letter writing.
Then he went to his examining rooms to attend to some
heart patients. Only when his duties were finished did he
summon the entire community by bell and join in the great
outburst of rejoicing that was touched off by the announce-
ment.

Schweitzer is one of the world's supreme optimists. The
encouragement people everywhere have given his work has
convinced him that the world is not so completely material-
istic-minded as it is said to be. He believes that there is more
"idealistic will power" in men and women than ever comes
to the surface, that there is a vast, untapped reservoir of
Christian feeling locked in human hearts. "To unbind what
is bound," to channel this underlying reverence for life into
a powerful expression of positive, everyday conduct—that is
the supreme mission of the human race.

And in his campaign to drive this mission home to people

everywhere, this man, nearly eighty years of age, labors vigorously, aggressively, single-mindedly, even today. To friends who warn him to ease his "killing" pace, arguing, "You cannot burn a candle at both ends," Schweitzer replies, "Yes you can, if the candle is long enough."

10

Father of California

JUNIPERO SERRA

〰〰〰〰〰〰〰〰〰〰〰〰〰〰〰〰〰〰〰〰〰〰〰〰〰〰〰〰〰〰〰〰

JUNÍPERO SERRA was a Franciscan friar who became one of the founding fathers of our country. It is more appropriate perhaps to call Serra one of the "foundling" fathers, for few men of his stature have received such little recognition by posterity. At the very time that George Washington was winning independence for the thirteen Atlantic colonies, Serra was directing the colonization of the Pacific Coast. He came of the race of Cortez and De Soto, inheriting their ardor for a crusade; but with this difference—his marching orders were the Sermon on the Mount.

In the orchard of the monastery of San Fernando in Mexico City in 1768, two friars sat quietly beneath a cypress tree. They were Franciscans, dressed in the brown habit of their order, with a crucifix and rosary hanging from their waists. After a time, the Father Guardian put his hand on his companion's shoulder. His eyes above the high Castilian cheekbones revealed intense excitement.

"His Excellency José de Gálvez, the new *visitador generale,* has just arrived from Spain. Do you know what this means?"

"I have heard," answered the other, "that he has been sent to administer the King's revenues."

"Aha! That is the news manufactured for the ears of unfriendly governments. I have received secret instructions that reveal a different story. Gálvez has been sent here to meet a serious challenge. And he needs the help of our order. I have selected you to represent us."

The Father Guardian looked keenly at his companion as if he were observing him for the first time, although, in fact, he had known him for years. "Fray Junípero," he declared warmly, "you have been a godsend to us. You have been the guiding spirit of our Indian missions. And now the opportunity of your life awaits you."

He rose to his feet. "Señor Gálvez wishes to give you the details of your assignment personally. I suggest you leave at once for Santa Ana where he has his headquarters."

Fray Junípero Serra stood up and accompanied the Father Guardian to the gate. It was noticeable that he limped. He had been crippled years before as the result of the bite of a poisonous insect.

In addition to teaching in Mexico City, this lame little friar had preached among the native Indians, traveling thousands of miles on foot over rocky mesas and arroyos, paddling up jungle streams for days at a time without daring to stretch his limbs because of the jaguars and pumas prowling the banks.

Father Junípero had not always been a missionary. Indeed, until the age of thirty-six, he had lived the quiet, sheltered life of a professor of philosophy in his native Majorca. He had gained a distinguished reputation and had

won many academic honors. Then suddenly, to the dismay
of his colleagues—and over their objections—he gave up this
life of security and rushed off to the New World to enroll as
a missionary friar.

Never once during the hardships he later experienced
serving among the Indians of the Sierra Gorda and the
Apache tribes did he utter a word of complaint. On the
trip overseas to the New World he had made clear his attitude toward personal suffering. When a fellow passenger had
protested the shortage of drinking water aboard ship, he had
replied, "I have found a remedy for thirst, my friend. It is to
eat very little and to talk less. That does not waste the
saliva."

Fray Junípero rose to the very top of his profession during
his service in New Spain. Now, at fifty-five, he was *presidente* of the missions in Lower California, an area that today
is part of Mexico.

Immediately after his conference with the Father Guardian, Fray Junípero set out for Santa Ana where Señor Gálvez
had temporarily established his lodgings with a wealthy
dealer in pearls.

Gálvez was a gracefully proportioned Malagan with
shrewd bold eyes. He greeted the padre warmly.

"*Ava Maria Purissima!* You Franciscans are certainly a
hardy lot. Señor Presidente, I have heard stories about your
missionary labors. But—begging your pardon if I am allud-
ing to a delicate subject—I hadn't realized that you accomplished all this with a crippled leg!"

"My lameness has not prevented me from doing my duty."

The other smiled. "No, of course not. Well, here is the
news briefly. We have received a report from our intelli-

gence in St. Petersburg that Russia has crossed from Siberia over to the Aleutian Islands and is reaching out for the fur trade in North America. It is a well-known fact that the Empress Catherine is hungry for new seaports. And we fear that she may already have begun explorations down the California coast.

"To prevent California from falling into Muscovite hands, I have immediate orders to march north to garrison San Diego and Monte Rey. Incidentally, Monte Rey will provide a relief station for our galleons from Manila."

He unrolled a map and pointed to the ports. "As you know, Vizcaíno discovered both harbors 166 years ago, but no white man has set foot in New California since. I have no knowledge of the temper of the Indians. Frankly, I haven't the slightest idea whether we'll arrive there with our scalps. I pray God it will be a bloodless occupation. That, Señor Presidente, is your assignment—to insure that it will be."

The Spaniards, since the coming of Cortez and Pizzaro, had become past masters at launching expeditions in the New World. They had occupied Lower California as early as 1533, and it was from this base that the present expedition into New California was to be undertaken. Missionaries of the Franciscan Order had accompanied the earliest *hidalgos* into New Spain to reduce the harshness of the conquest. They had been the first religious order to send friars into Mexico. And after the expulsion of the Jesuits, they had established their own missions in *baja* California. As *presidente* of the California missions, Father Junípero was in an ideal position to influence history.

The preparations for the present expedition into New Cali-

fornia were thorough. Cattle were slaughtered to provide the
necessary meat. Many varieties of seeds from Spain were
labeled carefully and packed away in the holds of ships to
be planted in the wilderness. One hundred and twenty-five
pounds of garlic were stored together with quantities of red
pepper and dried chocolate to be converted into a delicious,
almond-flavored drink. Engineers, a surgeon, a baker, a
cook, and a tortilla maker boarded the *San Carlos*. Carpenters and blacksmiths climbed aboard her sister ship, the
San Antonio, and companies of soldiers assembled to make
the journey by foot.

Father Junípero limped back and forth on his game leg,
making his own preparations. From the missions in Lower
California, he collected seven large church bells, pictures of
the Virgin, *purificadores*, silver vials for the sacred oil, goblets and censers for the churches to be established in New
California. The trip to collect these furnishings aggravated
his ulcerated ankle. When he set out for Velicatá to join the
expedition, he had to be lifted bodily onto his mule.

Gaspar de Portolá, the commander of troops under whom
he was scheduled to march, found him stretched out in bed.
He shook his head dubiously.

"Father, I cannot take along an invalid. You will only
hamper us on the trip."

But Father Junípero insisted on his right to come. He had
already recruited a party of Franciscan friars to work under
him in New California; in fact, they had already proceeded
to San Diego with the sea units of the expedition, and he was
determined to join them at any cost.

Portolá finally yielded. "I'll have a stretcher built, and
you'll be carried by the Indian converts accompanying us."

The friar protested vigorously. "That is no solution. I cannot permit the Indians to carry me over the mountain trails. They will be tired enough."

"How will you come then, Father!" exclaimed Don Gaspar sharply.

The friar considered the matter from every angle. Then he summoned Jean Antonio Coronel, the veterinarian.

"Son, can you cure my leg?"

"Reverend Father, I can only heal the sores of beasts."

"Then let us suppose, in this emergency, that I am one of your charges. Give me the medicine you would use for a mule!"

Jean Antonio laughed. *"Nombre de Dios!* If it will give you pleasure, I'll do it."

He prepared an ointment of tallow and herbs and applied it to the padre's leg. Perhaps the cure was psychological—at any rate, the pain lessened considerably. Fray Junípero rested quietly that night, and the following morning he was able to ride his mule although the wound remained open.

On the 16th of May, 1769, the column under Portolá, the fourth and last to depart, set out for San Diego, five hundred miles to the north. Under a brilliant morning sky, a picked squad of *Soldatos de Cuero* led the march, carrying axes to hack a passage through the underbrush. Behind them rode the military escort in sleeveless jackets fashioned from several layers of deerskin as protection against Indian arrows. Mounted on Castilian horses, the riders wore leather aprons fastened to their saddles, unfolding to the ground to protect the thighs against the semitropical underbrush. Each soldier carried a flintlock carbine cased in leather, a sabre, and a lance. The pack trains followed, together with the muleteers, Fray Junípero, and the Indian converts.

Following carefully prepared maps, the column traveled over parched ravines in the direction of the Contra Costa, climbing rough mountain trails and making difficult descents. No sooner did the weary travelers gain one difficult summit, nourished by the hope they would see level plain ahead, than they were disheartened by the view of a chain of mountains just beyond. All day the sun beat down unmercifully. Camp was pitched for the night where it seemed likely that holes could be dug for water. But often the shovels merely turned up mud. Then there was only what little water remained from that carried in skin bags from the previous camp.

The extreme dryness and transparency of the air threw the landscape out of perspective and deceived the eye as to distances. On occasion they saw sheet lightning rise from the blistering ground into the sky, and a huge cactus or a *garambullo* standing monster-like against foreshortened stretches of plain. They passed through dense cottonwood, over slippery *brancas* whose banks abounded with prickly pear six feet high, and through marshland choked with tule, encountering in clearings Indian *rancherias* that had apparently been hastily abandoned at their coming. Once they came upon an Indian cemetery where the grave of the local chief was marked by a grass cape unfurled from a pole.

Portolá enforced strict discipline among the troops. When the Genoese cook, a man with a choleric temper, ran his knife through a she-ass who had blocked his path, he was sentenced to pay four times the value of the beast out of his salary, and to walk the rest of the way on foot.

"*Madrecita*," swore one of the soldiers at the campfire that night. "A mule is a treasure not easily spared on a journey like this! The cook's throat should have been slit from ear to ear."

"Yes, Don Pedro," retorted a companion. "And who would do your cooking for you in this accursed wilderness—St. Joseph?"

Around a score of campfires they sat in groups, polishing their broad swords and carbines, sipping chocolate, each with thoughts of the gold he would find at San Diego—riches enough to send him home a gentleman. Each was obsessed with the fabulous success story of Cortez and Pizarro, and each conveniently ignored the tragedy that had attended so many other quests for gold.

They continued on their way, passing into country that grew progressively greener, through valleys of juniper trees and *madroñes* that bore yellow berries the size of a large chickpea, over hills studded with redwoods and mountains of pure, moist earth without a patch of stone. They descended into canyons whose sides abounded with poppies and where wild grapes clustered on the vine.

Bueno! This was God's country. One morning the "leather jackets" held between their fingers the queen of all flowers, known to them as the Rose of Castile.

Indian scouts alerted their tribes to the arrival of the Spaniards. The natives swarmed in numbers around the encampment, friendly and with childlike curiosity. They wore their hair in perukes plastered with white clay. Fray Junípero welcomed them on behalf of the travelers, although, for some time now, he had been in severe pain. The long miles on muleback had exhausted him, and his ankle was once again an angry ulcer. But he superintended the feeding of the visitors, introducing them to Castilian delicacies, and in return he accepted their baskets of atole and pinale, and bags made from wildcat skins. They plagued the father with their demands. They begged him for his robe, sandals, rosary. Once they made off with his spectacles. "The Lord knows I had some time getting them back," he wrote in his journal.

On traveled the column during hot, rainless days, wending its way through pastures of wild oats and patches of sycamore, over earth so finely powdered that the mules and horses skidded as if caught in a landslide.

Finally, on the morning of July first, forty-six days out of Velicatá, the salt of the sea was in every man's nostrils. The last hill was gained, and below—beyond shining sand dunes and the kelp of San Diego Bay—rode ships flying the Spanish flag.

But when the troops reached the encampment, they sensed that something was wrong. The commandante, Captain Rivera y Moncada, welcomed Portolá with a mournful face. "*Amigo mio*, I have terrible news!"

The water supply on the *San Carlos*, one of the two ships that left Velicatá for San Diego, had become contaminated. This, combined with a shortage of fresh provisions, led to an outbreak of disease. By the time the *San Carlos* reached port, every man aboard, including the captain and the ship's physician, was down with scurvy or dysentery. Tents were hastily erected by the crew of the sister ship which had arrived at San Diego earlier, and the sick were carried to them.

The dysentery spread rapidly in the encampment. For

fourteen terrible days those who were still able to get about dug graves. The night was filled with prayers for the dying.

The epidemic was finally checked only after the arrival overland of Captain Rivera with the first column of foot troops. Rivera vigorously took charge, removed the ailing far from the area of pestilence into clean, fresh huts, instituted rigorous methods of sanitation, and nursed many of the survivors back to health. But the losses were appalling. Almost half of the entire expedition's strength of 219 men was wiped out.

It was with particular sadness that Father Junípero celebrated Requiem Mass for the dead. The soldiers discharged their carbines into the air, substituting the smell of gunpowder for incense and the sound of musketry for an organ. On this location, Fray Junípero made plans for building his first mission in New California, dedicated to a medieval Spanish saint—San Diego Alcalá.

The officers now met to discuss the carrying out of José de Gálvez' second directive—the garrisoning of Monte Rey. Since the number of healthy sailors was inadequate to man both ships, it was decided to proceed overland with foot troops. The *San Antonio* was sent back to San Blas with a skeleton crew for fresh provisions and reinforcements. Father Junípero was left at San Diego to supervise the nursing of the convalescents. Portolá set out to find the bay of Monte Rey, aided by Vizcaíno's map and an account of the voyage of 1602.

But a frustrating thing happened. Although Portolá came practically to the edge of the body of water he was seeking, he failed to sight it. For several weeks he crossed and recrossed his tracks in the vain search, on occasions camping only a few miles from Monte Rey. Meanwhile, his troops suffered severe hardships. Sixteen soldiers succumbed to scurvy and had to be strapped to the backs of mules. Provisions were low, and the men were reduced to eating wild berries. Finally, Portolá gave orders to turn back to San Diego. When he arrived, he heard alarming news. The *San Antonio* had not yet returned with provisions from San Blas, and the supplies on hand were dangerously low.

He called a conference of officers and stated the facts bluntly. *"Nombre de Dios!* There are times when the wise soldier concedes defeat. Monte Rey has not been found. I am convinced that this port has been silted up by the shifting sands in the hundred and sixty-seven years since Vizcaíno sighted it. The *San Antonio* has not arrived and who knows if it will? Perhaps they have already forgotten us in San Blas. With our supplies running out, there is but one thing to do to protect the lives of the men."

He regarded the assembled officers grimly. "We must quit New California!"

Don Fernando Rivera y Moncada nodded his head in agreement. "We cannot struggle indefinitely with evil luck," he said. "This expedition has lived under a blight from the outset. Let us start back for Velicatá now, while we still have enough food for our bellies."

Portolá turned to Lieutenant Don Pedro Fages, a shy, lean man with burning black eyes. "And you, Lieutenant. How do you feel?"

"I agree. The morale of my troops will soar when they hear of this decision."

Not a dissenting voice was heard.

As Don Pedro had prophesied, the news was greeted by

the troops with wild approval. Men wept and hugged one another for joy. They had found no precious metal, only death, on this terrible adventure. *Gracias a Dios!* Back to Velicatá—to a life of certainties!

And then, as Don Gaspar de Portolá turned to the job of preparing for the homeward trip, an elderly man limped into his headquarters.

"Señor Commandante, we must not abandon California."

"Fray Junípero," responded Portolá with the patience of a father dealing with a child, "if we remain much longer, we'll be eating wild herbs from the fields."

"The *San Antonio* will arrive with supplies. I am sure of it!" replied the padre. He reminded Portolá that it was a hundred and sixty-seven years since Vizcaíno had first sailed up the coast of California, and that if the present expedition withdrew, conceding defeat, it was likely to be years or even generations—given the dilatory attitude of officials in Madrid—before a Spaniard would be sent to New California again.

"That can mean only one thing—by default it will go to the Muscovites. The Empress Catherine will pounce on San Diego!"

Fray Junípero's voice trembled. His features grew intense. "In any event, even if you leave California, Señor Commandante, I will remain!"

Don Gaspar laughed. "Indeed, do you propose to live all by yourself in the wilderness?"

The padre was serious. "I will stay with the Indians if they are willing. And, if they choose to do away with me—*dum spiro, spero.* I came to establish missions. I shall not go back."

He continued to drive home his points. "In laying plans for the missions, I studied the maps with Señor Gálvez. I am convinced that Monte Rey exists at the site designated by Vizcaíno. Señor Commandante, remain here at least nine more days. I grant that the entire venture depends on the arrival of supplies. If the *San Antonio* doesn't arrive within this period, you will at least depart with a clearer conscience."

He added shrewdly: "Suppose it should be discovered after all that Monte Rey exists exactly where Vizcaino placed it. Will His Majesty in Madrid be quick to forget— or forgive—the error?"

Portolá bit his lip in vexation. The thrust had gone home. "Very well, Father. You may have your nine days. We will remain for you to say a novena. In the meantime, I'll send Rivera with an advance column to Velicatá and continue my packing."

Father Junípero walked among the troops, speaking with men of every rank, inspiring them with the flame of his own zeal. And he formulated plans of his own in case the worst happened. He paid a visit to Captain Gila of the *San Carlos* and persuaded him to remain, if necessary, after Portolá departed with his troops.

"I know the supplies will come. We can go ourselves by sea and search for Monte Rey."

Each morning he walked to the headland and looked out over the water for the *San Antonio*. As the final day of Portolá's stay in California approached without any sign of the ship, the priest prayed with utmost fervency. The will power that had turned this least physically qualified of missionaries into the controlling force of the crusade in New Spain was

now being put to a severe test. On his knees, he recalled how
he had given up his professorship in Majorca and what it
had cost him to make this decision. And he remembered,
too, the time he had held a burning taper to his flesh until
the smell horrified his congregation in order to demonstrate
how a man, if called upon, could endure pain. His was an
uncompromising spirit.

On the ninth morning, he went down to the headland as
usual and remained all day, watching the horizon. And then,
just before twilight, he saw the faint outlines of a ship. But
the vessel continued to move northward, oblivious to the
men who had rushed in large numbers down to the water's
edge. With the coming of evening it was lost to sight
altogether.

During the night the encampment at San Diego was torn
with discussion. Had the captain blundered past the port?
Would he discover his mistake and return? Instead, of the
San Antonio might it have been a ship of another nation?

When the sun rose again, there was no sign of the vessel,
and all that anxiously spent day the horizon was empty.
Father Junípero alone remained confident. He pleaded with
Portolá to postpone his departure for a few days. The dis-
traught commandante had no longer the will to resist. His
very career now depended on his avoiding an historic error.

He shrugged his shoulders. "Four, five more days, then."

And then, on November 24th—the fifth day after the sight-
ing of the ship—a cry from watchers thrilled the encampment. "*Jesus Maria!* She is returning!"

Under a brilliant noon sky the *San Antonio* rode into port
and fired a salute. Her hold was loaded with provisions. On
deck was a full complement of soldiers, sailors, artisans. Her

mail pouches carried letters from José de Gálvez and the Viceroy himself. Juan Perez, the skipper, explained to Portolá why he had at first bypassed San Diego. Gálvez, confident that the expedition had reached Monte Rey, had ordered him to sail there directly. But when he was two hundred and fifty miles from port, his water supply ran short, and he landed at Point Conception to refill his casks. Here, Indians informed him that there were no white men north of this area. Accordingly, Perez turned and made sail for San Diego.

"It would have been serious indeed," he declared to Portolá, "if you had quit California. You would have had some explaining to do to His Excellency!"

It took no further urging now for the commandante to set out for Monte Rey. On his previous trip he had erected three crosses on the headlands to direct future explorers. His second cross had been planted on the heights of the very bay he had been seeking. This time he arrived at the water's edge. Eight days later, Fray Junípero, together with artisans and sailors, debarked from the *San Antonio* which had been guided into the harbor at Monte Rey by a bonfire. The padre fell on his knees and chanted the *Veni, Creator Spiritus*.

Determining to make Monte Rey the headquarters for his missionary activities, Fray Junípero hung a silver-throated bell on a stout branch of a tree, the first step in the establishment of a mission.

"Why do you do this?" asked a soldier. "There is no church as yet, and we have seen no Indians here."

"I hear them coming," answered the father optimistically.

As an essential in dealing with the Indians, he insisted that the mission be independent of military control. Five miles from the garrison and the sea, he chose his site along the bank of the Carmel River—"Carmel" was the Hebrew word for garden. For miles around, rosemary and scented lavender mingled fragrantly with the salt of the sea. Cypresses two hundred feet tall and over six feet in circumference unfolded gray moss from their sturdy branches. In the distance stood the scalloped outlines of the Santa Lucia Mountains, olive green in the mist that came in from the bay. And here it was that the Mission of San Carlos Barromeo was built.

It consisted of a main adobe building with a roof of dried mud on horizontal timbers, a chapel whose walls were whitewashed with lime, a storage room for agricultural implements, flour, maize. There was a barracks for the several soldiers assigned in case of an Indian attack, a corral for the livestock. The entire enclosure was surrounded by a palisade whose gates were locked at night—a meaningless precaution since, owing to a shortage of nails, the timbers of the stockade were not fastened in many places and could be forced without much effort.

Father Junípero slept on bare boards in a corner of the chapel, his only blanket the hide of an ox.

At Monte Rey itself, a garrison of fifty soldiers was left behind under the command of Lieutenant Don Pedro Fages. They built a *presidio* comprising the commandante's quarters, a barracks, a storehouse, a jail, and a corral for the horses and mules. The settlement was enclosed in a palisade on which four bronze cannons were mounted.

When the soldiers finished building the presidio and the mission, time hung heavily on their hands. There was very little to occupy them, only the regular turn at guard, the burnishing of their weapons, the grooming of the horses which they kept in twenty-four-hour readiness for mounting if the alarm were sounded.

"*Nombre de Dios!*" exclaimed a little Basque with fierce eyes. "I enrolled in this army to make my career. After seven years I find myself still a private, just a grade above a muleteer—and lost in this damned California where the berries are abundant but white women do not exist. How long shall we be stuck here?"

"Easy, easy, Carlos," replied another. "All is not hopeless. No doubt, in time, the commandante will receive enlightenment from God and order a shipload of decent, warm-blooded señoritas to populate this New California. How can you build a new world without my little dancer from Barcelona?"

The Indians who gathered in curiosity around the mission and the *presidio* were notorious thieves. Back in San Diego they had snatched everything they could get their hands on when the Spaniards' backs were turned—even the blankets from the sick in the hospital and the sails and rigging of the *San Carlos.* They worshipped a coyote as the god, Chinigchninich, who came down periodically from his lair in heaven to teach them many things, particularly how to dance. Their young men did not become warriors until they were whipped into unconsciousness and then placed on a nest of ants. Stirred up to virulence by the beating of sticks, the ants swarmed over their victim and into his eyes, ears, nose, and mouth. If the ordeal was borne without a murmur, the young man was admitted to the ranks of fighting men. In combat, they cut off the hands, feet, and head of a captured enemy.

For the most part, these Indians (there were four principal tribes in Monte Rey—the Mutsunes, Escalens, Runsilens,
and Achastlens) were lazy and unambitious in contrast to
the Indians on the Atlantic Coast. Most of the time, they
preferred to dress themselves in thick mud rather than exert
themselves hunting for skins. These were the savage children whom Father Junípero hoped to turn into useful part-
ners in the task of converting California from a wilderness
into a civilized community.

To lure the Indians into the mission he had one powerful
argument—food. It was much more pleasant for an Indian to
fill his belly with the Spaniards' food than to hunt through
the forests for game. Significantly enough, the Indian women
were the first to enter the mission in numbers. Victims of
tribal polygamy and the brutality of the males, they were
introduced to a life that afforded them protection and a
status of dignity. Serra exercised great influence over them
and, through them, over their children, many of whom,
born and raised in the mission and knowing no other existence, became devoted followers of Christianity. The Indians
were attracted to the story of Jesus chiefly through the picturesque paintings that hung in the mission.

Once, when an Indian squaw was shown a painting of the
Mother and Child, the simple-hearted woman bared her
breasts: "Please, Father, I would like to nurse the baby," she
said.

Fray Junípero began by teaching the Indians to say one
simple phrase, *"Amar a Dios*—Love God." And this became
a universal greeting among converts. He followed this by
teaching the Lord's Prayer and other basic prayers. The Indians spoke a language that contained the sounds of the

Latin alphabet, and it was relatively easy for them to learn simple Spanish. However, neither Father Junípero nor his assisting friars were blessed with the gift of tongues. Moreover, each of the neighboring tribes spoke a language that differed just enough from the others to make the task of learning it even more trying. But the padres eventually mastered the tongues with the persistency they showed in everything.

Father Junípero's ambitions for New California were practically limitless. Having established missions at San Diego and Monte Rey, he now proceeded to develop a cordon of settlements along the perimeter of the Spanish occupation. Each site was located about a day's journey from another. "I'd like a traveler to be assured of a nightly lodging, a good hot meal, and a fresh horse," he told his friars. "I want nothing less than to civilize the entire coast."

He recruited from the Franciscan Order two padres for each mission he founded. These fathers had a prodigious assignment. They preached, baptized, married, buried, and attended the sick and dying at any hour of the day or night. In addition, they supervised all agricultural activities, tucking up their frocks and personally setting an example of energetic labor.

Under the guidance of the missions the more intelligent Indians learned to become blacksmiths, carpenters, and tanners. And they developed great mechanical skill. The children were a particular concern of the padres. Each mission had a schoolroom, and in the early morning and late afternoon when the older folk were at work, children five years and older were assembled for instruction.

With all its shortcomings, the California mission was an

extraordinary experiment in peaceful, socially constructive conquest. It is a supreme example on the American continent of the white man's willingness to deal with the Indians in a Christian manner, and it was due largely to the shrewd humanity of Father Junípero.

A life spent in a mission outpost was a very lonely one. The padres were all above average in learning and many were highly cultured men. Some had been professors of philosophy and masters of art in Spain. Father Junípero arranged to have two padres assigned to each post so that one civilized mind, weary of continual contacts with the Indians, might be refreshed with the companionship of another akin to it. The padres had no knowledge of the great events of history taking place in the outside world; their only contact with Spain was through the ship that arrived yearly at Monte Rey and the visits of Father Junípero, when he related the news and gossip he had received by mail.

The *presidente* of California missions thoroughly enjoyed the visits he paid regularly to his assistant padres. He dined with the fathers overlooking the terraces they had cultivated, and talked of the sparkling gardens back home in Majorca; or he ran his fingers over a volume from the bookshelf and recalled the well-stocked library of the Lullian College where he had taught philosophy.

"How many of our order have suffered for God in New Spain!" remarked Fray Luis Jayme, a fellow Majorcan, during one of Junípero's visits to San Diego. He was thinking particularly of the large number of padres who had been murdered by the Mexican Indians since the coming of Cortez.

"It is not easy to die in a land thousands of miles from

one's birth. But the Lord has called us. The thornier the road, the more worthy a steppingstone into eternity."

Fray Jayme, in these remarks, was expressing the tension that existed at his mission of San Diego. Of all the unconverted Indians, the savages in the neighborhood of San Diego had proved the most intractable. When Fray Junípero had first arrived here in 1769, his company had been attacked by a column of Diegunos attempting to rob it of supplies. Father Junípero had won them over temporarily by forgiving them and restraining the soldiers who were bent on punishing them.

And now, on the evening of November 4, 1775, as Fray Luis Jayme prayed to the Holy Virgin, he had a premonition of trouble, as if this prayer were to be his last on earth. It was some time before peace settled into his heart.

Fray Junípero, as we have seen, before moving on to Monte Rey, had dedicated the site for San Diego in 1769 and had assigned Fray Jayme and his companion, Fray Vincente Fuster, to be its permanent directors. The mission was situated four miles from the garrison. So intently had the padres desired to impress the Indians with their peaceful nature that they requested the military authorities not to build a palisade around the settlement. The military, harassed by shortages in materials and only too glad to cut expenses, yielded to the friars' wishes and the mission was left unfortified.

There were nine white men in the mission in addition to the friars—three soldiers and a corporal on detached duty, two blacksmiths and a carpenter, and two young boys, the son and nephew of the commandante. Several hundred Indian converts lived in an enclosure a few hundred yards away. During the summer two neophytes disappeared from the mission, and rumors reached the Spaniards that they were calling on *rancherias* for miles around, repeating a lie calculated to rouse the tribes to fury. They claimed that the Spaniards were kidnaping Indians and using force to convert them. However, the military, discounting the reports, did nothing.

Shortly after night rolled in over the dunes—on November 4th—several hundred Indians assembled from the various *rancherias*—for an assault on the mission. They moved silently forward in two columns just before midnight, rushed the church and chapel, and ransacked the priestly robes, ornaments, and vessels. Within seconds they set aflame practically every building in the mission.

Fray Luis Jayme was among the first of the residents to awaken. Calmly he advanced toward the howling, shrieking savages, greeting them with *"Amar a Dios, hijos!"*—Love God, my children!" He was immediately pounced on, stripped naked, and dragged away. His head was crushed with clubs, his body pierced by a dozen arrows. Even after he was dead the Indians continued to outrage the corpse, disfiguring it completely before flinging it into a ravine.

Fray Vincente Fuster took the two young boys entrusted to him and ran with them across the courtyard to the barracks where the soldiers had set up a defense. The carpenter Jose Urselino, who had been asleep in the barracks, gave spirited assistance. An arrow struck him. Crying out to the attackers, "May God forgive you!" he fell wounded.

In another part of the mission one of the blacksmiths was killed while reaching for his sword. His fellow smithy leaped behind the bellows, took aim with his musket, and fired at the Indians, killing one of them. Then he retreated to the barracks, where he joined Fray Fuster and the soldiers.

The entire company of survivors were now together. But the flames forced them to seek cover elsewhere. Carrying the wounded carpenter with them, they ran to an unfinished adobe hut which had been used as a kitchen and had so far escaped the general conflagration. There was no roof to the building except for branches placed overhead by the cook to keep the sun from beating down on him. The Indians shot their flaming arrows through cracks in the walls. The survivors finally succeeded in plugging up the openings with barrels, boxes, and bundles, but not before every man was wounded. Only one man, the corporal of the guard, was able to continue firing. The blacksmith and one of the soldiers—wounded though they were—loaded and reloaded muskets and passed them to him in a steady relay, while the corporal barked orders to trick the savages into believing he had a considerable force of men behind him. The others smothered the fires touched off by the flame-tipped arrows.

Fray Fuster suddenly noticed in a corner a bag containing fifty pounds of gunpowder, only yards from the falling brands. *"Nombre de Dios!"* cried one soldier who saw the sack at the same moment. The father threw himself on the bag, draping his robe around it. In his excitement he was temporarily unaware of the agonizing pain in his shoulder where a piece of adobe hurled by an Indian had ripped open the flesh. All around him the arrows continued to drop. The fringes of his robe were scorched by the heat, but he prevented the powder from exploding.

For hours the assault continued. But the defenders put out the flames wherever they arose and held their ground.

And then, just before dawn, there was a sudden quiet. The attack ceased. Dismayed by the stubborn resistance in the hut and fearing that the white men would receive reinforcements from the *presidio* when the sun rose, the Indians withdrew and scattered into the hills.

As the morning lit up the ruins and the bodies of the dead, several of the Indian converts who, with the rest of their group, had huddled terror-stricken in their quarters during the attack, approached the hut and called to Fray Fuster.

"Father, we have searched the arroyo. We have found our friend."

Fray Fuster rose and accompanied them outside. He looked down on Fray Luis Jayme. The features were beyond identification. Only a few scattered places where the skin was not torn or encrusted with blood, and the hands, which strangely enough remained whole, indicated that he was a white man. Fray Fuster directed the converts to build stretchers for the friar and the murdered blacksmith, and the living walked with the dead four miles to the *presidio* whose occupants had passed the night unaware of the attack.

Couriers were sent to headquarters at Monte Rey with news of the catastrophe.

Captain Rivera, the commandante, assembled a company of soldiers and arrived at San Diego to track down the instigators of the attack and mete out a punishment that would serve as an example.

Early one morning shortly after Rivera's arrival, Fray Fuster opened his eyes and was aware of someone kneeling by his bed. He looked into the face of an Indian. There was something familiar about it, and this recognition disturbed the padre, for it did not belong to any of his converts.

Fray Fuster rose to his feet. Suddenly he knew. The Indian was one of the two neophytes who had fled the mission during the summer and had stirred up the *rancherias*. He stared at the renegade.

"You—you dare to return!"

"Father," said the Indian in fluent Spanish, "I stole in during the night and waited for you to awaken. You are the only one I have courage to come to."

The padre drew back. "You spread terrible lies! You caused the murder of innocent men!"

"Father, I will confess to you exactly as you have taught me to. I was, in fact, one of the leaders of the attack."

The muscles of Fray Fuster's throat tightened. "I see. And now that the soldiers have arrived with their muskets to punish the wrongdoers, you tremble. Very shrewdly you sneak back into the mission and throw yourself on my mercy, believing that I, of all people, will protect you because I have taught forgiveness!"

He motioned for the Indian to rise, and looked into his face. "You are right. I *will* protect you from the white man's bullets. We cannot wipe out the horror of your crime by employing violence on our own part. There are other ways you will be punished for your sin. Come."

He put his hand on the Indian's shoulder and led him to one of the few buildings that had escaped destruction. "Here is our church, my son. For centuries men have sought sanctuary at the foot of the altar. As long as you remain here no soldier will seize you. I will send you food."

He walked toward the kitchen, his face betraying no hint of what had occurred.

Yet the secret was soon out. Several neophytes who had caught a glimpse of the refugee at the altar spread the word, and before long the entire settlement had learned of his return.

Captain Rivera marched up to the building with a detachment of soldiers. He was about to enter when Father Fuster spoke out. "Señor Commandante, the Indian is under the protection of the Church!"

Captain Rivera turned impatiently. "Are you insane, Father? Why do you want to protect this red devil?"

"You will teach him nothing by killing him!"

The commandante shook his head. "*Hombre!* Do you think I do not know the rights of sanctuary? This building is not a church. It was erected as a warehouse."

"It was formerly used as a warehouse, Señor Commandante. But we have placed our altar and sacred vessels in it. Now it is our church."

Father Fuster put his hand on Don Rivera's arm. "Your punitive expedition will prove useless. We are dealing with children. Here is a God-given opportunity to teach them charity."

The commandante answered sarcastically, "This charity is fine for you and Jayme. But what of us ordinary men? What about the relatives of the blacksmith who died in the massacre? Would they propose to let the Indians go unpunished?"

Fray Fuster was silent for a moment. "There is no distinction between padres and ordinary men. Since you have brought up the subject, I'll tell you something. José Urselino, the carpenter, was in the thick of the fighting. He died five days later from his wounds. Now, he was an ordinary man. He had managed to save a little money. But he was all alone in the world. To whom should he give this money? As he lay tossing in bed the night before his death, he called for me and made out a will. He named as his heirs the Indians who had taken his life!"

When Fray Junípero received the news of the massacre at San Diego, he supported Fray Fuster's policy toward the Indians. Despite the continued protests of the military, he wrote a strong letter to the Viceroy in Mexico City, urging that the punitive expeditions be stopped. "For centuries these savages have lived by the code of violence. Can we expect them to change overnight? Let us teach them the lesson of forgiveness for which Father Jayme gave his life. Let us demand atonement and leave the final verdict to God."

His plea was successful. Captain Rivera, who had spread his net over the countryside for the malefactors, and had dragged in Indians for confinement and floggings, was ordered by the Viceroy to release his prisoners. The mission at San Diego was rebuilt under the personal supervision of Father Junípero.

The padres exhibited such an enlightened policy in their social dealings that it is not surprising the missions grew steadily in prestige and influence, playing a decisive historic role. In the early years, however, they were vulnerable in one respect, to the point where their very existence was threatened: Their supply lines were undependable. Before they became self-sufficient they depended on Mexico to replenish their supplies. Whenever these supplies were slow in coming through, the missions were left destitute.

Early one spring, Father Junípero summoned the friars to council. It was obvious that he had serious news. In his hands he held the latest mail from Mexico City.

"I have just received word of a change in Viceroys. His Excellency, Antonio Maria Bucareli, has succeeded Signor de Croix. And he has ordered that the naval base at San Blas be closed."

The friars were stunned. It was from San Blas that the supply ships sailed for the New California missions. To shut down the port was tantamount to shutting down the missions.

"His Excellency Bucareli, in going over the budget," explained Fray Junípero, "has been disturbed by the high cost of maintenance of the shipyard and the expenses of building vessels there. He recommends that hereafter we be supplied entirely by mule trains traveling overland from Guayamas."

He looked at each of his brethren. Here were men who had toiled and suffered for years with him—among them old Fray Juan Crespi, called by his associates *"El Beato*—The Blessed."

"The mule trains are slow," continued the *presidente*. "The number of men required to escort them through unfriendly country will make the cost to the treasury much more burdensome than the upkeep of San Blas. I predict that if San Blas is shut down, the closing of our missions will soon follow. Without a proper supply of food, we cannot win converts."

He put aside the letter and paced up and down the chamber, speaking quietly as if thrashing the matter out with himself. "But it's more than a matter of winning converts. It is a question of building a new civilization on the shores of the Pacific. When will the officials in New Mexico and Madrid realize that the only price to consider is the price of losing this!"

Fray Crespi spoke up. "Father Junípero, you must see His Excellency personally. You alone can persuade him not to commit this folly."

"It is a long trip to Mexico City for a man of my age. Suppose I do not live to get there?" He smiled resignedly. "But, of course I will go," he said.

He sailed for San Blas, taking along with him for companionship a young Indian convert. The overland trip from San Blas to Mexico City—a distance of five hundred miles— had to be made by mule. He carried a breviary and a few provisions. At night he slept in the windowless palm-leaf huts of Mexican peasants; he took his breakfast cross-legged on the floor beneath the images of saints.

Passing from the heat of the valleys into the chill of the mountains, the father and his companion both fell ill. They were forced to halt at Guadalajara, a hundred and sixty miles along the way. Both were so near death that the Last Sacrament was administered. But they rallied and gained strength.

The father patted the hand of the Indian beside him who had accepted this suffering with stoicism. "Be assured, son. It is not much further to Mexico City. Had you died because of my insistence that you accompany me, I could never have forgiven myself."

The Indian turned his face toward the priest and said simply. "And, Father, suppose *you* had died? . . ."

As soon as they were physically able, they continued on their way. But at Queretaro, eighty miles further east, Father Junípero's strength again failed, and he was carried into a Franciscan monastery. Here he lay prostrate for weeks. Finally, however, he recovered sufficiently to pass from the pine-girdled slopes of the *cordillera* into Mexico City.

Don Antonio Maria Bucareli, the new Viceroy, had the cynical eyes of Cyrano de Bergerac and the long tapering fingers of an El Greco *caballero*. The blood of French and Italian nobility was in his veins. He greeted the old friar with a quizzical look that changed to one of tolerant interest and finally grudging respect as the father proceeded to argue his case.

Fray Junípero convinced him that San Blas should be kept open, and he expanded on his theme. "Your Excellency, too long have our settlements been looked upon merely as military outposts. I tell you they must be regarded as the seeds of new colonies. Send us wives for our soldiers. They have been too long without them. Even the Indians are amazed at the absence of white women and are asking if marriage is a custom among Christians! Send us married farmers, mechanics, workmen. When we have babies born on this new American soil, then it will really be ours!

"Another matter—the military insists on extending their control over the mission Indians. But I maintain that we padres, who taught the Indians to love God, must continue our fatherly management of them. The development of California must be a civilian, not a military undertaking."

Bucareli agreed with the recommendations. He advised that the father draw them up in writing to be laid before the Board of War and Finance in Madrid for a final decision. Then, for the sake of his own peace of mind—there was no telling what the persistent old fellow would ask for next— Bucareli politely, but firmly, hinted to the padre that he was doubtless needed at Monte Rey and should plan to return at the earliest opportunity. "Father Junípero may be a saint," he muttered to friends, "but he certainly is a troublesome one!"

Junípero's recommendations were accepted by the Spanish government. At his suggestion, a call went out for families to colonize New California. They were offered land, livestock, and agricultural implements; in addition, each man was given four yards of ribbon for a homemade hat "as grand as any worn in Spain." The ladies were supplied with six yards for their hats.

Fourteen years before, when the naming of the first missions had been discussed, Junípero had remarked to Gálvez, "What about our father, St. Francis? Is he to have no mission?"

And Gálvez had replied, "If he wants a mission, let him show us his harbor."

Shortly thereafter, Portola, on his futile search for Monte Rey, had reached the shores of an impressive body of water further north and had dutifully named it "The Bay of St. Francis—San Francisco."

It was to this *Estero de San Francisco* that one hundred and thirty-six colonists now set out overland under the leadership of Don Juan Bautista de Anza, a *hidalgo* in the tradition of Cortez. There were twenty-nine women in the group. As the travelers stopped at various *presidios* on the way, soldiers tumbled out of barracks to stare at the *señoras*. Many of them hadn't seen a Spanish woman in seven years or more. Even the sentinels, as they paced back and forth, turned their necks and strained their ears to catch the delicious sound of female chatter. *Nombre de Dios!*

The journey was an ordeal for these pioneer women. Frequently they had to dismount from the mules and press through the underbrush on foot. Their arms and legs bled from the thick-knotted chaparral. Sometimes it required two and three of them working furiously by turns to milk a cow, for the breed that was being transported to California was a particularly stubborn one.

Three babies were born on the trip. The colonists traveled for months through sage and forests of redwood, through fields of scented *yerba buena* and red-berried cascara; and, finally, after a period of rest in Monte Rey, they arrived at the dunes of San Francisco.

The sight of the waters thrilled them as it has thrilled travelers ever since. "This is the harbor of harbors; nature's masterpiece," Anza wrote. And one of his lieutenants, Font, added, "I have seen . . . many noble anchorages; but nothing to surpass these safe and spacious waters with their commanding heights. A city built here might rival any seaport in Europe."

Continuing to act on Fray Junípero's recommendations, the Spanish authorities organized other projects of colonization. About a hundred and twenty miles north of San Diego, land was cleared and families were offered a monthly cash allowance, an advance of livestock, seed, and clothing to settle the *pueblo de la Reina de los Angeles*.

In 1781, forty-two soldiers with their wives and a sprinkling of artisans and mechanics became the pioneer colonists. That same year Los Angeles was founded, thirteen colonies, four thousand miles to the east, were engaged in critical battles of their War for Independence, and a new nation was in the process of being born. Within eighty years —or the span of a lifetime—Los Angeles and Boston would be joined under a single government.

Father Junípero's missions entered a period of striking growth. Before his death there were nine of them, accommodating approximately four thousand neophytes. There was San Juan Capistrano with its groves of palms, oranges, and bright-berried pepper trees, its gracious stone corridors to which the roses clung; San Luis Obispo, with its orchards of olive trees, famed throughout the countryside, and vineyards from which the most delicious wine in New Spain was pressed. There was lovely San Gabriel—one of the richest of the missions—surrounded by Barbary figs and prickly pear that burst into purple fruit for the thirsty wayfarer; San Antonio de Padua, celebrated for its pine nuts; San Diego and San Buenaventura, with cool arcades fragrant with blossoming almond and peach trees; San Carlos, Santa Clara, and San Francisco, whose whitewashed adobe and richly colored tiles sparkled in the clean blue air.

Neither padre nor Indian had any rigid ideas of architecture, and together, with the instinct of inspired artists, they developed and expanded for their needs buildings so individual, yet so exquisitely in harmony with the California landscape, that they have been the delight of painters and tourists ever since.

One of the glories of the missions was their bells. And

Father Junípero knew the tone of each as intimately as a human voice dear to him. Indeed, if he happened to approach a mission just before the Angelus, he would dismount from his plodding mule and limp ahead on foot in his impatience to be with a favorite and hear the silvery tones again. Cast in the furnaces of Mexico or Peru, each was named for a saint. Sea captains vied with one another for the privilege of transporting these bells to New California, for they were believed to be certain protection against shipwreck. No ship that carried them was ever lost.

In his last years, Fray Junípero continued to make the Pacific coast hum with his activities. After a busy day out in the world, he would pass most of the night in prayer. The soldiers who lived near the chapel murmured, *"Por Dios! When does the father take thirty winks!"*

Toward the end he developed a chest ailment that caused him spasms of suffocation. But when surgeons wanted to cauterize his chest—the therapy prescribed in those times—the friar shied away at the prospect of being bedridden even for a day. Whenever the physicians called, he would suddenly recall that he had to baptize a new batch of converts, or dedicate a mission bell, or discuss a project of agriculture with his board of friars. The surgeons followed him up and down the coast. Each time he was cornered he raised his hands. "Let's not bother. It might make me worse!"

Imagine their anxiety, therefore, when one day, approaching him as usual, they were greeted without protest. The old friar had resigned himself to the cauterization. Here was clear evidence that he had given up on himself.

He was seventy-one now. His work was completed. Largely because of his efforts, California had not been abandoned by Spain. After his death, his successors, carrying out his policies, increased the number and influence of the missions. At their height, over forty thousand converts were productively employed in them.

Although Mexico in 1822 overthrew the rule of Spain and secularized the missions, the seeds of Christian civilization and economic security had been sowed to such an extent that when California was occupied by the Americans, they found a land of irrigated fields, cultivated vineyards, and settlements of peaceful Christian Indians who for generations had carried on seven-eighths of the Pacific Coast's industry and trade. In a direct sense Father Junípero founded, settled, and saved California for the United States.

He awaited the end calmly in the arms of his Indian convert who nursed him with touching devotion.

An unconverted Indian woman, eighty years old, visited the dying man to say goodbye. He remembered her well. Some years before, planning to develop a chicken farm, he had imported a brood of chickens, the first introduced into New California. But the Indian woman, together with her son, had plundered the coop one night. The woman was apprehended, but the friar forgave her. And now, on this final visit, Father Junípero went into his cell and came out with the only blanket he had.

"Take this as a remembrance of me," he said.

"No doubt you are paying her for the chickens!" remarked an assistant friar.

In August, 1784, the *presidente* was laid to rest in his friar's robe in the grounds of San Carlos Borromeo. A second robe he had kept in reserve with which to patch his "best" garment was distributed, piece by piece, to the soldiers of the *presidio* who preserved each shred as a saintly relic. A pair of his sandals was presented to the commandante, a handkerchief to the doctor who had attended him.

There is a legend that one night in the middle of the last century a band of Spanish sailors put into Monte Rey secretly, opened the grave, and carried Fray Junípero's bones to Spain for reburial. Like many legends, this one dies hard. The fact is that the Presidente of California Missions rests today in the American soil to which he had given so much of himself.

11

Martyr on the Oregon Trail

NARCISSA WHITMAN

IN THE spring of 1832, four "Flathead" Indians traveled a thousand miles over the Rocky Mountains and walked into Saint Louis. General Clark, the Superintendent of Indian Affairs, showed them the sights of the city and presented them with gifts. As they were about to leave for their home in Oregon, one of their number, Chief "No Horns on His Head," declared to the General in the idiom of his people:

"My brothers sent me to get the white man's Book of Heaven. You make my feet heavy with the burden of gifts ... but the book is not among them."

In 1807, the explorers Lewis and Clark had arrived in Oregon and told these Indians about the Bible. Since then, fur traders had come among them, promising that missionaries would be sent to teach them the white man's religion. For years the savages waited patiently, discussing the subject around their campfires. But no one came.

And now the visiting chief continued reproachfully, "When I tell my poor blind people ... in the big council that I did not bring the Book, no word will be spoken by our old men or by our young braves. One by one they will rise up and go out in silence. My people will die in darkness, and they will go on the long path to the other hunting grounds. No white man will go with them and no white man's Book will make the way plain. I have no more words. . . . How can I go back with both eyes closed? How can I go back blind to my blind people?"

This touching, childlike appeal of the "Flatheads" was reported in the press and circulated by letter. And over the next few years it stirred feelings in religious circles everywhere. It focused the attention of missionaries on the little-known land beyond the Rockies.

In Amity, a village in upper New York, a blonde, queenly young woman of twenty-seven who taught physics at Miss Willard's fashionable academy took out a sheet of pale green, sweetly scented stationery and wrote to officials of the Presbyterian Church of which she was a member, "I would like to offer my services as teacher to the Indians."

The authorities were shocked. For an unmarried female to ask to go out among the Indians was more revolutionary than if she had demanded the right to vote. Women just didn't make such requests in America in 1809. But then Narcissa Prentiss was not an ordinary woman. She was beautiful, blessed with the type of features that forty years later the painter Rossetti would immortalize, and had a glorious singing voice. She had been born to wear exquisite lace dresses, to add luster to the social salon. Yet from her earliest years she behaved with the intellectual freedom of a man. At Miss Willard's Academy she taught, of all things, science, at a time when women were supposed to be concerned only with poetry, sewing, and eligible suitors. She enjoyed the zest of conflict and communion with vigorous intellects.

The authorities of the American Board of Missions decided to investigate this Miss Prentiss from Amity who had asked to work with the Indians. They sent Dr. Marcus Whitman to meet her. This young physician whose brown hair was already streaked with gray, whose shoulders were pressed forward as if to thrust him perpetually into trouble, had practiced medicine for four years in Canada after graduating from the College of Physicians and Surgeons in western New York. He, too, had expressed a desire to go among the Indians beyond the Rockies. However, missionary work was a man's job. Perhaps he would be successful in talking Miss Prentiss out of her unwomanly desire.

The result of the meeting turned out to be quite different from what he had planned. The bachelor doctor failed to persuade the young school teacher to abandon her project. Instead, he talked her into marriage.

When Narcissa again presented the mission board with a request to go to Oregon, no longer as a single woman, but as a missionary wife, there were no objections.

Narcissa was married in a dress of black bazaine, in a little neighborhood church. "We had to make love somewhat abruptly," she declared. "And we must do our courtship now that we are married." She was twenty-seven. Marcus was twenty-nine. The wedding was a social event; the daughter of Judge Stephen Prentiss traced her ancestry back to seventeenth-century New England, and so did Dr. Whitman.

The bride and groom traveled by wagon to Fort Loup, Missouri, where they joined the American Fur Company caravan, having received permission to accompany it on its yearly expedition to the Rocky Mountains. They made the trip with another Presbyterian missionary couple, Henry and Eliza Spalding.

The American Fur Company was a hustling community of seventy men and four hundred horses and mules, keyed to a strenuous camp life. Whitman had misgivings about bringing his bride on the trip. Crossing the prairies was no easy feat for a woman—and Narcissa looked so delicate in her pleated dresses and neckerchiefs. But Narcissa felt safe in the company of this powerfully built young physician whose physical strength was such that he had once caught a three-year-old steer under the jaw and one horn, had lifted it into the air, and thrown it on its back, holding it down single-handedly while it was branded.

At daybreak on May 2, 1836, the mules stirred restlessly and cries of "Arise! On your feet!" broke into the sleep of the encampment. After breakfast, the company started out across the plains. Narcissa began the journey on horseback, riding side saddle, but from time to time she switched to their Conestoga wagon, resting on top of the luggage. At night she slept in a tent of bedticking on Mackinaw blankets. She had an India-rubber life preserver along for protection when fording rivers.

In the prairies, where timber was practically non-existent, they built their cooking fire with dried Buffalo dung. Narcissa wrote in her journal: "I suppose Harriet [her sister] will make a face at this, but if she were here, she would be glad to have her supper cooked in any manner in this . . . country."

While crossing the plains, they lived almost entirely on

buffalo meat, washing it down with broth thickened with flour. The cattle supplied milk, and sometimes Narcissa brewed tea or coffee.

The trip was not without its dangers. On one occasion, a herd of buffalo emerged without warning from the hills and stampeded toward the company. Although the men closed ranks immediately and poured out a deadly fusillade, the herd continued its headlong rush. The horses and mules stamped and snorted and strained to break harness and scatter. Only at the last instant did the buffalo veer from their path, plunging a few yards to right of the travelers.

The column entered the Rockies by the South Pass, and on the Fourth of July crossed the Continental Divide. They celebrated the occasion by kneeling in prayer. On July 6th, they reached the great trading rendezvous in the Rockies, in the vicinity of the Green River near what is today Daniel, Wyoming.

The rendezvous was a riot of color and business activity, much like a huge country fair. Here Indian trappers and representatives of the fur companies east and west of the Rockies gathered to barter in skins. Mountain men dressed in buckskin, their hair worn long in Indian fashion, a blanket thrown jauntily over their shoulders, carrying knives, pipes, and pouches, rode in with their Indian wives whose babies were lashed to the saddle. The mountaineers swapped stories with one another, describing their Indian fights, their ambuscades and marvelous escapes, the buffalo feasts they had attended since the last rendezvous. The average lifespan of a trapper in these mountains dominated by hostile Indians was not more than five years. He made the most of each moment of relaxation.

During the period of trading, a truce went into effect between the white men and the tribes of unfriendly savages. The trappers and traders, together with the Indians allied to them, formed three sides of a huge ring. The enemy tribes, in closed ranks under their own protective guard, formed the fourth. An old brave selected by each tribe met the agents of the fur companies in the center of the ring and bartered his people's beaver skins.

On the morning of departure, the huge encampment, stretching for ten miles along the Green River, was transformed into a hive of activity. Tents were struck, temporary log cabins disassembled, provisions packed. Thousands of mules and horses were whipped into marching columns. Goodbyes were said. The caravans of fur companies left for their home stations, the Canadians singing their boating song, the English, Mexican, and American Fur Companies following with their own native airs. And the Indians left for their villages beyond the mountain.

The mountaineers, many of whom had not seen a white woman for years, made a great deal of fuss over Narcissa and Eliza. They strenuously urged their husbands to turn home with them. The American Fur Company, under whose protection they had proceeded this far, was scheduled to return to Saint Louis. From here to the Pacific Coast, through mountain passes bristling with warlike Crow and Blackfeet Indians, the missionaries could rely only on the protection of scattered parties of trappers trekking seaward. "It will be murder to attempt the trip with a woman," warned the mountaineers. They even hinted that they would call on civil authorities to prevent the missionaries from proceeding. But Narcissa and Eliza insisted on continuing.

The experts also warned Whitman that he would be unable to continue further with his wagon. "No man has ever succeeded in taking a wagon west of the Rockies," they said. They urged him to sell it at Green River, and proceed over the mountain trails on horseback.

But the doctor was stubborn. "If there is any chance whatsoever that I can take the wagon through, I must do it. It will be a great talking point for families who would like to come out to Oregon, but who await proof that they can transport their household belongings over the Rockies."

And so the Whitmans set out with a party of traders, taking the southern route toward the coast six hundred miles away. The journey over the mountains was an arduous one, and Whitman was forced to compromise on his wagon. He turned it into a two-wheel cart, packing away the second pair of wheels and the axle. But he succeeded in bringing the wagon to Fort Boise, Idaho, the first time anything on wheels had penetrated that far west.

The party moved through great patches of sunbaked desert and sagebrush. The cattle almost went mad from the gnats and sand flies, and were induced to go forward only with the greatest difficulty. The books that Narcissa and her husband had taken along grew wet and lumpy from many river crossings. But the most difficult river to ford was the Snake River in Idaho, whose course was so winding that it had to be crossed twice. This river was a fishing post for Indians, and the travelers found a canoe made of willows and rushes moored to the bank. Narcissa and Eliza placed themselves in it with their saddles, and two Indian scouts on horseback swam across, towing the canoe with ropes. However, when Marcus tried to get his cart across, it overturned in midstream; the mules became entangled in the harness and almost drowned. Finally, with a strong rope and two stout swimmers guiding it from behind, they managed to get it ashore. The cattle were swum across, lowing and snorting in panic.

The monotony of travel was relieved now and then by little surprises. Just beyond the Snake River the company passed the Hot Springs, in which Narcissa boiled a piece of salmon in five minutes. They fed on delicious hawthorne berries as large as cherries and sweet as juicy ripe apples. They found a plant that looked like an onion and tasted like a fig—the *cama,* which the Indians cooked on red-hot coals until it turned black.

One morning in the middle of August, Narcissa entered in her journal: "Last night I put my clothes in water and this morning I finished washing before breakfast. This is the third time I have washed since I left home." Six months before!

Toward the end of August, the Whitmans left the parched sand and sagebrush country and climbed the Blue Mountains, exhilarating in the fragrance of the pines and the cooling winds. The horses were weary and sorefooted. Their unshod feet dragged painfully over the broken black basalt of the mountain slopes. On August 29th, the travelers had their first sight of the Columbia River, and five days later they arrived at Fort Walla Walla, an outpost of the Hudson's Bay Company. Here they rested for several days.

Regaining their strength, they embarked by boat down the Columbia River for Fort Vancouver, the headquarters of the Hudson's Bay Company and the largest white settlement in Oregon.

On the way, they met "Flathead" Indians. A squaw horrified Narcissa by showing her a papoose whose head was bandaged tightly to a board. The mother explained that infants were bound this way for four months until their heads were flattened into a shape considered fashionable by the tribe.

One afternoon, while resting on the bank of the river before setting out over a portage path, Narcissa related in her journal: "I felt something unusual on my neck. I put my hand under my cape and took out two . . . fleas. . . . To my astonishment, I found my dress black with these creatures. . . . This sight made me almost frantic. . . . I climbed up the rock in pursuit of my husband, who soon saw and came to me. . . . On opening the gathers of my dress around the waist, every plait was lined with them. . . . We brushed and shook and shook and brushed for an hour, not stopping to kill, for that would have been impossible. By this time they were reduced very considerably, and I prepared to go to the boat. . . . I found the confinement of the boat distressing on account of my miserable companions, who would not let me rest for a moment in any one position. But I was not the only sufferer. Everyone on board was alike troubled, both crew and passengers. As soon as I was able to make a change in my apparel, I found relief."

In early September the missionaries arrived at Fort Vancouver. "This is the New York of the Pacific!" declared Narcissa, in her enthusiasm to convey what the modest little settlement meant to weary travelers. The thousand-mile trip from Fort Loup, Missouri, was concluded. Narcissa and Eliza Spalding were the first white women to cross the American continent.

Oregon, at the time of the Whitmans' arrival, was a country abounding in rich natural resources. From the time that Captain Robert Gray had explored the Columbia River in the interests of Boston businessmen, the territory had been a hotbed of rivalry between British and American fur traders. A stream of trappers, traders, and adventurers had passed overland into Oregon to make a quick fortune in beaver skins. By 1821, the British-owned Hudson's Bay Fur Company, with headquarters at Fort Vancouver, had become the chief commercial power in the territory, operating it as a vast preserve under the imaginative and resourceful leadership of the Chief Factor, Dr. John McLoughlin, as picturesque a character as the Northwest has ever seen. However, apart from the Hudson's Bay Company outposts and a mission established by Methodists in the Willamette Valley two years before the Whitmans' arrival, Oregon remained a wilderness. It was as little known to the average American as the mountains of Tibet.

Marcus left Narcissa at Fort Vancouver for several weeks while he set out to locate a site for his mission. He decided to settle among the Cayuse Indians, allied to the "Flatheads," on the bank of the Walla Walla River, twenty-five miles north of the Hudson's Bay Company fort. The Indian name for this region was *Waillatpu*—"the place of the tall rye grass." Grass here grew in large coarse bunches to a height of five feet.

When Narcissa arrived at Waillatpu, she found that her husband, with Indian labor, had already built a house and a lean-to with a stout chimney and fireplace. The floor, too, had been laid. But there were as yet no windows, no bed, table, or chairs. These were added during the first year of her housekeeping.

Narcissa led a lonely, isolated life. Her nearest neighbors were the Spaldings, who had established a mission ninety miles to the south. The only other American settlers were the Methodist preachers, three hundred and fifty miles away. Apart from these and the Hudson's Bay Company representatives, there were no other whites in Oregon.

Communication with home was extremely poor. Mail from the eastern seaboard was despatched by vessel from Boston all the way around Cape Horn to the Hawaiian Islands, then rerouted across the Pacific to the mouth of the Columbia River and upstream to Fort Walla Walla. Narcissa had to wait two years and four months before she received her first letter from her family. And then there was a wait of another three years before she received an answer to her correspondence. The newspapers she read were at least two years old.

The Cayuse Indians among whom the Whitmans had settled were a small tribe numbering no more than three hundred. They were sensitive, arrogant, and quick to avenge what they considered a slight. From the outset, the doctor had trouble giving them medical treatment. They held him responsible for the lives of his patients, threatening to kill him if any died under his care. One old chief hovered menacingly over him while he treated his squaw for lung trouble. Fortunately she recovered.

Gradually Whitman succeeded in gaining their confidence, and he was no longer threatened with retaliation for deaths beyond his control. Narcissa intrigued the Indians with her singing; they came from miles around to hear her interpret their songs. They were thrilled with her charm, and with the colorful print dresses she wore.

The Whitmans received five hundred dollars a year from the American Mission Board. This sum had to cover not only their salary, but all mission expenses as well. It was little enough to go on. Narcissa converted her kitchen into a classroom and gave English lessons to forty Indian children. She summoned them to study by hand bell, and served them fresh pitchers of milk at the end of the lesson. The Methodists in the Willamette Valley generously supplied her with books.

The Whitmans lived frugally. Narcissa saved the seeds of all grapes and apples for planting in the fields. During her early years of housekeeping, cattle was too scarce in Oregon to be used for food, and horseflesh was the only meat she served. It wasn't until four years after her arrival that the first cow west of the Rockies was killed for food—a twenty-year-old toothless female who was too old for milking. She was slaughtered at Fort Walla Walla and a cut was sent to the Whitmans.

In some respects it was easier to deal with the Cayuse than with many of the eastern tribes. They had no access to whiskey, as had the savages east of the Rockies. Narcissa could leave her clothes out on the line all night, for they weren't in the habit of stealing. On the other hand, her husband encountered trouble when he tried to teach them how to irrigate their crops. Too lazy to dig trenches of their own, they tried to divert his water to their own use. When he put a stop to this, they dammed up his supply in anger. But despite this petty hostility, he succeeded in developing a productive farm, raised many vegetables, planted an apple orchard, and set up a grist mill to provide the mission with flour.

In Narcissa's twenty-ninth year, the bleak life of the Whitmans was brightened by the coming of a child. She was the first white baby born west of the Rockies, and her parents called her Alice Clarissa.

Within a few days after giving birth, the mother was on her feet again, caring for her baby. She sang to her for hours. "Her hair is light brown," Narcissa wrote to her family when the child was several months old. "And we think she will be like her aunts, Jane and Harriet. She is plump and large, holds her head up finely, and she looks about considerably. She weighs ten pounds."

And when the child was two years old, her mother reported, "You see, Alice came and laid her dirty hands on this paper and gave it a fine mark. I send it as it is, so that you may have some of her doings to look at, and realize . . . there *is* such a child in existence."

The child loved the outdoors. When her parents visited the Spaldings, she rode the entire way with her father on his saddle.

One Sunday in June while Narcissa was setting the table for the holiday meal, she realized that the little girl had disappeared from the house. Suddenly she recalled that Alice had said a few minutes before, "Mama, dinner is almost ready; let Alice get the water." Narcissa noticed that two cups were missing from their place on the table. At the moment of this discovery, a hired helper came into the kitchen and reported that he had found two cups by the bank of the river that flowed a short distance from the home. Filled with anxiety, Narcissa rushed from the house.

Marcus laid aside the book he had been reading and followed her. When they reached the river, a search was organized in which several Indian converts who had joined the Whitmans for Sunday service took part.

At first the search revealed nothing. Narcissa turned toward the house in the hopes that the child had wandered back into the kitchen. Suddenly an old Indian wading close to the bank stumbled into a matted clump of underbrush, reached down, and extricated a limp body, calling out, "The child is found!" Narcissa rushed to the spot; Marcus was already there. Alice had tumbled into the stream and had become entangled in the roots of the coppice. She was dead at the age of two years, nine months.

The Spaldings traveled to Waillatpu when they heard the news. Henry Spalding read the funeral service as the Whitmans buried Alice on the plains, a little to the north of the mission.

The slowness of the mail reopened the wounds of grief. A year after her child's death Narcissa received letters of congratulations from her family on the child's birth. Dresses and shoes Narcissa had ordered for her arrived from the East two years too late.

The tragedy strengthened the determination of the Whitmans to remain in Oregon. Before the death of their daughter, their disappointment over the unfriendly attitude of the Indians had weakened their spirit, and they had talked more than once of returning home. But now that Alice was buried at Waillatpu they no longer had the heart to break their ties. "We are bound up with its destiny!"

Aware of the great richness of its forests, the navigability of its rivers, its strategic position on the north Pacific, the

Whitmans were more and more convinced that Oregon was a land in which thousands of their countrymen, cooped up in the mills and factories of eastern cities, could profitably begin life anew. "What a country this would be for the Yankees," wrote Marcus to his colleagues at home. "Why not tell them about it?"

But this territory that figuratively cried aloud to be populated was the subject of extraordinary misconceptions among Americans. This misinformation was vividly reflected in a contemporary article appearing in a Kentucky newspaper. "Of all the countries on the face of this earth, Oregon is one of the least favored by heaven. It is the mere riddlings of creation. It is almost as barren as the desert of Africa, and quite as unhealthy as the Campania of Italy. . . . Russia has her Siberia, and England has her Botany Bay, and if the United States should ever need a country to which to banish its rogues and scoundrels, the utility of such a region as Oregon would be demonstrated."

Whitman felt that someone who was acquainted with the Oregon territory first hand should go back East and tell the people the truth. The territory was then being jointly administered by the United States and Great Britain under a ten-year treaty which was approaching its termination. After the terminal date, the chances were that the region would pass into the possession of Great Britain, who dominated it commercially, unless Americans roused from their lethargy, moved into it, and claimed it for the United States by the right of colonization.

In the fall of 1842, instructions reached the Whitmans which brought their plans to a climax. Since their arrival in Oregon, another Presbyterian mission had been set up to the south of them. But dissension had arisen among the personnel. The board in the East decided to assign Whitman to this mission, and to abolish the settlement at Waillatpu.

"But we cannot abandon Waillatpu," Whitman told his wife. "Quite apart from our work with the Indians here, this mission is too strategically located to surrender. It is on the direct overland route from the East, and when settlers start coming over the Rockies—and they will come soon, Narcissa, you can be sure of that—our mission will provide a stopping-off place where they can rest and replenish their provisions before continuing to the Willamette valley. In our modest way we are an important link in the chain of circumstances that can bring Oregon into the possession of the United States."

"Then go East," urged Narcissa. "Explain why we cannot leave here."

To go East meant leaving Narcissa alone among the Cayuse Indians for a year at least, something that Marcus did not relish. And yet he couldn't take her through the Rockies in the dead of winter. Finally, however, strengthened by Narcissa's promptings, he decided to make the trip.

He set out by mule with a settler, A. L. Lovejoy. When he reached Fort Hall, he was told by a Hudson's Bay Company representative that the regular route over the Rockies was blocked by Indians on the warpath. However, he determined to go forward, taking a detour south through Salt Lake City, Taos, and Santa Fé.

It was a grim, heartbreaking journey. A severe cold spell had gripped the entire West that fall, accompanied by snowstorms that made travel almost impossible. Four days out of Fort Uncampagra, in Utah, the men were unable to proceed further through the drifts, and they sought shelter in a deep ravine until the storm slackened. When they emerged, their guide announced that the snowfall had so changed the aspect of the country that he had lost his way. After wandering about in confusion, they returned to Fort Uncampagra.

When they came to the Grand River, they discovered that it was packed solid with ice except for a lane of open water down the middle. The guide warned that crossing would be risky, but Whitman trotted his mule over the ice and plunged him into the open water, sinking beneath the surface with the animal. The powerful current bore him a considerable distance downstream before he succeeded in making his way to the far shore and clambering out on the bank. Lovejoy and the guide, following the doctor's example, forced the pack animals into the stream and gained the opposite shore. They then dried out their frozen clothes by a fire before proceeding further.

As they continued eastward, their provisions diminished, and a horse and a mule had to be killed for food. On January 3rd, exhausted and ill, Whitman reached Bents' Fort on the Arkansas River. Within a month he was in St. Louis. Here he rested with friends before proceeding east to meet with his missionarry colleagues and thresh out the issues that had motivated his trip.

In the meantime, Narcissa was passing the months of his absence in anxiety. Her isolation from everyone but Indians kept her nerves constantly on edge. "His society was my life," she wrote of her husband. "While I had him I never knew that I was lonely. Now, I am restless and uneasy . . .

anxiously looking forward, struggling between hope and fear."

Her eyes had grown weak, and she suffered continual headaches. She wrote to Marcus reminding him to buy her two pairs of spectacles.

One midnight she sat up in her bed with a start, awakened by a scraping noise at her door. Someone was trying to force the latch! At first she thought she was imagining things. She lay back and tried to go to sleep. Then she heard the noise again. While she listened horrified, the door moved open a few inches. She sprang from the bed, rushed to the door, and slammed it shut. Suddenly she felt a weight pushing against it. With all her strength she tried to close the latch, but the person at the other end was gaining—forcing it relentlessly open. She screamed for assistance. At the sound of the footsteps of the mission help responding to her call, the intruder, an Indian muffled in a blanket, turned quickly and fled into the night.

Narcissa discovered that the dining room door had carelessly been left unlocked, giving the intruder his chance to enter. Not until John the Hawaiian, one of the mission helpers who arrived in answer to her cries, had placed his bed within earshot of anyone attempting to approach her door did Narcissa retire.

When news of the attempted attack reached Fort Walla Walla, friends came out to the mission and took her back with them. Writing about the experience afterwards, she declared, "Had he persisted I do not know what I should have done. . . . I did think of the poker. Thanks be to our Heavenly Father. He mercifully delivered me."

Several weeks after Narcissa had left the mission, a party

of Cayuse stole up to the Whitman grist mill and set fire to it, burning it to the ground. Several hundred bushels of grain were destroyed. "All of our living came out of the mill," Narcissa wrote home. "The sensible folk among the Cayuse feel the loss deeply and they will feel it still more when they want their wheat ground. We hope it will be a lesson to them."

These were the things Narcissa endured during her husband's absence. But her letters to him were bristling with spirit. "Stay as long as it is necessary to accomplish all your heart's desire respecting the interest of this country."

Marcus Whitman's trip has given rise to speculation among historians as to whom he actually saw and just what he accomplished. Friends of his reported that he obtained an appointment with President Tyler himself, with whom he discussed the importance of keeping Oregon out of the hands of the British, rebutting the views of Secretary of State Daniel Webster, who, it was rumored, was prepared to trade away America's interests in Oregon to England in return for fishing rights in Newfoundland for his New England constituents. Most historians, however, believe that Whitman, upon returning East, attended only to missionary matters, and that he had no dealings with the government.

Two things are certain, however. Whitman persuaded the American Mission Board to retain the strategically situated Waillatpu settlement, and he played an important part in leading the first emigration over the Rockies the summer after his trip East. On his arrival, he was pleased to note that the job of "selling" Oregon to Americans was already being carried out by people of similar mind. The publicity had brought results.

In the winter of 1842-43, hundreds of Americans, convinced at last that Oregon was the place to stake out a future, loaded their families and worldly belongings into their Conestoga wagons and gathered at a place ten miles west of Independence, Missouri, for the great overland trek. Although settlers had been trickling into the territory for several years, it was this expedition of 1843, numbering eight hundred and seventy-five men, women, and children, and two thousand horses and cattle, that launched the great migration into Oregon and inaugurated one of the most inspiring chapters in American history.

Whitman joined the expedition and, to a very great extent, was its guiding spirit. He rode up and down the column of covered wagons, encouraging the drivers, tending the sick. Once, when a pregnant woman became due for her delivery, he guided her husband's wagon out of line, pitched a tent, kindled a fire to heat water, delivered the baby, and drove the parents up to the encampment where the others had settled for the night. His constant advice to the weary was "Travel! Travel! Nothing else will take you to the end of your journey. . . . Nothing is good for you that causes a moment's delay!"

At the Laramie River, the melting snow raised the water to such a level that to ford it seemed impossible. Ferries were made out of wagon beds, and Whitman swam across the river with a line about his waist, fastening it to the opposite shore. Along this line the ferries were towed across safely.

When the travelers arrived at the Platte River, Whitman swam back and forth at intervals for three days until he located the best place for crossing. Under his instructions, more than a hundred teams and wagons were chained to one another—the weakest ones in the center, the strongest ones leading—and the entire column, two miles long, reached the opposite bank without a single vehicle sinking in the quicksand.

When the emigrants arrived at Fort Hall, Idaho, they were given the usual warnings by British officials. Wagons would never get across the Rockies, they declared. This was in some measure propaganda put forward by the Hudson's Bay Company to discourage American colonization, and yet there is no doubt that there was an element of sincerity in the advice. Many of the emigrants were impressed by the arguments. One of the leaders recorded in his journal, "We had now arrived at a most critical period in our . . . journey, and we had many misgivings as to our ultimate success."

Marcus Whitman returned from a scouting trip to find the company torn with dissension. Some of the emigrants were ready to abandon the Oregon venture altogether. He assembled the company and vigorously assured them that they *could* cross the Rockies with their covered wagons and household belongings. He explained that he had done this very thing seven years before. "Believe me, I will take you through!" he promised. Once they reached the Columbia River, he declared, they could proceed by raft to the Willamette Valley where they intended to settle. "Do not abandon your wagons and do not sell your cattle. Your livestock will make you a living in Oregon."

Marcus Whitman's strong voice settled the issue. The company continued with its wagons, and, as the missionary had promised, many of them managed to get through to the Willamette Valley.

When the column reached the Gronde Valley, east of the Blue Mountains, Whitman received a message from Mrs. Spalding urging him to come to her mission as speedily as possible to treat a serious illness. And so the doctor went on ahead, leaving the emigrants under the guidance of his Indian convert, Istickus, who piloted them safely over the Blue Mountains to Waillatpu, where they rested for several days before proceeding to the Willamette Valley.

With the arrival of this expedition, the future of Oregon was no longer in doubt. Americans now greatly outnumbered the British in the territory. A year later, another party of emigrants set out from Missouri bolstered by the knowledge that their predecessors had been able to bring their wagons over the Rockies. A provisional government was formed in the Willamette Valley to represent the Americans until the United States should formally extend its jurisdiction. This came about on June 15, 1846, when, under a new treaty with Great Britain, all territory south of the Columbia River was formally joined to the United States. The 49th parallel remains the American boundary in the Northwest today.

Gone were the times when Henry Spalding could write, as he did after his pioneer journey with the Whitmans, "Never send another woman over those mountains, if you have any regard for human life." In every letter home Narcissa spoke glowingly of Oregon and its future, urging her family and friends to begin a new life in the territory. "Multitudes are flocking to this land. . . . And our anxious desire is that the salt of the earth should be found among them."

Much that Marcus Whitman accomplished for Oregon was made possible only because of Narcissa's courageous support. Although she was never again to give birth to a child of her own, she opened her heart wide to the motherless children of emigrants who died on the trail to Oregon and to the offspring of trappers who had become separated from their Indian wives. Among the children she cared for was the motherless daughter of Jim Bridger, the celebrated mountaineer. She took in a two-year-old half-breed, David Malan, whose mother, driven hysterical when her Spanish husband deserted her, had abandoned him in a well. From the emigration of 1844 she added to her household seven orphans whose parents had died on the trip. "You must learn to work," Whitman told the two older boys. "I am poor and can give you nothing but an education. This I intend to do to the best of my ability."

Narcissa cared for an assortment of grownups as well. As the Whitmans had foreseen, Waillatpu became the chief rehabilitation center for the emigrants, many of whom arrived for lengthy stays. At one time Narcissa kept house for thirty-eight people. The missionary couple gave up their bedroom to an emigrant who had just given birth to a baby and moved their own beds into the dining room. Five additional emigrant families were crowded into the kitchen. An "uninvited" mountain man named Alex slept near the stove.

Passing Indians frequently stopped here for a meal, and they made such an outrageous noise eating from their trenchers that Narcissa had to send the children outdoors so that their laughter would not offend the savages.

And so the beautiful girl from Amity, New York, who had had dreams as a child of becoming a great concert *diva*, toasted by America and Europe, became instead the mistress of a boardinghouse in the lusty West. Instead of receiving wreaths of flowers from admirers after a performance at La

Scala, we find her writing thanks to her brother Edward for several gifts he had sent from the East. "I had hopes of finding one little article . . . that is needed more than most any other because it cannot be obtained here; *pi-la-ain,* the Indians call it—louse trap."

The American colonization of Oregon fulfilled the highest hopes of Narcissa and her husband. And, at the same time, it was the indirect cause that led to tragedy. The Cayuse Indians in the neighborhood of the Whitman mission were angered by the infiltration of white men; they feared that they would be dispossessed of their land. The sachems met in council and issued threats of reprisal.

The Whitmans were well aware of the danger. "All the talk among the Indians is war, war," Marcus wrote home to his colleagues. "Some of the colonists in the Willamette wish Dr. White [the government representative for Indian affairs] to build a strong fortification in the center of the settlement; others wish him to take an armed force to the interior."

Indeed, it was learned that on the eve of the great migration of 1843, the "Flathead" Indians had secretly sent an emissary to tribes east of Fort Hall, urging them to massacre the emigrants on the trail. Fortunately the conspiracy came to nothing.

An incident that further sharpened the tension took place in California. A young chief of the Walla Walla tribe was murdered in a quarrel with an American. The Indians all along the Pacific Coast were aroused. Whitman called a council of the Cayuse and put a question to them bluntly.

"I am your friend. But you are threatening the lives of white men. You say we have come to rob you of your possessions. That is not true. I for one am willing to give up the

mission and go home, if you so desire it. Vote among yourselves, and tell me whether you wish me to remain or leave."

A vote was taken, and all but two or three favored the
Whitmans' remaining at Waillatpu. Thereafter, whenever
friends urged them to return to the East, Narcissa would
refer to the vote. "We'll stay as long as a majority of the
Cayuse want it."

This was the situation when, in the fall of 1847, in the
tenth year of the Whitman mission, a Canadian half-breed
by the name of Joe Lewis turned up at Waillatpu without
shoes or clothing. He had crossed the Rockies with a party
of Oregon-bound immigrants, but they had become so dis-
gusted with his disagreeable personality that they had left
him behind at Fort Boise, and he had made his way to the
Whitman mission alone. Narcissa received him with her characteristic kindness, gave him a shirt and shoes, and fed him
in her kitchen. Marcus hired him for the winter as a laborer,
against the advice of his assistants who were suspicious of
the half-breed's behavior.

Shortly afterwards, on a Saturday morning, as Whitman
was preparing to leave an Indian village where he had
treated several sick patients, his convert, Istickus, came to
him with alarming news. "Joe Lewis is making trouble for
you. He has been telling my people that you are going to
poison them so that you can give their land to white colonists. I fear my people will do you harm. You had better go
away."

When Marcus arrived home, Narcissa sensed that he was
deeply worried. Finally he told her what Istickus had said.
In belittling it, she expressed a lightheartedness she didn't
feel. She was as troubled as he was.

The following morning an Indian died. Marcus attended the funeral and noted with concern that only several savages were present. The Indian settlement was mantled in an ominous silence. "I cannot understand what this means," Marcus said to Narcissa when he returned.

Shortly after dinner, he was told that two Indians wished to see him in the kitchen. When he walked in, Ti-lau-kait, a chief, engaged him in conversation. The second Indian, Tam-a-has, edged around behind the doctor. Suddenly he drew a tomahawk from under his blanket and struck Marcus on the head. The first blow stunned him and snapped his head to his chest. The second toppled him to the ground.

At the sound of his moaning, Narcissa rushed into the kitchen. The Indians had vanished. She dragged her husband to the sofa and managed to get him on it. To her frantic questions, her feverish attempts to revive him, he mumbled inaudibly. He died without regaining consciousness.

Suddenly, as she got to her feet, an Indian appeared at the window. He aimed his rifle at her and shot her in the stomach. Narcissa crumpled to the floor. Then with a last ounce of energy she struggled to her knees and prayed to God to protect her foster children. She died as the blood poured from her lips.

Eleven men and boys at the mission were also murdered that afternoon. The buildings were burned to the ground.

This was the end of the adventure that had begun thirteen years before, when a young woman sat down and wrote a letter on green, scented stationery for permission to serve as a missionary among the Indians.

America was shocked by the massacre. Five hundred and thirty-seven men from Oregon volunteered to march on the

Cayuse and punish the murderers. In searching through the charred ruins of the mission at Waillatpu, they came upon scattered tufts of Narcissa's lovely blonde hair. This alone remained after her.

At the time of the raid she was only forty-one. Had she stayed in the East, she could have cultivated her musical talents, or continued on tranquilly, securely, as a teacher at Miss Willard's Academy for girls. And she would still have won our respect. But then she would not have been Narcissa Prentiss Whitman.

12

Crusaders for Today

1. TOYOHIKO KAGAWA

〰〰〰〰〰〰〰〰〰〰〰〰〰〰〰〰〰〰〰〰〰〰〰〰〰〰〰〰〰〰

From the great industrial slums of Kobe, on the Japanese mainland of Honshu, an almost totally blind consumptive, a man the doctors gave up for dead forty years ago, calls out in the age-old words of Jesus: "Whosoever will come after me, let him deny himself, and take up his cross, and follow me; whosoever will save his life shall lose it; but whosoever shall lose his life for my sake and the gospel's, the same shall save it."

He is Toyohiko Kagawa, the patron saint of the handicapped. The son of a wealthy Japanese aristocrat, a consultant to prime ministers of several administrations, a man who has earned a fortune on his own, Kagawa has lived much of his life in the Kobe slums of Shinkawa, sharing his rooms with hoboes, lunatics, and the chronic unemployed. He has given away practically every cent of his earnings. "Religion is not a theory," he declares. "It is life."

Practically all the great missionaries of the past have come from the West. And many of them have devoted their lives to teaching the gospel in the Orient. But Kagawa has taken

309

a long step toward repaying the debt. This frail Oriental mystic is an inspiration not only to the Japanese, but to all people who respond to a great clarion call of the spirit.

Kagawa was born out of wedlock, the illegitimate son of a dancing girl. His father was a diplomat, a political bigwig, and a close advisor to the Emperor. A playboy who frequented the night spots, he squandered the family fortune, dissipated his health, and died when Toyohiko was four; his mother passed away within a year. Entrusted to the care of his father's neglected widow, Kagawa passed a childhood that left scars in him for life. He was unwanted and unloved. His foster mother often beat him and confined him in the outhouse.

But when Kagawa was eleven, his uncle took charge of him. He sent him to a boy's boarding school at Tokushima to prepare him for the Imperial University at Tokyo and a career in diplomacy.

English was one of the subjects the boy studied at boarding school. To obtain practice speaking it, he attended classes held in Tokushima by Dr. Henry Meyers, a Presbyterian missionary from America. Dr. Meyers was attracted to this sickly looking student who was without question the loneliest, saddest boy he had ever met. He invited Kagawa to his house, took him for walks, and had long talks with him. Once, during a stroll, the missionary pointed to the sky turned scarlet with the sunset.

"Can the power that created such beauty have the heart to neglect human suffering on earth, my boy? No one who lives underneath the sunset need despair of God." Under his tutelage Kagawa became a Christian.

When the time arrived for him to enter the Imperial

University, he told his uncle that he was not interested in a diplomatic career. He wanted instead to live a humble life ministering to the unfortunate. His uncle, in a terrible anger, threw him out of the house and cut off his financial support. However, Toyohiko's friend, Dr. Meyers, stood by him, and entered him in the Presbyterian Seminary at Kobe.

Here, while studying for the ministry, Toyohiko contracted tuberculosis. He was sent to a health resort on the sea coast. His friends were convinced that this seriously ill young man would not live out the year.

During his stay on the coast, a fishing boat was wrecked in a storm, and all hands were swept overboard. Kagawa stumbled from his room down to the shore, and in a pouring rain helped launch a rescue boat through the heavy surf. Later, the young consumptive was found crouched against a rock, in utter exhaustion, coughing up blood. He was carried to bed, a fire was started, and the village folk stood by anxiously, awaiting the arrival of death.

But Kagawa refused to die. By some miracle of will this fragile young student, not yet twenty, hung on to life. His cheeks gradually took on a bit of color; soon he rose from bed and returned to the city. He came back to Kobe not to rest, not even to study—but to labor in the slums.

In the Shinkawa slums, nearly twelve thousand people were pressed into eleven city blocks. Frequent epidemics of smallpox, cholera, and typhus had turned the area into a pesthole. Of sixty-two babies born in Kagawa's neighborhood in his first year there, forty-five died. Nine or ten people were often crowded together in a single room no larger than a prison cell.

This man who was alive only because of stubbornness arrived on Christmas Day, 1909, and moved into a small alley room without windows or furniture. It was vacant only because it was believed to be haunted; a murder had recently been committed there. His neighbors in the miserable alley knew at a glance that he was not one of them. Why had this ascetic looking student with the manners of an aristocrat come to Shinkawa? They suspected that he was either a police spy or a madman.

Kagawa immediately offered shelter to vagrants who had nowhere to sleep. His first lodger was a tramp covered from head to foot with a contagious skin disease. The second was a paroled convict hounded by remorse over a murder he had committed, who shrieked aloud in nightmares as he slept at Kagawa's side. The company was increased by a tubercular in the final stages, a lunatic, and an alcoholic rotting with syphilis. At one time, ten outcasts lived together under Kagawa's roof. Kagawa tore down one of the walls to provide more space. Once he was pushed out into the street, where he spent the night.

Kagawa not only housed and fed a constant turnover of vagabonds, but he nursed them and taught them to read and write. His little room was a combination dormitory, hospital, and school. He took a job sweeping chimneys, and the wages from this, together with a small allowance from the seminary, comprised his entire income.

One night he slept with a tramp who was suffering from the eye disease, trachoma. Kagawa caught it and almost lost his sight. To this day he is nearly blind, and it is a painful effort for him to read print, even through powerful lenses. Yet he is an inexhaustible student and a prolific writer.

During his early years in the slums, Kagawa married a

young girl with the charming name of Spring. She had been
an employee in a bookbinding shop. No bride was ever faced
with a more difficult job of housekeeping than Spring
Kagawa when she moved into Shinkawa. She not only had
to keep home for her husband, but for his derelict lodgers—
and she had to do it on a budget equal to fifteen dollars a
month.

Before he was thirty, Kagawa's life underwent an unexpected change. A newspaper publisher, touring the slums
one afternoon to gather material for an article, was directed
to the oddest specimen in the neighborhood, Kagawa. In the
course of the interview, the publisher drew from Kagawa
the information that he had been spending his spare hours
working on a novel. The manuscript was written on wrapping paper, food-can labels, the margins of newspapers. "I
began this novel when I was dying of tuberculosis in a fishing village," explained Kagawa. "I wrote down everything
that came to mind, using any paper I could get my hands on.
I have called the book *Across the Death Line*, because I
myself have crossed the line, and only the great misery and
need of the world have brought me back."

The newspaperman took the manuscript home with him.
Across the Death Line was published first as a newspaper
serial, then as a book. Instantly it became a sensation. Re-
viewers acclaimed Kagawa as a brilliant new talent. People
queued up at bookstores all over the nation to buy copies.
Printing after printing of the book sold out, and the royalties
poured in, to the astonishment of the young man in Shinkawa. Publishers besieged him with offers for contracts.

To his friends who showered him with congratulations,
Kagawa replied, "Now I have discovered how to earn money

to carry on my work here. And if the public wants a new book from me, I'll give it one. I'll write about life in the slums and make people writhe with shame. Perhaps then, Shinkawa will be abolished."

With his earnings, Kagawa financed himself to an exhaustive study of settlement work. He traveled to America and studied for three years at Princeton University, earning a degree as doctor of theology.

Now that he was a man with a reputation, Kagawa's friends expected him to join the faculty of a university or become associated with a prominent church, or at least live the comfortable, easy-going life of the successful writer. They were wrong. Kagawa moved right back into the slums.

"There is nothing more zestful," he declared, "than to walk through the world unhampered. If possessions abound, there is a haunting fear that they may be stolen. . . . If you pride yourself on being erudite, you are cut to the quick if someone makes light of you. Stripped to the skin. . . . That is the way to walk!"

That was the way Kagawa continued to walk. Another book followed the first, and then another, created out of his own personal experiences and the misery of the people around him. And the demand for his writings continued strong. He has written more than fifty books, plus a vast number of newspaper articles and essays on social and religious topics. And yet, from a financial standpoint he remains a poor man, for all his earnings have gone into his social work. Most of his incredibly large output has had to be dictated, since his diseased eyes are swathed in bandages for hours and days at a stretch. Also, he continually suffers

hemorrhages of the lungs. In one of his most active years—
1930—he experienced nine such hemorrhages.

His great campaign to abolish the slums bore fruit after
fifteen years, when the government yielded to Kagawa's
persistent prodding and launched a project to wipe out the
worst slum areas in the six largest cities of Japan—Tokyo,
Osaka, Kobe, Kyoto, Yokohama, and Nagoya. Today, in
place of these slums, there are sanitary, low-priced dwellings,
playgrounds, settlement houses, and nurseries for the children of working mothers.

On September 1, 1923, a tremendous earthquake turned
northern Japan into a shambles. At noon, while housewives
were cooking lunch, the earth was convulsed with tremors.
Within seconds Tokyo and the neighboring seaport Yokohama lay in ruins. The fires in the charcoal braziers were
overturned, caught up by the wind, and turned into an
enormous conflagration. Hundreds of families were snatched
by the police out of the ruins and herded into an area of
several square blocks that was believed to be out of the path
of the flames. But the wind suddenly shifted, and the place
of refuge turned into an inferno, destroying every last person.

Before that tragic day was over, more than a hundred
thousand Japanese had died. The industrial plant of the
nation was demolished. The government turned to Toyohiko
Kagawa and invited him to organize a program from Tokyo
City Hall. The little scholar with the thick spectacles accepted and became a crusading force behind the nation's
social and industrial recovery.

Time and again, Kagawa has been summoned by the government to supervise projects to put the nation's economy on

its feet. In the winter of 1930, during the height of the depression, Kagawa was drafted by the mayor of Tokyo to head the city's Social Welfare Bureau for the relief of the unemployed. He appeared at his desk in the $1.85 laborer's suit which he wore in the Shinkawa slums. His fellow bureaucrats were shocked; they preferred trying to save the country in dinner jackets over cocktails.

Kagawa's social philosophy is blunt and uncompromising. "Unless Christ is made the center of the social movement, the world is doomed."

Assisted by pastors, evangelists, and missionaries of all Christian denominations in Japan, he has spearheaded a "Kingdom of God" movement to translate the spirit of the gospel into the day-by-day economic, political, and social life of Japan. "Love," he insists, "is the law of life."

His missionary followers have gone into every community, setting up industrial conferences among employers and laborers to adjust their differences over wages, hours, and working conditions in harmony with the spirit of Jesus.

Spiritually, Kagawa is very close to Tolstoy—that other celebrated apostate from the nobility. "God dwells among the lowliest of men," Kagawa writes in his *Meditations.* "He sits on the rubbish-pile among prison convicts. He stands at the door begging bread. He joins the beggars at the place of alms. . . . He stands in line with the unemployed in front of the employment bureaus. Therefore, let him who would meet God pay a visit to the prison cell before going to the church. Before he goes to the temple let him visit the hospital."

He is an internationalist, possessing, nevertheless, a fierce pride in the people of his own nation. When the Japanese

Army invaded Manchuria, he stood before a Chinese audience in the International Friendship Club in Tsinan and declared, "I believe you Chinese must hate me because I am a Japanese. . . . Therefore do not consider me a Japanese, but a Christian." And then he added, "And yet, if you want to hate Japan, hate me also!"

Kagawa is a rare combination of mystic and realist. He shares, for instance, Gandhi's abhorrence of a soulless, materialistic civilization. And yet, unlike the Hindu leader, he has no wish to abolish modern machinery and return to an economically primitive way of life just because the can opener has been unable to solve man's spiritual problems. He feels that the machine can yet be domesticated; that it has already given the individual greater leisure than he has ever before enjoyed, and that the problem is to educate him to use this leisure properly. "There is nothing so dangerous as growthless freedom," he says. He believes that teachers should cram fewer facts into the heads of the young, and spend more time instilling in them the art of living.

This crusader of the Orient emphatically rejects the Communists' use of violence in dealing with Asia's social and economic problems. "All the . . . experiments of history that were based on violence rather than love have ended on the rocks. Love alone can create a just social order." He points out that the French and Russian revolutions, both accomplished through force, imposed a rule of materialism that destroyed all spiritual and moral values. To the philosophy of Marxism he opposes the dynamics of the gospel: "If we take it seriously, live it adventurously, we will be able to do far more than Russian Communism ever dreams of doing in building a better world."

Kagawa's work in the slums led him into the field of factory reform, where, through his influence, legislation was passed eliminating unsanitary conditions, reducing work hours, and guaranteeing a living wage. He initiated an economic rehabilitation program for handicapped workers, providing them with capital to start small businesses of their own.

And then he turned his attention to agriculture, developing a program to keep the farmer happy and productive. He provided for instruction in up-to-date agriculture techniques, the establishment of village clubs for social life, day nurseries for children, and a cooperative credit system to enable the farmer to possess modern machinery.

In struggling for the minds and hearts of his countrymen during a very critical period in human affairs, Kagawa has given his health, his earnings—everything he has—to his crusade. He has made many enemies and has been in frequent physical danger. During a lecture tour, Communist agitators broke up his meetings in Los Angeles and New York. Free thinkers have denounced him as a traitor to the workers. Various political leaders have called for violent action against him. In 1921 he was jailed by the government for his part in organizing labor; out of this experience came one of his most poignant novels, *Listening to the Voice in the Wall.* In World War II he was again imprisoned, this time for his opposition to Japanese militarism. However, after the signing of the peace treaty, Prince Higashi-Kuni, Prime Minister of the new Japanese government, aware of Kagawa's wide influence, invited him to join the cabinet. Kagawa preferred to carry on his spiritual campaign as a political independent, but he did act as a consultant to the Department of Public Welfare.

Many groups with an ax to grind have at one time or another vilified Kagawa. Yet this man who refused to die of consumption at twenty, who has lived a third of a century with trachoma and diseased kidneys, who has outlasted attacks, imprisonment, starvation, and self-imposed poverty, doesn't scare easily—not even at sixty. Today he is campaigning as vigorously as ever to sell the world *total* Christianity as the only alternative to *total* war.

2. MEN OF MARYKNOLL

Today, among the oppressed millions of Asia, other crusaders are fighting the battle of civilization. Hundreds of Americans have left their farms and factories, offices, banks, and universities, have parted from their families and severed personal ties to enlist in a great fighting army mobilized for "R-Day"—the reclamation of the underprivileged.

They are the Men of Maryknoll, the Catholic Foreign Mission of America. The seminary in which they are trained is a striking symbol of their mission. It is a gray stone building with carved Chinese roofs and pagoda-shaped towers overlooking the Hudson, outside Ossining, New York, thirty miles from the skyscrapers of Manhattan. In many of the refectories and corridors hang the framed works of Oriental artists. Overlooking the baseball diamond where young seminarians field grounders and knock out home runs is a statue of the Mother and Child under a pagoda. And near by, a huge Oriental gong sounds its solemn note whenever a new group of missionaries is about to depart for the East.

The American boy from Broadway and the hinterlands feels, the moment he enters Maryknoll, that the East and the West are one, that nothing is foreign to God.

These young crusaders have been setting out from the banks of the Hudson for thirty years now. During this period, the political map of the world has been reconstructed many times; war, depression, and revolution have uprooted millions of people. Yet year by year the Maryknoll Mission has grown progressively greater in scope and influence.

It all began as a dream in the hearts of two vigorous priests, Fathers Thomas Edward Price and James Anthony Walsh, back in the days when Victor Herbert was writing his early musical hits and Woodrow Wilson was still a college professor.

Thomas Price was a "Tarheel" from North Carolina who had faith in cotton, corn, and the God who made all men. The son of a newspaper editor, young Tom—he was more often called by his middle name "Freddie"—got to know God earlier than many men. When he was sixteen he took passage on a steamer that was shipwrecked off Cape Hatteras. Nearly everyone aboard was lost. But Price, who couldn't swim a stroke, clung to a piece of wreckage and was picked up after several hours in the water. At first he was believed to be dead, but restoratives brought him back to consciousness.

Price entered Saint Mary's Seminary in Baltimore and became the first North Carolinian ever to be ordained a priest.

He was assigned to a rural parish covering more than three hundred square miles in the eastern section of the state. He was continually on the move. He passed the night in the open fields, in barns, or in the log cabins of the poor, sleeping on a sheepskin within walls plastered with mud. He developed severe rheumatism from his exposure to all kinds of weather.

The backwoodsmen were devoted to this clergyman who ate with relish their own cornbread and coffee, their razorback bacon heavy with juice, and who quoted the latest prices on hogs. He made friends with men of all creeds. When he organized a fair to raise funds for his parish, his heaviest contributions came from Jewish citizens of Goldsboro.

Father Price did not expect his catechumens to drop their work and travel long miles to him. He went to them, explaining the gospel as they reaped the cotton and planted corn, as they rested for a moment on a fence, or wiped away their sweat under the shade of a tree. His humorous blue eyes were irresistible. His anecdotes sent the "Tarheels" into gusts of laughter.

He would frequently catch a train between stations simply by signaling the approaching locomotive. There wasn't an engineer in the area who didn't recognize Father Price. The engineer would bring the train to a halt, wait for the priest to get aboard, sound his whistle, then continue his run.

Eventually, Father Price bought a horse and buggy to carry him on his travels. His mare, "Nancy Hanks," had the temper of a mule. She was particularly difficult to start and stop. Once, after loading up his buggy with groceries and vestments for the church, he instructed a bystander to rub Nancy's nozzle with a few grains of sand, his customary way of getting her to move. But the onlooker, interpreting his instructions too liberally, poured a handful of sand down her mouth. Father Price succeeded in halting the stampeding mare only after all his sugar, calico, coffee, and half a dozen bottles of altar wine had been dumped overboard.

Father Price was not an eloquent speaker. His own simple, busy life was his finest sermon. He wore patched clothes that were hand-me-downs from some of his former classmates. He edited a little magazine, *Truth*, for his parishioners, printing it on an old press in the rectory kitchen. As the deadline for the publication drew near, he would hustle about his parish duties with manuscript pages bulging from his coat pockets. He jotted down ideas and corrected his copy at odd moments—in railroad stations, on trains, in the backwoods shack of a parishioner.

For years Father Price had nourished an ideal—the establishment of a great missionary movement that would send young Americans to all corners of the globe. Then, in 1910, while attending the Eucharest Congress in Montreal, he met a man who had been thinking along his own lines. This man was Father James Anthony Walsh from Cambridge, Massachusetts, a crusading journalist with a pen as forceful as his heart was large. The two men immediately became friends.

Thirteen months after the meeting, with the backing of ecclesiastical officials, the two priests leased land for a seminary in the town of Hawthorne in lower New York State. They gave up their previous duties to devote full time to the experiment. In a particularly raw January, they set up headquarters in a cottage that at first had no electric lights.

Water had to be pumped from a well. Walsh cooked the meals. Price stoked the furnace. Frequently they ran out of bread and out of oil for the lamps, and the well ran dry.

The first nine months were spent recruiting a faculty and raising funds. With the coming of spring, the priests looked for more desirable land, and they purchased ninety-three acres of woodland and pasture near Ossining overlooking the Hudson River. Dominating the property was a hill on which there was a farmhouse and a barn. The priests named the mission Maryknoll—the Hill of Mary.

In the meantime, six young men had entered as pioneer seminarians. In addition to the usual courses taught at a seminary, they were given special training for a life requiring physical labor as well as intellectual dexterity. They "toughened up" by scrubbing floors, doing repair jobs, raising livestock, plowing and planting the fields.

Father Walsh has written vividly of the homely problems with which they were faced. "It took us some time to find a baker whose horse would climb the hill to see us. Eventually, we obtained a . . . horse, 'Billy,' who could walk more rapidly than he could run, but who never shied at least at a hill . . . and a dog whose fourth leg went bad occasionally, but whose night bark never failed."

The founders established a six-year curriculum for training missionaries. In 1917, as the education of the pioneer seminarians reached its final stages, Father Walsh traveled to the Orient to survey possible areas to which they could be sent. The misery that he witnessed in China convinced him that here was a logical field. "The struggle of some poor human beings to keep life in their bodies," he wrote after visiting an orphanage at Mukden, "makes a man almost ashamed to eat a square meal."

He arranged for his Maryknollers to serve in Yeungkong in South China, under the jurisdiction of the Canton Vicariate.

On his return to the States, plans were made to send several graduates to Yeungkong. Father Price insisted on leading the contingent personally, but his colleagues felt that he was too old to go. He was in his fifty-ninth year; furthermore, he was a chronic sufferer from rheumatism and had been warned by physicians that he might become permanently crippled. The long rainy season and high humidity of South China would only aggravate his condition. But the Carolina "Tarheel" stubbornly resisted all efforts to sidetrack him, and he was reluctantly given the assignment.

In the fall of 1918, Price and his fellow missionaries embarked from San Francisco at the very moment that doughboys by the thousands were loading into transports bound for France. The departure of the Maryknollers to wage a different kind of battle in the Far East was an unobtrusive event.

Upon the arrival of the missionaries, the Chinese foreign office changed their American names to corresponding Chinese sounds to simplify passport identification. Price was given the name "Pou-ri-ce," which in English meant "Universal jewel is here." But this was too much for Price's modesty. He dropped everything but the "Pou"—"Universal." Hereafter, he was known everywhere in China as Father Pou.

To reach Yeungkong in Kwantung Province, the missionaries traveled to Canton. Here in the harbor at midnight

they scrambled on hands and knees over neighboring junks
to find their boat. The "cabin" which had been assigned to
them was merely deck space. They had to spread their bed-
ding on the floor. "Tonight we leave for Yeungkong on a junk
de luxe," Father Price noted in his diary. In the course of
the trip they transferred to a freighter having no accommo-
dations for passengers. As they shaved next morning, the
salt spray drenched them to the skin. When they were
twenty-five miles from Yeungkong, the temperamental captain suddenly, and for no known reason, refused to take
them any further. He put into a cove. They had to engage
a sailboat for the rest of the way.

They reached Yeungkong a few days before Christmas and
moved into a two-story brick house with a red-tiled roof.
For the Christmas holiday the Chinese Christians in the
area, numbering a thousand, organized a gala celebration.
They hired a band to serenade the missionaries, exploded
firecrackers in their honor, and invited them to a banquet
of chicken, duck, and shrimp.

In the few months after his arrival, Father Price traveled
extensively to familiarize himself with the living conditions
of the people. But his vitality was spent; determination
alone kept him going. One thing that gave him particular
trouble was the Chinese language. Although he applied himself energetically, he was helpless before the maze of characters and sounds. After several months, the most he was
able to say was "How do you do?" and "God bless you!"

His rheumatism caused him agony. But only in his diary
did he reveal the extent of his suffering. "I am full of pains
—all over. Where it will all end is hard to say. . . . I can see
nothing clear ahead. It looks like being invalided here."

But he was spared that fate. Less than a year after his arrival, before the Yeungkong mission was even fully organized, the priest suffered a sudden attack of appendicitis. He was operated on at a hospital in Hongkong, but failed to rally from the operation. He passed away in September, 1919.

He died before his dreams for Maryknoll materialized. But Father Walsh, who survived him by seventeen years, witnessed the harvest of his labors. Under his direction the Maryknoll Mission broadened the scope of its activities to include many backward regions of the globe. Today, more than a thousand missionaries—lay brothers, seminarians, and sisters (women, too, have ranged themselves under the banner of Maryknoll)—are serving not only in China, Japan, and Korea, but in the Philippines, Hawaii, South Africa, and South America.

Dozens of typical Maryknollers come to mind. Any of them might have been raised on the very street of the reader of this book. There is Father Patrick Sweeney of New Britain, Connecticut, director of the Gate of Heaven, a leper asylum in southern China, who crawled under gunfire to bandage the wounds of his lepers during an attack by Japanese soldiers; Father Daniel McShane of Columbus, Indiana, head of an orphanage in Loting, who died of smallpox he contracted from one of the Chinese children he took in from the streets; Father Jerry Donovan of McKeesport, Pennsylvania, who penetrated into the mountainous regions of Manchuria, bringing food supplies to villages that had never before seen a white man. Called "the Laughing Father" because of his sense of humor, he was kidnapped by

Chinese bandits and found strangled in a snowdrift at the base of a hill.

There is Father Bernard Meyers from Stuart, Iowa, who was trapped between Nationalist and Communist armies fighting for the city of Kochow. Asked by the Nationalist general to try to arrange a truce parley, he walked through a heavy artillery barrage into the opposing camp and persuaded the commander to come to terms. There is Father Lloyd Glass of Cresco, Iowa, who has devoted his life to rehabilitating "dead end" kids in boys' towns throughout southern China; and Father "Sandy" Cairns, born in Glasgow but raised in Worcester, Massachusetts, who ran a Japanese naval blockade from Sancian Island with rice and powdered milk for the residents of the Chinese mainland.

When the Sino-Japanese War broke out in 1937, and bombs were dropped on Loting, Father Robert Kennelly, a Maryknoll missionary from Norwalk, Connecticut, jumped behind a tree near the wall of his compound. His thigh was hit by a bomb fragment. From a nearby dugout a nun emerged, dashed to the house for her first aid kit, and returned to Father Kennelly. As she was about to dress his wound, a second bomb landed a dozen yards away, knocking the medicine bottle from her hand. Then a third bomb exploded, turning the house into a shambles.

"There goes our supper, Father," the sister said, as casually as if she were announcing the time of the day.

And in places where war has not come—the South African veldt, the highlands of Chile, the Ecuadorian jungle, the mountains of Peru—Maryknoll missionaries in recent years have been directing the battle against human misery, challenging the superstitions of the witch doctors, bringing food, education, and spiritual dignity to the forgotten man.

"Progress through pain is a spiritual law." The man who made this statement was Bishop Francis X. Ford, one of the first group of Maryknollers who arrived with Father Price at Yeungkong. In 1922 he was robbed by Chinese pirates on the Loting River. Two years later he barely escaped with his life when pirates again boarded a steamer on which he was traveling, murdered the captain, and looted all valuables. On still another occasion he was captured by brigands near Chankiang. During World War II he remained in China serving in areas continually menaced by Japanese troops. In December, 1950, he was arrested by Chinese Communists on the trumped-up charge of espionage. He was marched to prison with his hands tied behind him; the people he had served for thirty-four years pelted him with garbage and beat him with sticks and ropes. He died in jail after a little more than a year's confinement, his black hair having turned completely white, his body wasted to a skeleton.

"Progress through pain is a spiritual law." The young Americans who depart annually from the banks of the Hudson to make life more decent for their fellows live by the words of this man who truly knew.

3. FRANK LAUBACH

ONE AFTERNOON on the Island of Mindanao in the southern Philippines, a bald-headed, broad-shouldered American missionary stood up in a former saloon and faced as ferocious looking a group of Filipinos as had ever congregated under a white man's roof. They were the dreaded Moros, warriors who in times past had given the United States Army some of the roughest fighting in its history. For twenty-five years no civilized man had dared to walk among them without a gun. But times had changed. On this particular afternoon, close to a hundred of the savages were sitting as meekly as nursery children at the feet of a gentle-mannered missionary, listening enthralled to what he had to say.

The American pointed to a large wall chart covered with bold-printed letters and brightly colored pictures. "Now, repeat after me, 'Ma, mi, mo, mu!'"

And each Moro obediently opened his mouth and recited, "Ma, mi, mo, mu."

From time to time natives put down the books they were holding, leaped to their feet with shining eyes and shouted, "Teacher, I can spell the words! I can really read. Listen to me!"

When the class was dismissed, a savage old fellow came up to the missionary and indicating that he wished to speak to him privately, beckoned him into a corner. This Moro was one of the most feared outlaws in Lanao.

"You are doing a great thing for me, Teacher. You are the

329

very best friend I have in this world. Is there anybody in Lanao you want assassinated? I shall do the job free of charge for you!"

"No, thank you, brother. Go home and teach others what you have learned here. That will make me happy."

Frank Laubach, the teacher who "loves these natives into learning," has taught the ABC's not only to Filipino Moros, but to Solomon Island head hunters, Haitian medicine men, New Guinea cannibals, Australian bushmen, and numerous other primitive peoples from pole to pole. He has been at this profession for twenty-five years now, and he won't be satisfied until a good proportion of the twelve hundred million people who are still unable to sign their names or read a newspaper are given the tools of literacy.

Laubach stumbled on his unique vocation as the result of a personal crisis. Born in Benton, Pennsylvania, a doctor of philosophy from Columbia University and an authority on slum settlement work, he arrived in the Philippines in 1915, and spent thirteen years as a Presbyterian missionary in Cayagan and Manila. Then in 1928 he received an assignment to go among the Moros of Mindanao. Upon arriving, he was confronted with a baffling situation; the Moros were unapproachable. He spent months in Lanao without gaining a hearing with them.

Day after day he climbed a hill in back of his cottage and prayed. Then one afternoon—as Frank Laubach tells it—"My lips began to move, and it seemed to me that God was speaking. 'My child . . . you have failed because you do not really love these Moros. You feel superior to them because you are white. If you can forget you are an American and think only how you can love them, they will respond.'"

That was Frank Laubach's sudden insight into things. "In that terrible, wonderful hour, I became colorblind!"

"If you want the Moros to be fair to your religion," he told himself, "be fair to theirs. Study their Koran with them."

He immediately sought out two Moslem priests (the Moros are a Moslem people) and told them through an interpreter that he wanted to study the Koran. He would, in return, teach them the Christian Bible. "We will share what we have," he said. The next day several priests came to his cottage with Korans under their arms. Laubach studied with them the teachings of Mohammed and in turn translated several Old Testament stories and the Gospel of St. Luke into Arabic.

And since he wanted to reach the common people as well as the priests, he applied himself to the study of the popular language, Maranaw. The task was by no means easy. Maranaw was a spoken language only; it had never been written down. Laubach listened to each word, and when he had discovered what it meant, he wrote it down phonetically. His teacher was an old Moro named Pambaya, who had been sentenced to twenty years in prison for murder but had managed to "beat the rap."

In learning Maranaw in this fashion, Laubach became the only man in the world to reduce it to a form in which it could be written and read. And he was inspired with an idea. Why not teach the Moros to read and write their language exactly as he was learning to do?

He immediately set about developing a system for teaching them. He reduced the language to its basic phonetic sounds, then presented it in a modified Roman alphabet.

Each key syllable was accompanied by a key picture, an object familiar to the people. Laubach knew that most illiterates have a highly developed sense of observation. The name of each object selected was the same as the sound of the syllable; very often the identity was established by the use of a pun.

Laubach developed three charts incorporating every syllable of the language. Converting a saloon on the United States Army post at Lanao into a classroom, he selected a group of illiterates for a test, and was amazed at the results. Several of the people actually began to read their language after no more than an hour of instruction. Others were able to pick out the words haltingly, slowly, but accurately, within a day. After thorough testing, Laubach discovered that the average illiterate learned the essentials of reading and writing in four or five days.

The reaction of these backward people, when the implications of what Laubach was doing for them became fully understood, was tremendously heartwarming. He won their confidence to a degree that amazed the other white inhabitants of the Philippines. Whole villages of Moros flocked to his classroom. Men and women emerged from their lesson, their faces wreathed in smiles, murmuring, "It is very easy. He was surprised at my bright mind." A chieftain brought six wives from his harem to be educated. One village Romeo lured a bevy of young ladies to class by writing a love letter to a young woman who had recently acquired her ABC's, informing her that her learning had turned her into positively the loveliest lady in Lanao. The girl showed the letter to all her female friends. And the rush for an education was on. One enthusiastic native used his newly gained education to write a long letter to the President of the United States, and he hounded Laubach until he translated it and mailed it to the White House.

The Moros were spectacular in their gratitude. When Laubach decided to purchase land on which to build a school for Moro girls, the native owner of the property paid him a visit and offered it to him free of charge. "I told my husband," declared his wife, who had accompanied him, "that if he did not give that property to you, I would cut his throat in his sleep."

Since Laubach could not personally teach the thousands who desired to learn, he instructed each of his pupils to pass on his knowledge to another. "Each teach one" became his slogan for mass literacy.

He was profoundly moved by episodes he witnessed. "At the church in Cavite, I taught one girl to read, and the next day she taught the chart beautifully to another girl in front of some thirty people. . . . The teacher was so overcome with joy that she wiped away the tears from her eyes with her red handkerchief as she taught. The women who watched her wept, and the men turned their backs and blew their noses." Chiefs came from distant towns, took lessons from Laubach, and departed with a colorfully decorated chart under one arm, a diploma under the other, and a broad smile on their face, to instruct their people back home.

A magazine put out by the United States Government awarded prizes to Moro communities in which the greatest number of inhabitants had learned to read and write within a specified period. One month the editor announced that the prize had been won by the Davao Penal Colony. "The prisons are becoming universities," he declared.

Before Laubach appeared with his charts, only 4 per cent of the Moros were literate, mostly priests and members of upper classes, who were educated in Arabic. Two years after Laubach began his classes, 20 per cent were able to read and write, and literacy was increasing at the rate of 12 per cent a year. Today, three out of four Moros are literate. They have one of the highest voting records of any group in the Philippine Islands.

Laubach prepared special literature for his new readers. He edited a newspaper containing articles on Christianity, summaries of world news, simple discussions of agriculture, sanitation, and other local problems. He published books graded to the reading skill of his audience. He opened folk schools in Mindanao. One of his star pupils translated a hundred pages of the Old Testament and prepared a booklet on the care of babies.

The degree to which Frank Laubach and his fellow Americans gained the affection of the Moros was impressively demonstrated during World War II, when thousands of natives signed a pledge to resist the attempts of the Japanese Army to overthrow the United States Government on Mindanao.

Frank Laubach's literacy campaign did not end with the Moros. He had, in fact, developed techniques to abolish illiteracy all over the world. Educational and missionary circles, and even governments, were quick to grasp the implications. Three out of every five members of the human race were disqualified from entering the market of skilled labor because they were unable to read simple directions for using a tool. Nine-tenths of the people in Asia were incapable of obtaining informed knowledge about political, economic, and social problems through the printed word. In India, which in 1947 had the responsibility of freedom suddenly thrust upon it, more than three hundred million people were unable even to read a candidate's name on a voting ballot.

"The most bruised people on this planet," Laubach declared, "the naked, the hungry, the fallen among thieves, the sick, the imprisoned in mind and soul, are the twelve hundred million illiterates."

Laubach's first invitation to apply his educational techniques outside Mindanao came from missionaries in India who for thirty years had "beaten their heads against the stone wall" of illiteracy. They asked him to come with his phonetic charts and, at the same time, warned him to expect "a task about equal to shoveling the Himalayas into the Indian Ocean."

When Laubach left Lanao on this new assignment, his Moro friends saw him off in a highly emotional manner. Five big truckloads of natives followed his automobile down to the seaport twenty-five miles away. "They swarmed onto the ship and spilled over the wharf. Every high *dato* (Moslem priest) in Lanao wanted to make a speech on how they were sending me to bring light to mankind and how this was to be the beginning of the emancipation of the human race. At ten that night, the captain blew his whistle to warn that he was about to cast off, but the Moros laughed and went on talking. The captain subsided for fear they would cut his head off."

Upon arriving in India, the missionary paid a visit to Mohandas Gandhi. The two sat down cross-legged on the floor, and Laubach unrolled a sample picture-syllable chart to explain his educational methods. He could hardly believe his ears when the sardonic old Mahatma declared, "I doubt whether India ought to become literate."

"You are the first one I've ever heard say that. What do you mean?"

Gandhi shrugged. "The literature you publish in the West is not fit for India to read. Look at what you are selling us on every railroad stand."

"You are right," Laubach admitted. "But on the other hand, millions of us admire you and have read your books with great blessing. If you had not written these books and if we had not learned to read, we should never have heard of you."

The thrust went home.

Since the languages spoken in India are more complex than Maranaw, Laubach had greater difficulty in constructing charts for the Indians than for the Moros. However, after exhaustive tests, he succeeded in developing an effective syllable-picture system, and the people responded to it with zeal.

Following his trip to India, Laubach was besieged with invitations to visit other countries. Practically overnight he became the world's foremost traveling salesman of the alphabet. To date, as a special representative of the Committee on World Literacy and Christian Literature, he has carried suitcases crammed with primers and sample reading charts to more than sixty different nations, teaching millions of illiterates to read and write in more than two hundred different languages. An artist accompanies him on his trips; for to unlock the mind of a Fiji Islander or a Chaco Indian, the painter's brush is as mighty as the pen. Laubach enters a language area, has a discussion with local educators to pick out the key words in their tongues, prepares his astonishingly effective word-picture charts for native teachers to employ in the "Each Teaches One" crusade, and then departs for another region.

He has brought his pedagogic wizardry as far as Dhamatri on the edge of the Indian jungle, where tigers have crossed the path of his auto and peered into the headlights at night. He has drilled phonetics into the heads of Egyptian "fellahin" within sight of the ancient pyramid of Cheops, "where the air seemed full of the spirits of millions of those slaves who had toiled in that sand five thousand years ago." In the marketplace of Zanzibar he has taught descendants of native African slave traders to write their names in Swahili.

Everywhere he has gone he has been welcomed with enthusiasm. In New Guinea, drum and bush signals telegraphed his arrival among the tribes. Two rival cannibal villages almost went to war over which should be taught by him first. African Zulus hiked hundreds of miles to get the new "injection against ignorance." At Baroda, Laubach was met by Hindus attired smartly in Scotch kilts who, after serenading him with bagpipes, escorted him in a parade to a large public square where four thousand children from thirty-five schools lustily sang a song he had prepared as a means of teaching phonetics, the words of which were painted on a large building behind them.

> *"Everybody's singing, ka, ke, ki, ko, ku*
> *All the boys are singing, ka, ke, ki, ko, ku*
> *All the girls are singing, ka, ke, ki, ko, ku*
> *All Baroda's singing, ka, ke, ki, ko, ku."*

Today, Laubach, in association with the Mutual Security Administration through the United States' Point Four Program, is working overtime to provide people with the essential education they require for minimum economic security. Frank Laubach has always been a *doer*. He knows that the people of Asia and Africa will never be won to our way of life by sermons alone.

"When we come to them and say, 'Listen to the story of Jesus,' they do not hear the story; they are interested in . . . *us*. The Bible they read in *our faces*. . . . If they fail to see Christ in us, they have no interest in our Book. Our kind words . . . do not convince unless they *cost something*. . . . This is a terrifying responsibility.

"Millions have accustomed themselves to living compartmentalized lives until they have developed into well-meaning, sincere, self-deceived hypocrites. . . . The greatest hindrance to Christ in non-Christian lands is that so many of us talk like Christians and act like heathens in our social and business relationships."

Laubach asserts that what the world needs today is not more good books, but good men and women who will live daringly and adventurously, "who will share the sufferings of the . . . South African gold miners, or the slums of Kobe." What the world needs is a "tremendous cooperative resolve to turn its back upon *self* and go with Christ to meet human need." An army so mobilized "would rock the world."

Laubach, Kagawa, the men and women of Maryknoll—here are outstanding missionaries of today who are fighting the vital battle of freedom in sectors of the world where millions of second-class citizens are being wooed by disciples of class warfare and Marxist revolution. And there are many other crusaders mobilized in this common cause. There is, for instance, the remarkable pioneer woman doctor in India, Ida S. Scudder, who established a system of roadside clinics and built one of the finest medical centers in all Asia, at Vellore. In addition to combating disease on her own, she organized a medical school for native women. And today hundreds of her graduates hold responsible medical posts in India, Burma, and Ceylon. She became so well known among the natives that letters addressed "Dr. Ida, India" have reached her without difficulty.

And there is Dr. Dillmann Samuel Bullock, director of an agricultural mission serving the government of Chile. On his huge experimental farm, the "Garden of Eden," the sons and daughters of Chilean peasants are trained to be able to manage farms of their own and thus raise themselves to positions of economic independence and social dignity.

There is that extraordinary Moravian missionary couple, George and Marguerite Heath, whose labor among the Miskito Indians of Nicaragua and the Honduras is an epic of modern adventure. After thirty-five years of service, George Heath went into retirement. But when no volunteers came forward to carry on his work, this man of fifty-five "whose snow-white hair and stooped figure made him look more like seventy-five" told the Mission Board, "If the conference feels it can use us, my wife and I are ready to go back." And back they went to live through a hurricane in a hut made out of slats of cabbage palms in the jungles of the Honduras.

Then there is Harold Stover Kulp, a descendant of Mennonites, who has done much to improve the living standards of the natives of Nigeria; and the celebrated Methodist, Eli

Stanley Jones of India, an intimate friend of Mohandas Gandhi, whose books on his experiences have been translated into twelve languages and into Braille.

But there are also many men and women who will never be famous. They are doctors, nurses, teachers and lay brothers, social workers and scientists, laboring among the pariahs of five continents to bring decency and hope into lives that have heretofore been without meaning. They belong to the company of David Livingstone and Jacques Marquette, Father Damien and Narcissa Whitman, Junípero Serra and Ann Judson, Charlotte Bompas and Wilfred Grenfell, whose heroic missionary careers have so effectively dramatized the epic of Christianity in action.

This book has dealt with only a part of this remarkable story. No one can foresee the final chapter. But this much is certain—as long as the human heart responds to the Sermon on the Mount, crusaders will continue to toil and suffer and persevere for their fellow men in every corner of the world in the spirit of the Teacher of Galilee.

CHARLOTTE SELINA BOMPAS

DR. GRENFELL

JACQUES MARQUETTE

YUKON R.

Dawson City

Seagway

MACKENZIE R.

Fort Simpson

NORTH

Athabaska

NARCISSA PRENTISS WHITMAN

Fort Vancouver

AMERICA

COLUMBIA R.

Ft. Walla Walla

MISSOURI R.

ARKANSAS R.

Monte Rey

San Diego

Santa Ana

Mexico

MISSISSIPPI R.

Sault Ste. Marie

Quebec

Three Rivers

LABRADOR

Ossining

MARYKNOLL MISSION

MOLOKAI

HAWAII

FATHER JUNIPERO SERRA

FATHER DAMIEN

Pacific

Ocean

SOUTH

AMERICA

IRE

Atlantic

Ocean

DR. ALBERT SCHWEITZER